The Voyage of
Christopher Columbus

By the same author
The Spanish Traditional Lyric
The Hound and the Hawk: The Art of Medieval Hunting

as editor
Juan de Mena, *Laberinto de Fortuna*
T. E. May, *Wit of the Golden Age*
(with P. Bacarisse and I. R. Macdonald)
Pero López de Ayala, *Libro de la caça de las aves*

The Voyage of
CHRISTOPHER
COLUMBUS

---

*Columbus' Own Journal of Discovery
Newly Restored and Translated*

John Cummins

St. Martin's Press
New York

To Susan, Hamish and Ewen

THE VOYAGE OF CHRISTOPHER COLUMBUS: COLUMBUS' OWN JOURNAL OF DISCOVERY. Copyright © 1992 by John Cummins. All rights reserved. Printed in the United States of America. No part of this book may be used or reproduced in any manner whatsoever without written permission except in the case of brief quotations embodied in critical articles or reviews. For information, address St. Martin's Press, 175 Fifth Avenue, New York, N.Y. 10010.

Library of Congress Cataloging-in-Publication Data

Columbus, Christopher.
   [Diario. English]
   The voyage of Christopher Columbus : Columbus' own journal of
   discovery / newly restored and translated by John Cummins.
      p.   cm.
   Translation of: Diario.
   "A Thomas Dunne book."
   ISBN 0-312-07880-3
   1. Columbus, Christopher—Diaries.   2. America—Discovery and
exploration—Spanish.   3. Explorers—America—Diaries.
   4. Explorers—Spain—Diaries.   I. Cummins, John G.   II. Title.
   E118.C725   1992
   970.01′5′092—dc20   92-4012
                                                                           CIP

First published in Great Britain by George Weidenfeld and Nicolson.

First U.S. Edition: May 1992
10 9 8 7 6 5 4 3 2 1

Contents

Acknowledgements

My thanks are due to my colleagues in the University of Aberdeen, Jim Forsyth (Russian), Bob Ralph (Zoology), Jeffrey Stone (Geography) and Chris Wilcock (Plant Science), for assistance with specific points and for the loan or gift of textual material. I have received invaluable help from the staff of the Aberdeen University Library, especially from the Photographic Service and from Colin McLaren and Myrtle Anderson-Smith of the Special Collections section.

The help of Jorge Urrutia in Seville, Guillermina Cenoz and Fernando Huerta in Barcelona and Annamaria Venturi in Genoa eased the progress of my research considerably. I am also grateful to my publishers, and particularly to Allegra Huston and Natalina Bertoli for their supportive interest and suggestions for textual improvements.

Above all, as ever, I thank Liz Weir, the best of secretaries and a patient teacher of the electronically bemused.

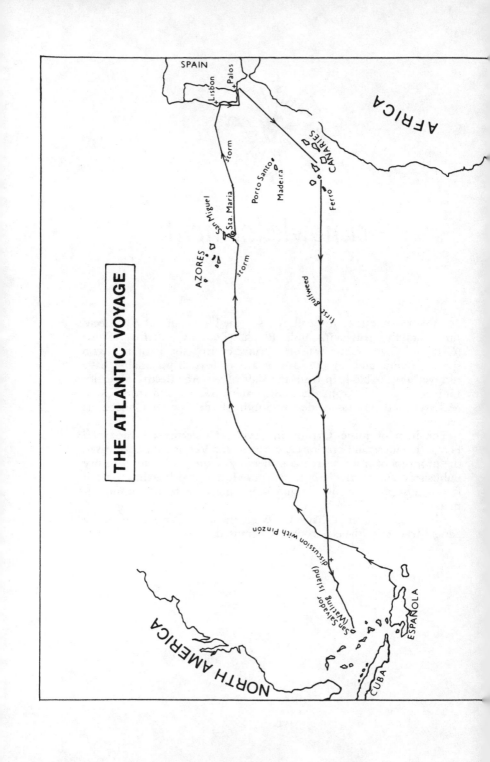

THE ATLANTIC VOYAGE

SPAIN

Lisbon

Palos

AFRICA

CANARIES

Storm

Porto Santo

Madeira

San Miguel

Sta. Maria

Ferro

AZORES

Storm

first gulfweed

discussion with Pinzón

San Salvador
(Watling Island)

NORTH AMERICA

CUBA

ESPAÑOLA

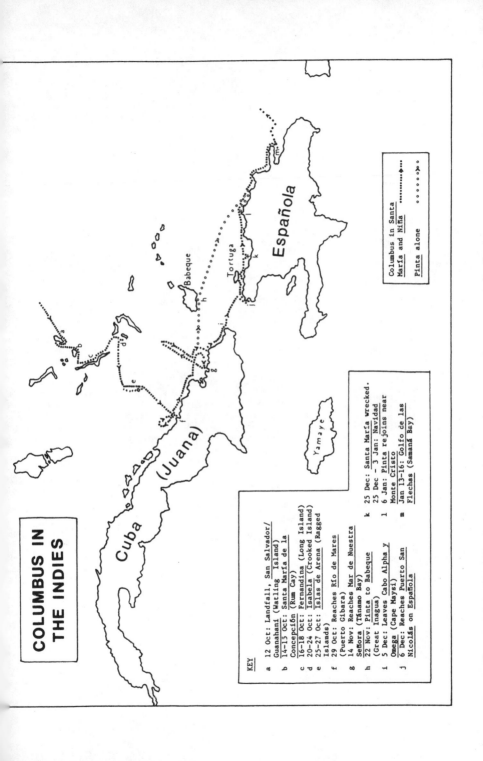

COLUMBUS IN THE INDIES

Cuba (Juana)

Española

Babeque

Tortuga

Yamaye

KEY

a 12 Oct: Landfall, San Salvador/ Guanahani (Watling Island)
b 14-15 Oct: Santa María de la Concepción (Rum Cay)
c 16-18 Oct: Fernandina (Long Island)
d 20-24 Oct: Isabela (Crooked Island)
e 25-27 Oct: Islas de Arena (Ragged Islands)
f 29 Oct: Reaches Río de Mares (Puerto Gibara)
g 14 Nov: Reaches Mar de Nuestra Señora (Tánamo Bay)
h 22 Nov: Pinta to Babeque (Great Inagua)
i 5 Dec: Leaves Cabo Alpha y Omega (Cape Maysí)
j 6 Dec: Reaches Puerto San Nicolás on Española

k 25 Dec: Santa María wrecked.
   25 Dec – 3 Jan: Navidad
l 6 Jan: Pinta rejoins near Monte Cristo
m Jan 13-16: Golfo de las Flechas (Samaná Bay)

Columbus in Santa María and Niña ••••••••••

Pinta alone ∘∘∘∘∘∘∘∘∘∘

The Voyage of
Christopher Columbus

1492: An End and a Beginning

From our viewpoint in the world we have inherited, a world shrunken by technological advance and robbed of its mystery by scientific enquiry, we see 1492 as the date of a great beginning; an expansion of man's acquaintance with his planetary environment on a scale so great that it was not exceeded until he escaped the gravitational pull of the earth. Whatever Columbus thought he had discovered on 12 October (and only later voyages revealed the startling presence of a continent), the reorientation of European eyes westward which followed his return in the following spring was the prelude to a substantial proportion of the now mythicized elements which form our historical culture. The Conquistadors followed, and returned with tales of El Dorado. The riches which they brought home funded Spanish power in Europe, turned mediaeval reivers into *hidalgos* and paid for the art of Velázquez, Rubens and Titian, the craft of goldsmith, gunmaker and embroiderer, the overdressed galleons of the Armada and the literary glories of the Golden Age. Other, later myths came to enrich our vision of a continent of wonders, dangers and inexhaustible wealth: the Spanish Main; the slave trade; the great rivers; Cape Horn;

> Spanish port,
> fever port,
> port of Holy Peter.

The terrain of the Americas and the people who settled there, too, are part of our traditional culture. The Rockies and the Andes; the *pampas* and the Great Plains; jungle and palm tree; gaucho, cowboy, gold-miner and cotton-picker. Columbus's halting conversations with the Caribbean Indians began a redistribution of Europe's languages which has taken French to Quebec and Louisiana, Gaelic to Cape Breton, German to Pennsylvania, Welsh to Patagonia, Italian to Buenos Aires and New York, and Portuguese to Brazil. Above all, Spanish: over 200 million speakers now west of the Atlantic, the successors to the brave and hopeful thirty-nine who used the timbers of the Santa María, wrecked on Christmas Day, to build the first, shortlived foothold, the 'fortress and town' of Navidad.

In retrospect, then, a beginning. Spaniards celebrating that Christmas in Spain, however, even if they had seen Columbus's three little ships drop down the Saltés river with the tide in the blaze of August and knew their mission, would give thanks for the year as the time of a great, triumphal ending. On 2 January 1492, the King of the Islamic state of Granada had emerged from the gate of his capital, kissed the hands of Queen Isabella of Castile and King Ferdinand of Aragon, and thereby conceded that Muslim power in the Iberian peninsula was over. It was the end of the Spanish Middle Ages.

The taking of Granada was the finish of a campaign to reincorporate the whole of Iberia into Christendom, an aim pursued intermittently for almost 800 years. It is easy to imagine the euphoria of the King and Queen in the final weeks of the campaign as they realized that the legendary efforts of their predecessors, the kings and counts of Castile, Leon, Asturias, Galicia, Aragon, Navarre and Catalonia, were about to be crowned by their own success. Their marriage had bridged the one surviving gap between the long separated kingdoms of northern Spain; they were now about to achieve the final stage of the *Reconquista*. This intermittent southward thrust of crusading Christendom had survived alliances cemented and dissolved; Hispanic empires painfully gathered by war, diplomatic intrigue and loveless marriages, and dispersed by the erratic wills of dotards. Periods of half admiring coexistence with Islam had been repeatedly punctuated by conflict – sometimes by mere border forays in which a couple of mills were burned and a few cattle crossed the frontier; sometimes by major battles in which only the intervention of St James the Apostle and his host of white-armoured angels had enabled the Christians to hold the field and set up new southern ramparts of the Faith. The anti-Islamic impetus of these gradually expanding kingdoms had been made sporadic by the resurgent fervour of the enemy, sometimes bolstered from Africa, and by squabbles with Christian neighbours who were often royal siblings. Now the long struggle was over.

In the royal campaign headquarters at Santa Fe, near Granada, only a few days before the formal surrender of the city, Columbus received permission from the Queen to proceed with his project to seek a western route to the orient. The new beginning is tied so neatly to the ending, the sequence is so felicitous, that one resists making the point for fear of accusations of being facile. Those were, no doubt, good days in which to seek a favour from the euphoric monarchs, but Columbus's petitioning and lobbying for royal support of his scheme had been going on for years. In the busy days of the Granada campaign his plan was probably not in the forefront of the minds of the King and Queen.

This does not mean that they were unaware of the benefits which would arise from its success. If it worked, well and good. The costs emerged as relatively slight in the weeks which followed: three vessels, two of them small and in any case due to the Crown in payment of a civic debt, the other moderately sized; fewer than a hundred men; stores and trinkets. It was a small risk for a successful nation in comparison with the potential gains. Mediaeval Spain was at the furthest extremity of the trade routes from the orient, cut off from the sources of eastern luxury goods not only, like the rest of Europe, by frequently hostile populations of infidels, but also by better placed Mediterranean rivals, Venice and Genoa in particular.

Lately the ships of the King of Portugal had opened up a new source of gold and spices southward along the coast of Africa, and by rounding the Cape of Good Hope had revealed a valid sea route to the east, untrammelled by desert, brigand or tax gatherer. The vision of a direct (and, according to Columbus, short) western route from Andalusia to the Spice Islands and the gold-roofed cities described in mediaeval travel literature could not fail to appeal, and he would have had his authorization earlier but for the influence of conservative royal counsellors and Isabella's Catholic conscience about treaty obligations towards Portugal.[1]

The Queen's religious zeal, however, was a factor generally favouring Columbus. He was to seek a route to lands which might be expected not only to consolidate the strength of a newly united Spain with rich and cheaply transported imports, but also to provide a field for a lately accelerating and now thriving enterprise, the incorporation into Christendom of hundreds of thousands of waiting souls. Columbus himself was always aware of this aspect of the voyage, and always eager to stress it; indeed, in later life his conviction became a virtual mania.[2] After leaving behind the intrigue of the soft-fleshed men of the Spanish Court, and finding himself faced once again with the less ambiguous demands of course-finding and weather, he reveals in the Prologue to the Journal and in the more workaday later entries a breadth of historical perspective that enables him to link the aims of his voyage with the recent triumph of Spanish Christendom. The acquisition of gold and spices and the conferring of salvation: these two threads emerge repeatedly in the day-to-day descriptions of seafarer's task and island landscape, neither absent for long.

Hypocrisy, the cynical might say; and Bartolomé de las Casas, the priest through whose interest and diligence our closest approximation to Columbus's original Journal survives, is always ready to point out the contradictions inherent in the dual motivation.[3] But the strength of faith underlying the voyage is unquestionable. Columbus and his men say the *Salve Regina* together as the last act of their day; in their references to time they use the hours of the Church services: terce, vespers and compline;[4] wearied and desperate in the storm, they remember the seaman's favoured shrines in Andalusia and two of the great centres of mediaeval Marian pilgrimage, Our Lady of Guadalupe and the Virgin of Loretto; after their safe deliverance, their first act is to walk through the February wind to the nearest church to give thanks to the Virgin, clothed only in their shirts (whether their faith was shaken by the immediate result, seizure by the Portuguese, we can only surmise). In conspicuous sites in the Indies Columbus sets up crosses, a physical indication that the islands are now possessed not only politically but spiritually. Again one thinks back to the early days of the Reconquest: when a Christian nobleman came down from the Cantabrian mountains to repossess an area of the empty lands left by the Moors as a buffer zone in the upper valleys of the Ebro or the Duero, he naturally established a military outpost, a *castellum*,[5] but normally a monastery too, often giving the richer land near the river to the monks. This hand-in-hand progress of the secular and the religious was carried southward, and then into the new lands across the Atlantic.

Columbus had no space aboard for priests, but the priests soon followed, and it is clear that in the early days of empire the indigenous populations of the Americas were looked on by Spaniards not versed in theology as something akin to the Moors. This view was probably accentuated as soon as the Conquistadors met, on the one hand, serious opposition, and, on the other, the astonishing creations of the builders and craftsmen of the mainland. For the real veterans among them, men hardened in their youth by the long campaigns of the Moorish wars, those marches through the hostile lands of Mexico and Peru, the alien complexions, the curious tongues, the pagan temples and richly worked artefacts, the constant stress on their role as the vanguard of God, must have seemed very much an extension of the Christian Reconquest of Spain.[6]

There is something of this even in the work of Las Casas, a great and scholarly defender of both the reputation of Columbus and the rights of the Indians. His admiration for the Admiral gives way to anger when he describes Columbus's arrogant assumption that the natives can be gathered and removed to Spain as examples of natural fauna, but the distinguishing factor of religion is fundamental to Las Casas too: whenever he has to allude to a group of Columbus's men in relation to the Indians, he calls them not Spaniards, but *cristianos*, Christians.

A man's signature tells us much about how he sees himself. In later life, even on family letters, Columbus conveyed his own view of his historical importance by analyzing his own Christian name:

> . S .
> S . A . S
> X . M . Y
> Xp̄o FERENS

The first three lines of this cypher are enigmatic,[7] but the meaning of the last is obvious. It is an analysis of the Latinized form of Christopher, split to show the meaning 'the bearer of Christ' (Xp̄o is the normal scribal abbreviation for *Cristo*). Columbus, aware of the legend of the saint who carried Christ across the river, expresses in his signature a high concept of his own significance as the man who bore Christ and his faith across an ocean.

His contemporaries were aware of this saintly symbolism. One of the finest maps of the world produced in the period immediately following the discovery of the Indies is attributed to Juan de la Cosa. At the western extremity of his map, just to the left of the newly discovered islands, he placed a picture of St Christopher carrying the infant Christ across the river. The thought of alluding to Columbus in this way may have come to him independently, but whether or not he was the Juan de la Cosa who sailed as master of the Santa María he probably had in mind Columbus's own association of his name with the legend of the saint.[8] The same link is the basis of murals in early colonial churches,[9] and probably of the painting in the Lázaro Galdiano museum which, it is claimed, shows Columbus kneeling before the Virgin. Partly clad in armour (possibly the armour of God of St Paul's *Epistle to the Ephesians*, but more probably symbolizing his elevation to the nobility), Columbus prays to the Virgin as he and his crew prayed to her to save their ship from foundering off the Azores. At his back, with a sponsoring hand on the explorer's shoulder, stands the great bearded presence of St Christopher.

Columbus's son Fernando, a man of literary interests who wrote a posthumous biography of his father, explains the link with the saint rather laboriously, and also draws symbolism from the family surname, which means 'dove' in Latin:

He was truly *Columbus* or 'dove', for he bore the grace of the Holy Spirit to that New World, revealing who was God's beloved Son to those who did not know Him, as did the Holy Spirit in the shape of a dove when St John baptised Christ; and because he bore the olive branch and oil of baptism over the waters of the ocean, like the dove of Noah's ark, to show that those people who had been confined in the ark of darkness and confusion were to enjoy peace and be incorporated into the Church.[10]

In the Journal Columbus never reflects on the implications of the fact that some of the essential aspects of the true Christian were more in evidence in the society he had found than in the one he had left behind. He mentions with astonishment the simplicity and spontaneous generosity of the Indians; their neglect of wealth which enables them to value a lump of gold at no more than a piece of broken pot, a glass bead or a sparrowhawk bell. He never goes on to wonder how these virtues have been achieved without baptism or the guidance of priests, and whether they will survive contact with rapacious men whose values are different.

Let us not be too hard on him for this complacency in his European values. In our own time there are devout souls who, wishing to benefit rather than exploit the naïve inhabitants of the Latin American forests, nevertheless believe that God will look askance on any man not wearing trousers. Five hundred years after Columbus his evangelistic aim is unfulfilled, and the inculcation of the civilizing values of Christendom continues to be a more complicated process than he and his age, in their own naïvety, anticipated.

The Orient and the
Ocean Sea

The extent of European knowledge and speculation regarding world geography at the time of Columbus's departure may be broadly appreciated by examining the globe of Martin Behaim, produced in 1492. Generally, and unsurprisingly, the accuracy of the delineation varies inversely with the distance from central Europe. Behaim states explicitly in a legend on the globe that he is updating Ptolemy, the main influence on late mediaeval ideas of the shape of the world. The principal element he drew from Ptolemy was that the world is, indeed, a globe, and in this respect Behaim was doing nothing startling in the context of his times. The idea, fostered by Hollywood, that opposition to Columbus was based on a generally held vision of a flat earth with an edge over which one could fall into a void is nonsense. Mediaeval astronomy, often erroneous and not yet clearly separated from astrology, was nevertheless a developed science, and the Ptolemaic concept of the earth as a sphere was widely familiar to both churchmen and laymen; indeed the churches were often the repositories of visual confirmation of it for the worshipping public. In San Gimignano in Tuscany, for instance, a typical fresco framed by an arch in the church shows the earth as a sphere with the other heavenly bodies rotating in crystalline layers around it.

Behaim claims to be expanding Ptolemy with details from thirteenth- and fourteenth-century travel books and with information recently gathered by Portuguese explorations in which he took part himself:

You must know that this depiction represents the whole extent of the earth in both latitude and longitude, measured geometrically. It is based partly on

7

Ptolemy's book entitled *Cosmographia Ptolomei*, and for the rest on the accounts of the knight Marco Polo, who travelled from Venice to the orient in 1250, and also in accordance with the description given in 1322 by that respectable scholar and knight John Maundevile in a book on the eastern lands unknown to Ptolemy, with all their islands, which are the source of spices and precious stones. But the illustrious Dom João, King of Portugal, sent his ships to the south in 1485 to explore all the rest of the world, and I, the author of this globe, was on that voyage of discovery.[1]

It has been suggested[2] that Behaim's globe may have been produced under Portuguese royal influence to publicize Portugal's discoveries and consolidate her claims to empire, and that similarities between it and the world map of Henricus Martellus Germanus may indicate that the latter was produced for the same purpose and was then used as a partial basis for the globe. The Martellus map, too, amalgamates Ptolemy with an imaginative representation of the orient based on mediaeval travel writings and with material based on the Portuguese discoveries in west and south Africa. Like the globe, it must be post 1488, for it refers to the voyage of Bartholomew Dias.

In the Journal entries for 24 October and 13 November Columbus mentions spheres and *mapamundos* which he has seen, and if the Henricus Martellus map was widely reproduced it could possibly be one of the maps to which he is referring. There is dissent about whether copies of the Henricus Martellus map were hand-drawn or printed for general sale,[3] but as commercial chartmakers for an international market Columbus and his brother Bartholomew would certainly have had their ears to the ground for information on any such work. In view of Martin Behaim's known involvement with Portugal in the years immediately preceding the voyage, it is possible that the Behaim globe was one of the spheres examined by Columbus. Be that as it may, the Henricus Martellus map and the Behaim globe represent the current thinking of alert European cartographers at the time when Columbus was planning his voyage.

Various elements of these two representations are relevant to Columbus's project. The orient is shown as an area of a myriad islands, stated by Behaim to be the source of precious stones and spices. The globe shows the fabled Great Khan, the Mongol emperor who figures so prominently in Columbus's expectations. It also represents, very crudely, the overland trade routes to the east, but both the map and the globe reflect the crucial discovery by the Portuguese that Africa had a southern tip which could be rounded. Japan is prominent.

There is abundant evidence that reaching the orient was a difficult business, but this should not mislead us into thinking that all mediaeval Europeans saw it merely as a place of distant legend. The same dual incentives which lay behind Columbus's project, commercial exploitation and missionary zeal, had led to a surprisingly extensive overland penetration by Europeans in the preceding centuries. Marco Polo's journeys furnished the information on which late mediaeval ideas of the east, including those of Columbus, were largely based: golden pagodas; teeming cities; wharves and markets thronged with merchants; cargoes of gold, spices, jewels; the palaces and hunting parties of the Great Khan Kublai. It was an account translated and copied over and over by mediaeval scholars:

Inside these walls, which make up the boundary of four miles, stands the palace of the Great Khan, the largest that has ever yet been known . . . The paved foundation or platform on which it stands is raised ten spans above ground level, and a wall of marble, two paces wide, is built on all sides . . . The walls of the great halls and the apartments are decorated with carved and gilded dragons, figures of warriors, of birds and of beasts, with representations of battles. The inside of the roof is contrived in such a way that one can see nothing but gilding and painting . . . The outside of the roof is adorned with a variety of colours, red, green, azure and violet . . . At the back of the palace there are large buildings containing several apartments holding the private property of the monarch, his treasure in gold and silver bullion, precious stones, and also his vessels of gold and silver plate.

. . . Zipangu is an island in the eastern ocean, situated at the distance of about 1,500 miles from the mainland . . . its inhabitants are handsome, fair-skinned, and civilized in their manners . . . They have gold in the greatest abundance, their supplies being inexhaustible, but as the king does not allow it to be exported, few merchants visit the country . . . This is the reason for the extraordinary richness of the sovereign's palace, according to what we have been told by those who have access to the place. The whole roof is covered with a plating of gold, just as we cover houses, or more properly churches, with lead. The ceilings of the halls are of the same precious metal; many of the rooms have small tables of pure gold, of considerable thickness; and the windows also have golden ornaments. So huge indeed, are the riches of the palace, that it is impossible to give a true idea of them. In this island there are also pearls in large quantities, of a red colour, round in shape, and very large, equal in value to, or even exceeding that of the white pearls.

The sea in which the island of Zipangu is situated is called the sea of Chin, and so large is this eastern sea that . . . it contains no fewer than 7,440 islands, mostly inhabited. It is said that of the trees which grow in them, every single one gives off a fragrant smell. They produce many spices and drugs, particularly lignum aloes and pepper, in large quantities, both white and black. It is impossible to estimate the value of the gold and other articles found on the island.[4]

Graphic artists reinforced this literary vision. The *Livre des merveilles* is one of many testimonies to the influence of Marco Polo's journeys. It is liberally illustrated, and while the European miniaturist has little idea of the ethnic or architectural features of the far east (the Great Khan is made to look very much like Charlemagne or King Arthur; the fortresses could equally represent Tintagel or Carcassonne), his choice of subject matter is influenced not only by the need to depict the events of the narrative but also by the opportunity to excite wonder at the marvels to which the title alludes. The illuminations gild a vision already golden.

The richness and detail of *The Travels of Marco Polo* ensured its longlasting popularity, and its descriptions dominated the naïve European view of the orient up to and beyond the time of Columbus. (Its only rival is the *Travels* of Sir John Maundevile, whose assistance is acknowledged by Martin Behaim alongside that of Polo. Maundevile's is an inferior work, a sensationalist ragbag.)

The Travels of Marco Polo describes a conversation on religion with the Great Khan in which the question of Christian baptism arose. While not overenthusiastic about the proposal, the Khan evidently believed in spreading his bets in matters of faith. He saw nothing basically wrong with Christianity; his reluctance to embrace it exclusively was due to its failure hitherto to provide convincing local effects of the power of God.

'For what reason', he said, 'should I become a Christian? You yourselves must have noticed that the Christians of these countries are ignorant, inefficient people, who do not possess the ability to perform anything miraculous; whereas you see that the idolators can do whatever they like. They have the power of controlling bad weather . . . You have witnessed that their idols have the power of speech . . . If I were to become a convert to Christianity and profess myself a Christian, the nobles of my Court . . . would ask me what sufficient motives had caused me to receive baptism and to embrace Christianity. 'What extraordinary powers,' they would say, 'what miracles have been displayed by its ministers?'[5]

The Khan then proposed a formal trial of strength between the Pope's representatives and the local infidel priests:

'But please return to your Pontiff, and ask him, in my name, to send here a hundred persons well skilled in your faith, who when put face to face with the idolators shall have power to coerce them, showing that they themselves have the same art, but refrain from exercising it because it is derived from the agency of evil spirits, and shall compel them to give up practices of such a nature in their presence. When I witness this, I shall place them and their religion under an interdict, and shall allow myself to be baptised.'
. . . It must be evident from this account that if the Pope had sent out persons properly qualified to preach the gospel, the Great Khan would have embraced Christianity, to which, it is certainly known, he was strongly inclined.[6]

The Khan's request to the Pope, as described by Marco Polo, probably underlies Columbus's assertion in the Prologue to the Journal that emissaries had come to Rome from the far east to appeal for instruction in Christianity. Columbus says that the appeal had met with no response, and gives the impression of vast areas totally untouched by Christian influence or, indeed, by European feet. This is a considerable misrepresentation, though probably largely an unwitting one, which suited his own proposals. The trial of strength proposed by the Great Khan had developed from the late thirteenth century onwards, not in the stage-managed form of conquest by miracle suggested in the Marco Polo account, but as a missionary campaign which went hand in hand with commercial exploration.

European acquaintanceship with the far east, therefore, was not limited to the information available in the famous travel books. In the years between Polo's journeys and Columbus's voyage surprisingly large numbers of Europeans travelled to the east, and many lingered there for evangelical or commercial purposes. A high proportion of these were Italians, and a high proportion of the Italians, significantly in this context, were from Genoa, the birthplace of Columbus.[7] Even these, however, were far from being the first Christians in China: a branch of the Church known as the Nestorians, after the fifth-century founder Nestorius, had a strong missionary spirit and by the first quarter of the eighth century had established bishoprics in China. After reaching a low ebb in the tenth century the Nestorians revived in the thirteenth and fourteenth, and are mentioned as an established feature of Chinese society by Catholic missionaries in their letters to Europe.[8]

There were also formal contacts between oriental ambassadors and Rome, and Italian churchmen went bravely to the far east. In April 1278 a group of Minorite friars, Gerald of Prato, Anthony of Parma, John of St Agatha, Andrew of Florence and Matthew of Arezzo, were sent off to Cathay by Pope Nicholas III on an embassy to 'the Great Cham, the illustrious Emperor of all the Tartars'. There is no evidence of their arrival.[9] In April 1287 Rabban Sauma, an emissary of Khan Argun, was in Rome. Guided by a Genoese called Buscarelli he then visited Genoa, Paris (where he met Philippe Le Bel) and Bordeaux (where he met Edward I). He was received into the Catholic Church by Pope Nicholas IV in 1288.

In the same year a Franciscan called John of Montecorvino set off from Venice with letters of commendation from Nicholas IV to the King and Queen of Armenia, Khan Argun, the Great Khan Kublai and his rival, Kaidu of Turkestan. After reaching Tabriz, where he met Buscarelli and a man from Tuscany, Montecorvino decided against continuing along the overland route followed by Polo, and took instead a route involving two sea passages: one from Ormuz to the Malabar coast, and a second from Malabar to China. With him went two other Italians: a Dominican called Nicholas of Pistoia and a merchant, Peter of Lucalongo. Nicholas died in India, but Peter the merchant reached China with the friar. They were probably the first westerners to arrive in China by sea; harbingers of the many future voyagers in a joint endeavour in which, despite war, piracy and storm, the merchants generally found progress easier than the missionaries, but kept quieter about it. The two travellers exemplify the collaborative nature of the early exploration. When the friar John of Montecorvino began building his fine new monastery 'before the gate of the Lord Cham' in 1304, he did so on ground bought for the purpose by the merchant Peter of Lucalongo.[10]

This was part of an energetic Christian missionary campaign. In 1305 the Pope named Montecorvino Archbishop of Pekin, with instructions to build a cathedral using funds given by a rich Armenian woman and to organize the structure of the Church in China. Other missions followed frequently: Andrew of Perugia and six companions were sent as suffragan bishops in 1307; Peter of Florence and Jerome of Catalonia went out in 1311; Jourdain de Sévérac in 1321; Odoric of Pordenone spent several years in Pekin; John of Marignolli left Avignon in 1338 and remained in the east for fifteen years. Their descriptions reinforce those of Marco Polo: Odoric describes Canton as being three times as big as Venice, with more ships than the whole of Italy. In Tsiun-Cheu, which was 'twice the size of Rome', he and Jourdain de Sévérac saw a Franciscan monastery and just beside it a monastery with 3,000 bonzes worshipping 11,000 idols.

A letter from Montecorvino gives a vivid account of his early activities, and of the difficulties of the journey:

I have built a church in the city of Cambalec, in which the king has his chief residence . . . I have baptised there, as well as I can estimate, up to this time some 6,000 persons . . . Also I have gradually bought 150 boys, the children of pagan parents, and of ages varying from seven to eleven, who have never learned any religion. These boys I have baptised, and I have taught them Greek and Latin after our manner . . . As for the road hither I may tell you that the way through the land of the Goths, subject to the Emperor of the northern Tartars, is the shortest and safest; and by it the friars might come, along with the letter carriers, in five or six months. The other route again is very long and dangerous, involving two sea voyages; the first of which is about as long as that from Acre to Provence, while the second is as long as from Acre to England. And it is possible that it might take more than two years to accomplish the journey that way. But on the other hand, the first-mentioned route has not been open for a considerable time, on account of wars that have been going on. It is twelve years since I have had any news of the Papal Court, or of our Order, or of the state of affairs generally in the west.[11]

John of Montecorvino died around 1328, not only the first but also, apparently, the last effective Archbishop of Pekin. In 1333 a Friar Nicholas, professor of Divinity in Paris, was appointed to succeed him. He set off with twenty friars and six laymen; they were well received in Almalik, but there is no record of their having reached Cathay.

Around 1330 the relations between the Great Khan and the Catholic missionaries appear to have been cordial. The *Livre de l'estat du grant Kaan*,[12] said to be by the Archbishop of Soltania, John of Cora, gives a glowing account of the glittering pomp of the Khan's Empire and ends with a description of his generous support of the European missions:

The Grand Caan supporteth the Christians . . . and causes provision to be made for all their necessities; for he hath very great devotion towards them, and sheweth them great affection. And when they require or ask anything from him, in order to furnish their churches, their crosses or their sanctuaries in honour of Jesus Christ, he doth most willingly bestow it . . . And most willingly doth he suffer and encourage the friars to preach the Faith of God in the churches of the pagans . . .[13]

There are many references to the presence of men from Genoa in the east in the early fourteenth century. In 1321 Jourdain de Sévérac had the help of a Genoese to gather the relics of four martyrs in India; Andrew of Perugia, Bishop of Zaitun, mentions the influential position of the Genoese in the city in 1326; Andalo di Savignone, sent by the Great Khan as ambassador to Europe in 1338, was Genoese; in 1340 a Genoese merchant was martyred in Almalik. There are references to a Genoese presence in Turkestan, China, the Malabar coast.

The hardships of the journey to the east and the difficulties of communicating in strange tongues led to the composition of guides and commercial handbooks, and here too the Genoese participation is evident. The Biblioteca Marciana in Venice has a copy of a trilingual dictionary in Latin, Persian and Cumanian composed by a Genoese in 1303 for the use of merchants. There was obviously some naïvety of attitude towards distant tongues; missionary friars preached in Latin or Italian to uncomprehending Saracens on route.

A striking impression of how appealing the idea of a short sea journey to the orient must have seemed to anyone in western Europe, and especially in Spain, emerges from a commercial handbook written by another fourteenth-century Italian, Francesco Balducci Pegolotti.[14] He was a Florentine, but clearly much of his information comes from a

Genoese source, for he uses Genoese weights and measures in correlating oriental and western practices. He is very informative on the length and nature of the overland journey, recommending the following stages and modes of transport:

Tana (Azor on the Black Sea) to Astrakhan:

by ox-cart	24 days
by horse-carriage	12 days
Astrakhan to Sarai: by boat on the Volga	1 day
Sarai to Saraichik: by land or boat	8 days
Saraichik to Urgandi on the Oxus: by camel	20 days[15]
Urgandi to Otrar: by camel	34 days
Otrar to Almalik on the Ili river: by donkey	45 days
Almalik to Kanchau: by donkey	60 days
Kanchau to Quinsay (Hang-chau-fu): by horse and river	45 days
Quinsay to Cambalec (Pekin): method not given	30 days

Pegolotti is not consistently reassuring about the safety of the journey:

The road you travel from Tana to Cathay is perfectly safe, whether by day or by night, according to what merchants say who have used it . . . When the lord of the country dies, and before the new lord who is to have the lordship is proclaimed . . . there have sometimes been irregularities practised on the Franks, and other foreigners . . . You may reckon also that from Tana to Sarai the road is less safe than on any other part of the journey; and yet even when this part of the road is at its worst, if you are some sixty men in the company you will go as safely as if you were in your own house.[16]

A less equivocal description of the overland route is given by Pascal of Vittoria, a Franciscan who had much to suffer on his journey in 1338. First he had to reach Tana, the same starting point specified by Pegolotti. Writing to his brother friars in Vittoria from Almalik (still over a hundred days short of Cambalec), he describes how he and Friar Gonsalvo Trastorna went first to Avignon and Assisi:

And after that we embarked at Venice on board a certain carrack, and sailed down the Adriatic sea. We next sailed through the sea of Pontus, leaving Sclavonia to the left and Turkey to the right, and landed in Greece at Galata near Constantinople, where we found the father Vicar of Cathay in the Vicariat of the East. Then, embarking on another vessel, we sailed across the Black Sea, whose depth is unfathomable, to Gazaria in the Vicariat of the North, and in the Empire of the Tartars. Then traversing another sea which has no bottom, we landed at Tana.

His journey then followed the stages recommended by Pegolotti, though the timing varied and he certainly had his troubles. It must be said that he brought much of his distress on himself by his determined preaching, and that a merchant would have travelled more discreetly.[17]

Still, allowing for negotiating time, setbacks and weather, it was probably necessary to set aside the best part of a couple of years for a trading journey to China and back. From Spain, remember, one had to travel right across Europe or sail the length of the Mediterranean and the Black Sea before starting on Pegolotti's itinerary.[18]

With the fall of the Mongol dynasty, the cordial relations with the far east disappeared, and details of contacts in the fifteenth century are hard to come by. A list of the Catholic Archbishops of Cambalec includes men who occupied the see nominally until the 1480s, but says that some of these, including all the fifteenth-century incumbents, did not take up residence there.[19] The Nestorian Church lingered on in a decadent state, Metropolitans of China being appointed until 1490. In the case of John, nominated Metropolitan in that year, the charge appears to have been united with that of India, and the responsibility for China may have shrunk to a purely nominal one.[20] When Jesuit missionaries went to China in the sixteenth century they found only residual evidence of the previous Christian presence, whether Catholic or Nestorian.

Thus the reports about China which reached Europe in the fifteenth century were few and far between, and were based not on residential experience but on chance contacts with orientals made in the middle east or central Asia. An example is Ruy González de Clavijo, a Spaniard who went on an embassy to Samarkand in 1403. Timur Beg, ruler in Samarkand at the time, rearranged the seating at dinner to make the Spaniard sit above the Cathayan ambassador, since 'those who came from the King of Spain, his son and friend, were not to sit below the envoy of a thief and a scoundrel who was Timur's enemy'.[21] Clavijo gives interesting details about contemporary trade. The best of the merchandise coming to Samarkand was from China: silk and satin; musk and the medicinal rhubarb which Columbus subsequently thought he had found in the Caribbean; pearls, diamonds and rubies. Cambalu (presumably the same place as Cambalec, i.e., Pekin) was six months' journey from Samarkand, including two months crossing the Steppes. In the year of Clavijo's visit 800 camels came from Cambalu laden with goods for Samarkand. He also says, remembering or picking up who knows what oral legend, that the Emperor of Cathay used to be a pagan but had been converted to Christianity.

In the fifteenth century, indeed, there are indications of a break-down of European practical awareness of the east so complete that when relations were resumed with early Portuguese trading visits and the establishment of Jesuit missions in the sixteenth century it was by no means generally accepted that this new land of China was the same as the Cathay of the mediaeval accounts. In the account of the journey made in 1603 by Benedict Goes, a Portuguese Jesuit, with the specific aim of establishing whether the two were one and the same, Cathay is described as 'that famous Empire . . . the name of which was once familiar to Europe through the story of Marco Polo the Venetian, but had in the lapse of ages so fallen out of remembrance that people scarcely believed in the existence of such a country'.[22]

Late in the fifteenth century, therefore, Columbus could be excused for his statement about the unChristianized state of the east, which within the perimeters of his own lifetime was true enough. How much he knew about the great Genoese mercantile tradition which had assisted the Church in its oriental flowering in 1300–50 is impossible to assess – a few oral memories, perhaps, blurred and embroidered in the family traditions of neighbours. On the nature and sources of his personal vision of the east, however, we have reliable information in his own hand, as we shall see.

The orient, then, had begun to be explored, evangelized and even exploited two centuries before Columbus set sail westward, and its geography and wealth were reasonably well documented, though relations had become distant in the fifteenth century. The Atlantic, in contrast, had been explored only relatively recently, and to a very limited extent. Late mediaeval cartographers up to and including Martin Behaim included in their maps not only the Azores, the Cape Verdes and the Canaries as these groups were successively explored and colonized,[23] but also a range of other islands whose number, size, names and positions were based partly on legend and partly on the reports of deluded contemporary mariners.

One scholarly view was that in the far west the Atlantic was shrouded in an unwelcoming mist. St Isidore of Seville, the great seventh-century authority on virtually everything, refers to several island groups of antiquity including the Isles of the Blessed, the Gorgades and the Hesperides, but in his section *De Oceano* he writes that 'according to the philosophers there is no land beyond the Ocean, and the sea is bounded only by dense, cloudy air'.[24]

One of the most famous of the imagined islands was that of St Brendan. The main source of information on this seafaring Irish saint of the Dark Ages was a widely circulated work called the *Navigatio Sancti Brandani*. Originally in Latin, it was translated into various European vernaculars. It describes how in the sixth century the saint set off with a group of monks from their monastery at Clonfert, by the Shannon, in a sailing boat constructed with a wooden framework and an outer skin, like a large version of the modern *curragh* of the west of Ireland. They took forty days' supplies and made repeated attempts to sail westward across an Atlantic full of storms, magical birds and sea monsters. This Christian odyssey took them to a series of islands, including a green and beautiful one in the far west. St Brendan's island is shown on various mediaeval maps from about 1270 onwards, including the globe of Martin Behaim, who placed it in the mid-Atlantic, just north of the Equator. It is identified by sixteenth-century and more recent speculation with Barbados.[25]

Another island whose location changed from map to map was Brazil. It lacked the religious credentials and Homeric supporting legend of St Brendan's island, but was often depicted as being of substantial size, and was commonly shown as lying to the west of Ireland. Other cartographers place it in the west Atlantic on the latitude of Brittany. Voyages were still being made from Bristol in search of the island of Brazil in the late fifteenth century.[26] There are no signs that Columbus had any particular theories on the position of St Brendan's island or Brazil, or even any faith in their existence. More relevant to his plans, because of their consistent appearance on late mediaeval maps in a position remarkably close to the true position of the West Indies, are Antilia, the island of the Seven Cities, Satanazes and some smaller adjacent islands.

The name Antilia (Antillia, Anthylla, Antila) is first documented on a chart of 1424, and the island appears as a large rectangular presence on the western fringe of several late mediaeval charts. Explanations of the name have been varied and at times fanciful: the name of a city in Egypt, or a lake in northwestern Spain, or a village in Portugal; a deformed version of Atlantis, the legendary civilization which had sunk beneath the Atlantic waves. More convincing phonologically is the interpretation of the name as two Portuguese words, *ante*, meaning 'before', 'in front of', and *ilha*, 'island'. For anyone wishing to prove that Columbus was not the first to discover America, this etymology is a godsend; it is said to suggest, not only that one of the major Caribbean islands was known to European mariners, but that it was given the name Ante-ilha because they knew that behind it lay something else, i.e., the American mainland. The presence on some charts of an archipelago of islands of varying size, grouped near Antilia, is interpreted as suggesting that there had been previous exploration of much of the West Indies.

There was a strong legend in Iberia that there was an island in the far west occupied by Christians of Portuguese origin. This island, sometimes called the Island of the Seven Cities, is identified in some sources with Antilia. The Portuguese Crown sent expeditions in search of it in the fifteenth century, and Martin Behaim appears to have believed firmly in its existence when he produced his globe in 1492. He labels Antilia *Insula Antilia septe citade* and follows the name with a version of the legend: 'In the year of Christ 734, when the whole of Spain had been conquered by the pagans from Africa, the above

17

island of Antilia, called the Island of the Seven Cities, was populated by an archbishop from Oporto, in Portugal, six other bishops, and Christian men and women who had fled from Spain by sea with their cattle, belongings and goods. A Spanish ship got closest to it without being in danger in 1414.'

The strength of this legend is such that on the chart of 1424 specific place names are given to the seven cities of the island, and belief in its existence as a distinct entity continued well after Columbus's discoveries. In the fifteenth century the belief was bolstered by accounts of Portuguese or Spanish visits to the island, which was said to be rich in gold.[27] Columbus certainly knew of the legend, and according to Fernando it influenced him considerably.[28]

The 1424 chart shows three other islands in the Antilia group: two, labelled Saya and Imana, are insignificant in size, but the other, Satanazes, is not much smaller than Antilia and has five place names on it. It appears on other charts with its name varyingly distorted: Satanagio, Saluaga, Salvatga, Salirosa, etc. Islands named Roillo and Tanmar, sometimes with a few additional unnamed islets, appear in the Antilia group on other late mediaeval charts.

A largely undocumented but evidently lively belief in these islands probably received additional stimulation from the exploring zeal of the Portuguese in the fifteenth century. At a time of general illiteracy the orally transmitted reports of sightings received a credence which would not be accorded them today, and it is evident that Columbus himself took some of them seriously and thought of the islands either as potential stopping places for a passage to the orient or as being the detached easterly fringe of the continent of Asia.

Cristoforo Colombo

Look at the catalogue of any major research library, and you will find references to hundreds of books to do with Columbus. Because of the magnitude of his achievement, many of these are devoted to proving that he was born in this or that country, province or town. The Columbus pages of the British Library catalogue, for example, are strewn with nationalistic titles in various languages: *Columbus: Where was he born?*; *The Fatherland of Columbus*; *Christopher Columbus was born in Pontevedra*; *America was discovered by Catalans: Joan Cabot and Christopher Columbus*; *Christopher Columbus was Corsican*; *Columbus, Native of Toledo*; *Christopher Columbus was a Greek*; *Was Christopher Columbus a Jew?*; *The Portuguese Nationality of Christopher Columbus*; *Columbus was Spanish*; *New Proofs of Columbus's Catalan Origin*; *Marginalisation and Judaism in Christopher Columbus . . .* Five hundred years after the great discovery, as the countries of Europe fumble their way towards pride in a joint heritage, one may perhaps hope that such manifestations of nationalism will cease, but meanwhile the misguided waste of ink continues: in 1989 a local newspaper published articles claiming that the explorer was from Majorca, and early in 1991 he was claimed as a Norwegian aristocrat.

Columbus was Genoese. Contemporary historians who were personally acquainted with him say that he was Genoese,[1] and surviving documentary material links him firmly with Genoa. His son Fernando is a little vague about the explorer's precise birthplace, but is in no doubt about the fact of his origins in the Genoese area: 'Some, who wish to diminish his reputation, say he was from Nervi, or Cugureo, or Bugasca, which are small places on the coast near Genoa. Others, to increase his dignity, say he was from Savona; others that he was from Genoa itself.'[2]

The most telling assertion comes from Columbus himself. In the document entailing his estate, made before the third voyage, he asked his heirs 'to work always to enhance the reputation, welfare and growth of the city of Genoa', and to maintain a house there so that a member of the Columbus family might always live there as a native, 'for I came from there and there I was born'. He also asked his heirs to invest in the Bank of St George in Genoa.[3]

This document, of course, has been discounted by crackpots and chauvinists, but its reliability is now difficult to challenge.[4] If we still need convincing, we need only turn to a large volume published in 1931 by the city of Genoa.[5] The city fathers, justifiably irritated by counter-claims, sponsored the publication in photographic facsimile of a large collection of fifteenth- and sixteenth-century material, including notarial manuscripts alluding to various members of the Colombo family, of Genoa and Savona. The parties and witnesses to the transactions concerned include Cristoforo Colombo, his father, his paternal grandfather and other relatives.

Now, one might say that Colombo is not an especially rare surname in northern Italy, and Cristoforo not an especially rare Christian name, and that finding a Christopher Columbus in a city the size of Genoa is only a degree more difficult than finding a little María in Ravenna, as Sancho Panza would put it. But when one finds that the Christopher mentioned in the Genoese documents has been in Lisbon, is about to depart for Lisbon, has been to Madeira to buy a cargo of sugar, has business dealings with Genoese merchants who are subsequently mentioned in the wills of Columbus the explorer and his son, is widely known to have been absent from his house in Savona and to have been living for a long time in Spain, or is alluded to by his first cousins as Admiral of the King of Spain, one wonders how the claims of the explorer's non-Genoese origin continue to find a publisher.

The Genoese documents provide the basis for a picture of an enterprising, well respected and reasonably well off family of wool-dealers and weavers. In the third generation Christopher emerges in his twenties as a man to be trusted with the commercial and specifically the maritime enterprises of others. The documents provide the basis for the family tree shown opposite.

Fernando Columbus is vague about his father's ancestry, and all the indications are that Columbus himself, having made his way in the world largely by his own efforts, was reticent about it. Fernando hints at noble lineage, mentioning 'worthy persons of the family in Piacenza, where there are also tombs with coats of arms and epitaphs including the name Colombo'. He offers no details, and is equally vague later when he describes his father's parents simply as 'persons of

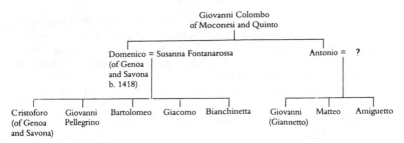

Giovanni Colombo
of Moconesi and Quinto

Domenico = Susanna Fontanarossa   Antonio = ?
(of Genoa
and Savona
b. 1418)

Cristoforo   Giovanni   Bartolomeo   Giacomo   Bianchinetta   Giovanni   Matteo   Amiguetto
(of Genoa   Pellegrino   (Giannetto)
and Savona)

worth brought down in the world by the wars and conflicts in Lombardy'.[6]

Giovanni Colombo, the explorer's grandfather, came from Moconesi, in eastern Liguria. In 1429 he was living in the village of Quinto, five miles east of Genoa, and had a son, Domenico, born in 1418. Giovanni had at least one other son, Antonio. In February 1429, not long before Domenico's eleventh birthday, Giovanni bound his son to a six-year apprenticeship with a weaver called William, from Brabant.[7]

In September 1440, aged twenty-two, with five years as a qualified weaver behind him, Domenico was granted the leasehold of a house in the Vico dell'Olivella, in Genoa, on land belonging to the monastery of Santo Stefano.[8] By 1447, still in his twenties, he was evidently a man of some civic prominence. A document survives in which the Doge of Genoa appoints him Keeper of the Olivella tower and gate, not far from his house;[9] another, dated 7 January 1450, orders the city treasurer to pay him the three-monthly stipend for himself, as Keeper, and his subordinates;[10] others refer to him as Keeper of the gate in October 1450 and November 1451.

Before 1451[11] Domenico acquired a wife, Susanna Fontanarossa, from the nearby valley of the Bisagno. Their first child, Cristoforo, was probably born in the autumn of that year. They subsequently had at least three other sons: Giovanni Pellegrino (alive in 1473 but probably dead, like his mother, by 1489),[12] Bartolomeo and Giacomo.[13] The youngest, Giacomo, was probably born around 1468.[14] There was also a daughter, Bianchinetta, who married a cheesemonger.[15]

The involvement in the wool and clothing trades continued. In 1460 Domenico acted as guarantor when his brother Antonio apprenticed his son Giovanni, named after his grandfather but called affectionately Giannetto, to the tailor Antonio Dellepiane. By 1470, now prominent among his fellow tradespeople, and described as 'master weaver of Genoa', Domenico signed an agreement with the clothiers' council of Savona, approved by the weavers' corporation of Genoa.[16] The family's link with Savona developed to the point where Domenico decided to move house there. Christopher appears as the witness of a will signed in Savona on 20 February 1472,[17] in which he is described as a 'clothier of Genoa', but in a similar document of the 20 March 1472, still 'clothier of Genoa', he and two other witnesses, both tailors, are apparently all included in the description 'citizens of Savona'.[18] In August of the same year Domenico and Christopher both signed a document acknowledging a debt for wool in Savona, Domenico being described as a 'clothier, resident in Savona'.[19]

In August 1473 the family was living in a house in the street of San Giuliano in Savona. On 7 August, in the *bottega* (shop) there, Susanna, Christopher and Giovanni gave legal form to their agreement to the sale by Domenico of the house near the Olivella gate in Genoa.[20] A document of 1483 shows that by then Domenico had returned to Genoa and was living in the Vico Dritto. The last evidence showing him to be still alive is probably a will witnessed by a Domenico Colombo on 3 September 1490, when he would have been in his early seventies. Domenico's sons maintained, or renewed, the connection with Savona, but the link subsequently became attenuated; in a 1501 document Christopher, Bartholomew and Giovanni are described as owning a house in the town but as having been long absent from it.

Information on Columbus's date of birth must be gleaned from allusions to his age in later documents. In a manuscript dated 31 October 1470 in which he acknowledges a debt he is described as being 'over nineteen years of age'.[21] When he appears as a witness in a court case on 25 August 1479, he gives his age as 'about twenty-seven'. These dates are a little confusing. If his age was nineteen on 31 October 1470, he must have been born between 1 November 1450 and 31 October 1451. If he was still twenty-six on 25 August 1479, but almost twenty-seven, he must have been born shortly after 25 August 1452. One way of reconciling the two pieces of data is to interpret the second as meaning 'twenty-seven, rising twenty-eight', which would indicate that he was born after 25 August 1451. We can say with confidence, then, that he was born after 1 November 1450 and before the end of 1452, and accept more reservedly the generally suggested dating of the autumn of 1451.

Of Columbus's boyhood and adolescence we know nothing beyond what can be collected from the sparse documentary information on family movements and occupation already surveyed. Fernando's life of his father claims that he learned his letters early and studied at the University of Pavia. The matriculation records of the University apparently provide no evidence to support this,[22] and the guarded phrasing used by Fernando suggests that, even if the claim is not totally spurious, Columbus's university education was not a prolonged one. But study he certainly did, somehow – enough to read and write Latin capably in later life, and:

Enough . . . to understand the geographers, to whose teachings he was greatly devoted . . . he also studied astronomy and geometry, since these are closely related sciences, dependent on each other. And since Ptolemy says in the beginning of his *Geographia* that to be a good geographer one must know how to draw, he learned drawing, so as to be able to show the positions of countries, and to form geographic bodies in the plane or in the round.[23]

Most books about Columbus include a picture of him. The scores of portraits of him are contradictory, and none have been authenticated as dating from his own lifetime. The one I have included is symbolic rather than representational. The Journal looks outward through its author's eyes; its greatest interest lies in the interplay between the vision in his mind and the reality he sees unfolding around him, and in his efforts to reconcile the two without losing the vision, in a situation of loneliness and semi mutiny. His physical appearance is secondary, and our own imagined Columbus is as valid a representation of him as any other portrait. The best assistance to our imagination is the passage in which his own son describes him:

A well-built man of average height; his face was long, with rather high cheekbones, and his body neither fat nor lean. His nose was aquiline, his eyes light in colour, and his complexion fresh and ruddy. His hair was fair when he was young, but turned grey when he was thirty. He was very restrained and modest in his dress, and temperate in matters of food and drink. He had an easy way with strangers, and was very pleasant with his household, though rather serious.

It will be seen that in most respects the portrait I have included is at odds with this description. However, it is in accord, at least, with the stress laid by Fernando on his father's God-fearing nature:

In religion he was so strict in fasting and prayer that one could easily have taken him to be a member of a religious order. He hated swearing and blasphemy; the only oath I ever heard him say was 'By St Ferdinand!' Even when he was very angry with someone the worst he would say to rebuke them was 'God take you!' He began everything he wrote with the words *Iesus cum Maria sit nobis in via*.[24]

In all this, there is not one word about the sea. The details of Columbus's change of profession are as obscure as his reasons. What is clear is that, having grown up in a respected and comfortably off family, he displayed a degree of commercial talent and trustworthiness which won him the confidence of prosperous fellow citizens, including some with maritime interests who were willing to offer him a role in their enterprises.

Fernando quotes a letter written to Ferdinand and Isabella in 1501 in which Columbus claims to have been at sea for over forty years.[25] If we were to take this literally, rather than as a rhetorical generalization, it would take Columbus's seafaring back to 1461, when he was only nine or ten years old. The Genoese documentary evidence already mentioned suggests that he was engaged principally in the woollen trade with his father until at least 1472. We must take the claim of forty years at sea with a large pinch of salt. Anyone living in Genoa, with family links to the coastal villages of Liguria, could not fail to imbibe something of the seafaring traditions of the area, especially if his family was engaged in any form of entrepreneurial trade, but if Columbus did go to sea before the age of ten, or even in his teens, it was probably a matter of a few coastal journeys or an occasional trip in a fishing boat rather than any serious service. A reference in the Journal, also quoted by Fernando, is probably more reliable, not least because it is obviously not a carelessly chosen round figure: praising the harbours of the West Indies in his entry for 21 December Columbus says that he has been at sea, without leaving it for any considerable length of time, for twenty-three years. This takes his seafaring back to 1470.

In the decade of the 1470s his horizons evidently expanded. Fernando's fourth chapter is almost as vague on the subject of his father's early voyages as is his second chapter about his ancestry. He excuses himself on the grounds that 'he died before I was bold enough to enquire of him about such matters, or, to be more truthful, at a time when such things were a long way from my childish mind.' Fernando, however, had evidently scoured his father's letters and writings and put together some helpful details.

He quotes another letter in which Columbus describes being sent to Tunis in a ship of King René of Anjou to capture the galleass Fernandina. He gives no date, but the name of the enemy vessel suggests that the voyage was part of René's long-running hostilities with Aragon, which continued into the early 1470s and for which he chartered Genoese vessels.[26] The letter claims that Columbus was captain, which seems extremely unlikely, not so much on the grounds of maritime inexperience (the master, rather than the captain, was responsible for the working of the ship) as because of his extreme youth.

It may seem odd that a young man in the woollen trade should suddenly find himself afloat and engaged in a foreign King's wars, but certain events of the mid-1470s reveal how just such a thing could happen. The island of Chios was captured in 1346 by Genoese privateers, and Genoa subsequently exploited and controlled the lucrative trade in Chian mastic, a soluble resin used in early medicine.

In 1474 and 1475 ships were fitted out by Genoese merchants for journeys to Chios in order to trade and to ward off the Turks. These merchants included Paolo di Negro and members of the Spinola family. In his Journal Columbus mentions having seen the mastic trees of Chios, and indeed grows obsessive in his conviction that the Caribbean gumbo-limbo is the same valuable tree.

Two other details suggest that Columbus took part in one of these Chios voyages, or a similar one. First, he had close connections with Paolo di Negro, whose heirs are mentioned in Columbus's will, as is Battista Spinola, the son-in-law of di Negro's trading partner. Secondly, the records of the voyage of the Roxanna, fitted out for the Chios voyage at Savona in 1474, by Gioffredo Spinola, mention that the soldiers and sailors aboard were accompanied by some 'tradesmen of Savona', including *tessitori*, weavers. Columbus was living in Savona at the time, was occupied in the cloth business, and had close contacts with at least one member of the family of Gioffredo Spinola. Whether or not we draw the conclusion that the Roxanna's voyage was Columbus's initiation into serious seafaring, it provides a good example of how a landsman whose trade and living had been based on the produce of *terra firma* could find himself on a swaying deck, with new ambitions fired by sunlit islands which not only delighted the senses but also offered rich argosies of profit to resolute men.

These Chios voyages, small affairs compared to many Genoese enterprises, nevertheless encapsulate the city's mediaeval achievements. In the view of modern Italians, the *genovese* is a man canny with money, like the English concept of the Scot. This semantic restriction traduces a mediaeval city and state whose tradition, not unsullied by greed, combined that greed with a clarity of purpose, a breadth of geographical vision and inquisitiveness, and a tolerance of hardship and risk in distant places, which must have commanded the admiration even of the envious. If not a single written word survived indicating Columbus's origins – if he had emerged from the blackness of history ready forged and tempered as the seafarer of his late thirties, and we had only his vision of a sea route to the Indies and the narratives of his voyages on which to base a wager as to his birthplace – our best bet would be Genoa.

If we were allowed to hedge our bets, our first alternative might well be Portugal. But this is taking us ahead of our story.

From the early 1470s onwards Columbus expanded his sea-going experience, initially, one presumes, within the Mediterranean, but also with at least one excursion to the far north Atlantic, at least one journey to Madeira, and at least one voyage in the developing trade with the Atlantic coast of tropical Africa. In this widening of horizons he was borne along by two historical currents: the search by the

Genoese for new Atlantic markets as their oriental connections shrank and their Mediterranean influence waned, and the rise in the power of Portugal, so favourably placed to develop and control maritime exploration southward.

Paradoxically, the Genoese control of the Mediterranean mastic trade was a decisive factor in Columbus's introduction to Atlantic navigation and the beginnings of the weakening of his links with Genoa to the level of nostalgia. His acquaintance with the merchant families of the city provided him with a role in a stirring voyage which crucially affected the course of his life. In 1476 a group including Paolo di Negro and the Spinolas put together a fleet to take a shipment of Chian mastic to Portugal, England and Flanders. Columbus went on this voyage, in a role unknown. Off Lagos in Portugal the ships were attacked by a combined French and Portuguese fleet. Several ships were sunk on either side, including the one on which Columbus was sailing. He is said to have been wounded in the battle, but to have seized a floating oar and made his way to shore and subsequently to Lisbon.[27] According to Fernando, as 'many of his Genoese countrymen lived in that city', he received a warm welcome.

How long he stayed on this involuntary visit to Portugal we do not know, but he must have returned quite quickly to the sea. Fernando mentions a note by his father saying that in February 1477 he sailed a hundred leagues beyond Thule, by which he probably means Iceland.[28] Columbus describes Thule as being the size of England, which rules out the Faroes, and mentions the trade between there and Bristol. It was possibly on this or a similar Icelandic voyage that he called at Galway, for, annotating one of the books he was reading, he describes seeing a man and woman with curious features adrift in a boat there.[29] He supposed them to be from Cathay. Why he or anyone should sail a hundred leagues *beyond* Iceland, especially in the late winter, it is difficult to say. He also mentions the extreme tidal range in Icelandic waters, over fifty feet. This is simply not true, and all in all the matter of Columbus's Icelandic voyage is beset by problems.[30]

The likelihood is that it was a trading voyage from Lisbon; once integrated into the Genoese community there Columbus was well placed to renew and develop the relationship of trust built up with the merchants of his home city and to undertake Portuguese commissions on their behalf. In the 1479 court case already mentioned Columbus, as witness, described a visit to Madeira in 1478. Paolo di Negro, the Genoese merchant involved in the Chian mastic trade and the abortive voyage which had brought Columbus to Lisbon, was in the Portuguese capital himself, having been commissioned by Lodovico Centurione to buy a cargo of sugar from Madeira. Columbus went to Madeira on di Negro's behalf, not as a sea captain but simply as an agent, and bought the sugar, which was then to have been loaded by a ship of unspecified nationality commanded by a Portuguese.[31] Columbus had been supplied with only a proportion of the purchase money, and when the rest failed to arrive the sellers withheld most of the sugar, hence the problems of Lodovico Centurione which gave rise to the court hearing.

Columbus's residence in Lisbon continued, or was resumed, in 1479. He gave evidence about the Madeira affair to the court in Genoa on 25 August, but in answer to the question as to whether he had to leave soon, he replied, 'Yes, tomorrow, for Lisbon.' The notary, nevertheless, describes him as a citizen of Genoa. Early historians state that he was engaged in a chart-making enterprise in Lisbon with his brother Bartholomew, who had arrived there before him.[32]

He did not abandon the sea for long, but he was ashore long enough to find himself a wife, and one of higher status than might have been aspired to by a foreign mercantile jack-of-all-trades. At some time in the late 1470s he met and married Felipa Perestrello e Moniz, the daughter of a nobleman, Bartolomeo Perestrello. The surname is Italian; the family originated in Piacenza but emigrated to Lisbon in the fourteenth century. Felipa's father, having taken part in the Portuguese expedition to colonize Madeira and the nearby island of Porto Santo in 1425, was made hereditary captain of Porto Santo. Felipa's brother, also called Bartolomeo, was captain of the island in the 1470s. We know that Columbus's new wife spent time on the island after their marriage, for their son, Diego, was born there, probably in or around 1480.[33] Columbus may have accompanied her, or he may have been away voyaging. Fernando says that his father lived for a while with Felipa's mother, who gave him her dead husband's charts and notes, and that at this time he took a great interest in the contemporary explorations being made by the Portuguese.[34] It would not be long before he gained first-hand knowledge of them; indeed, he may already have acquired it.

At some time, probably in the early years of his marriage, and before Felipa died in 1485, Columbus lived in Madeira, perhaps still engaged in the sugar trade with Genoa. Las Casas, describing the explorer's visit to Funchal in 1498, mentions the warm welcome he was given, being well known there because of his previous period of residence.[35]

To be part of the maritime society of Portugal in the 1470s would have quickened the spirit of any man, let alone one with the questing tradition of Genoa behind him. After colonizing Madeira and the Azores in the late fourteenth and early fifteenth centuries, and discovering the Cape Verde islands, with Genoese participation, in the 1450s, the Portuguese Crown had directed the explorations of its caravels southward along the coast of Africa. In 1469 a Lisbon merchant, Fernão Gomes, was granted the monopoly of trade with the Guinea coast on condition that he extended the exploration southward every year. By the mid-1470s this incentive had taken ships around the whole semicircle of west Africa, including the Malagueta coast which supplied the pepper mentioned by Columbus in the Journal. When the agreement with Gomes expired the Crown retained the monopoly of trade with what was now lumped together broadly as Guinea and with the coast further south, and Columbus had arrived in a Lisbon made lively and prosperous by the African trade which was bringing in cargoes of spices, slaves and gold.

We know that Columbus sailed in this trade, for he tells us so in the Journal. He mentions seeing mermaids off the coast of Guinea, and his marginal annotations to his books state twice that he has seen the castle of La Mina on the Gold Coast.[36] The establishment of this fortress in 1481–2 was one of the most significant events in Portugal's consolidation of her control of the African trade. By the treaty of Alcaçovas Spain had recognized Portugal's exclusive rights to explore the African coast, and the Pope granted indulgences to those who sailed to take part in the building of the castle. Its full name, São Jorge da Mina, St George of the Mine, embodies the dual nature of European fifteenth-century exploration, invoking saintly assistance in the protection of commerce, La Mina being the royal gold mine. Columbus alludes, by implication, to La Mina when he mentions its supposed Caribbean counterpart, the 'mine of gold' on whose whereabouts he repeatedly speculates.

In another of his marginal notes[37] Columbus writes of taking navigational sights while sailing to Guinea: *Nota quod sepe navigando ex Ulixbona ad austrum in Guinea notavi . . . altitudinem solis cum quadrantem et aliis instrumentis plures vices*. His failure to punctuate leaves us with a problem: that he sailed from Lisbon to Guinea and took sights of the sun with his quadrant is clear enough, but *sepe*, 'often', is ambiguously positioned. A grammarian would interpret the positioning of *sepe* before *navigando* to mean that he made frequent voyages to Guinea, but Columbus was no grammarian. Some biographers have interpreted *sepe* as accompanying *notavi*; Morison, for instance, concludes that he took many sightings on a single voyage. This, however, is to ignore *plures vices*, 'repeatedly', which certainly accompanies *notavi* and would make *sepe* redundant in Morison's interpretation. The passage could, therefore, mean: 'Note that in many voyages southward from Lisbon to Guinea I have taken repeated observations of the altitude of the sun with the quadrant and other instruments.'

A statement by Fernando[38] that his father was once in charge of two ships on a homeward voyage, and that he left one in Porto Santo and went on in the other to Lisbon, may be an allusion to an African trip. Certainly the fact that Columbus took with him a quadrant and other instruments (one of them probably an astrolabe) suggests that he was acting at least as an officer and possibly as master or captain when he took his sightings on the way to Guinea.

His conclusions from his solar observations supported a conviction crucial to his subsequent plan to sail westward to the far east. The marginal note continues: '. . . and I found that [my readings] agreed with Alfragan[39] that a degree is equal to $56\frac{2}{3}$ miles . . . so we may therefore conclude that the circumference of the earth on the Equator is 20,400 miles.' Whether this substantial underestimate and other marginal comments on the same lines were a cause or an effect of Columbus's project to sail westward, they are very germane to his own view of the validity of the scheme.

I have mentioned the world map of Henricus Martellus. If Columbus did set eyes on it (and he certainly saw a map which had important features in common with it) what interested him most was the size of the land mass of Europe and Asia compared to the extent of the area of water separating the west coast of Europe from Japan. In reading Columbus's marginal annotations to his own books, of which we shall have more to say shortly, one notices that he seizes avidly on any item indicating or exaggerating the length and hardship of the overland journey from Europe to the orient, or suggesting that a western passage by sea might be shorter than accepted opinion supposed. The Martellus map does both. The crucial factor is the scale of longitude: on fifteenth-century maps based on Ptolemy the longitude between Cape St Vincent in the west and the furthest limit of Asia in the east is 180 degrees, leaving half the circumference of the earth as water, largely vacant and almost entirely unexplored. Henricus Martellus expanded the land mass so that it occupied 270 degrees, leaving only 90 degrees of ocean separating Spain from the orient, and some of this had already been explored with the discovery of the Azores and Canaries, with which Columbus was by now well acquainted.

The logistical implications are obvious. European commercial navigation, even to foreign lands, was largely done coastwise; it seldom took mariners out of contact with the land for periods of weeks. The idea of a continuous voyage around half the circumference of the world, unbroken except for the chance of an occasional call at Atlantic islands dubiously charted and possibly legendary, was untenable. Even with constant fair winds the problems of water and stores, and their replacement with ballast as they were used up, would be daunting, and if the winds on the outward passage were fair all the way, how would one ever get home again? But reduce the distance by half, and shorten it further by taking on water and stores in the Canaries, and the voyage became something brave men could rationally contemplate.

Columbus, in fact, like Alfragan and Henricus Martellus, was hugely wrong, and those of his contemporaries who adhered to the more correct view of the distance to be covered were right to decry his plan as the product of self-deluding optimism. What neither he nor they could know was that a new continent would interrupt his outward voyage when it was really only half complete. Had it not been there to save both him and his fragile reputation he and his crews might have vanished without trace, like many others. That, or they would have turned for home in a mood of mutiny and recrimination and struggled with empty holds, half starved and thirsty, into some Andalusian port, to face ridicule and, in Columbus's case, a lifetime's debts.

In those brave days in Portugal, though, with a grand design forming in his mind, all was hope and optimism. Columbus was now a man in the prime of life, experienced in the control of others, and psychologically free from the confines of the Mediterranean. He had seen the sunlit waters of the tropical Atlantic, admired the sea-keeping qualities of the weatherly Portuguese caravels, and felt the steady northeast trade winds on his port quarter as his ship ran down to Africa. Alter course through ninety degrees, bring those same fair winds onto the starboard quarter, and the way lay open across an Atlantic shrunken in his mind by erroneous computation, wishful thinking, selectivity in the choice of geographical authorities, and an incipient sense of personal mission; an ocean bounded on its western side by Cathay, Japan and the Spice Islands.

Planning and Persuasion

> While he was in Portugal the Admiral began to speculate
> that if the Portuguese could sail so far southward, it
> should be possible to sail just as far to the west, and that
> one might expect to find land in that direction . . . He
> grew convinced beyond doubt that west of the Canaries
> and the Cape Verdes many lands lay waiting to be
> discovered.

Fernando Columbus, who wrote the above words, had access to his
father's library and writings, including some which have not survived.
Fernando was a scholarly man, who saw the bases of his father's project
in the writings of early geographers, cosmologists and travellers:
Ptolemy, Aristotle, Marinus, Strabo, Pliny, Pierre d'Ailly and Marco
Polo. However, we cannot be certain that all these works were
influential, nor indeed that they all formed part of the explorer's library.
He certainly owned some of them, and his copies of the books are
marked by copious underscorings and marginal comments in his own
handwriting. Many of these comments may be post-1492, though if this
is so it is surprising that only one of them alludes to his personal
experiences in the Caribbean (or, as he continued to think, in the orient).
In any case, their content is highly indicative of Columbus's trains of
thought and vision of the shape of the world.[1]

The books of most interest in relation to the voyage are the *Historia
Rerum Ubique Gestarum* of Pius II, the *Imago Mundi* of Pierre d'Ailly
and the *Travels of Marco Polo*, all in Latin, and an Italian version of
Pliny's *Natural History*. The view of the orient which emerges from
the originals is interesting in itself, and the wording of the comments

more so. The passages which specially interested Columbus were of three kinds: those describing natural wealth or rich artefacts (gold, precious stones, spices, porcelain, architecture); the allusions to curious ethnological features; and any sentences which either accentuated the difficulties and length of the overland journey to the east or suggested that the westward distance from Europe to Japan could be less than normally supposed.

The chronological relationship between his first and later readings of these works, the writing of the comments, and his voyages is difficult to establish. The comments may be interpreted as contributions to the development of the thinking which lay behind his project, or as a later, more defensive form of self-justification; Columbus continued to believe that he had reached the far east for some time after subsequent voyages by himself and others had accumulated evidence suggesting to the impartial that his discoveries were part of a new continent.

His marginal notes about natural wealth, especially in his comments on Marco Polo,[2] grow repetitive:

Gold and jewels in plenty . . . emeralds . . . In Trapobana there are jewels and elephants . . . Crison and Argirem have gold and silver . . . In India there are many things . . . aromatic spices, many precious stones, mountains of gold . . . rhubarb . . . lapis lazuli . . . precious stones . . . mines of silver . . . innumerable goods . . . gemstones and pearls . . . gold, silver, precious stones . . . cloth of gold . . . ginger, pheasants, wax in plenty . . . nutmeg . . . coral used as money . . . cinnamon, aloes and many other spices which are not brought to us . . . a lake of pearls . . . ginger, cinnamon, many aromatic things . . . turquoises . . . They cover their teeth with gold . . . Store of ginger, sugar, elephants, spices . . . rhubarb and ginger . . . lignum aloes, sandalwood . . . plates of porcelain . . . rubies . . . amber . . .

We can see him absorbing from these writers, and mentally embroidering, a vision of an advanced civilization with huge concentrations of people, a rich architecture and a seething maritime trade:

The city of Cambalec . . . is twenty-eight miles around . . . Nemptai . . . is thirty miles around, teeming with people. In other towns the houses, palaces, temples and all the other civic architecture are like those of Italy . . . rooms adorned with gold . . . beautiful palaces . . . innumerable ships and merchants . . . ships in great numbers . . . a thousand ships . . . fifteen thousand ships . . . The city of Synguy is sixty miles in circumference . . . Quinsay is the largest city in the world, a hundred miles around, with twelve thousand stone bridges . . .

This evidence about Columbus's reading explains much about the content of the Journal. He had desperate difficulties in his conversations with the Indians. It is obvious that wishful thinking played a role in his interpretation of their signs and noises, and that such thinking was often founded on elements which had impressed him in his reading of descriptions of the lands in which he thought he had arrived. Throughout his time in the islands his conviction is apparent that these are merely the undeveloped fringes of an oriental empire; that when he finds the mainland he will be among the buzzing markets and gilded palaces of his vision. He seizes eagerly on anything which will bolster his confidence: the gold, obviously, but also the fool's gold in the rivers; the mastic trees, aloe plants and medicinal rhubarb which were all really something else; the rich vegetation, which must surely yield endless spices, if he in his sailor's ignorance could only identify them; and any sign or sound made by the Indians which could be interpreted as an allusion to the presence of more sophisticated peoples over the horizon.

It is often possible to relate what he thought the Indians told him about other tribes and islands to specific passages in his reading which caught his attention sufficiently to call for a marginal remark. He is fascinated by cannibalism; his comments on Pius II, Pierre d'Ailly and Marco Polo include: 'Anthropophagi who eat human flesh . . . wild men who eat human flesh; their faces are ugly and loathsome . . . people who eat human flesh . . . In Synguy they eat human flesh.' This same obsession emerges in the Journal in his interpretation of what the Indians tell him; he writes several times that the people he has met are preyed on by cannibals.

He also claims in the Journal that the Indians told him about a pair of islands, one occupied solely by women, the other by men, who joined the women once a year for breeding purposes. This idea too probably springs from Marco Polo, to whose description of similar islands[3] Columbus draws attention in a marginal comment, though Behaim's globe also shows an Isla Masculina, populated only by men, in the Indian ocean. The Journal also tells us that the Indians mentioned a tribe with faces like dogs, an idea present in Marco Polo's description of the island of Angaman.[4]

The most important of the elements drawn from Columbus's reading which colour the Journal, in this case from his Prologue onwards, is the Great Khan, whose imperial power and fabulous wealth dominated the mediaeval European view of the east. He clearly caught the imagination of Columbus, who comments repeatedly on him in the margins of his books: 'The subjects of the Great Khan in Cathay . . . He went to war with ten thousand elephants . . . The Emperor the Great Khan, the lord of many provinces in Cathay . . . The Great Khan once ruled the greater part of Asia . . .' Columbus assumes that the tribe he calls the *Caniba* or *Canima*, who terrify the friendly Indians whom he first encounters, are the subjects of the

Great Khan, and are cannibals. His reading, the strangeness of the language, and his own wishful self-conditioning combine to produce a range of shifting and deluding semantic associations: anthropophagi; *Caniba*; canine-faced men; Great Khan.

Tradition, from Fernando onwards, also accords great importance to an exchange of letters between Columbus and a Florentine, Paolo Toscanelli. Little is known of Toscanelli or the reasons for his authority, but he had previously been contacted by a Lisbon canon, Fernão Martins, who sought advice at the request of the King of Portugal on the subject of maritime access to the Spice Islands; Toscanelli had written back in 1474, attaching a chart to his letter. Columbus heard of this and wrote to Toscanelli through an Italian intermediary in Lisbon, Lorenzo Girardi, sending him a small globe with an indication of his scheme. Toscanelli obligingly sent him a copy of his previous letter to Martins, with a duplicate chart.

The Toscanelli chart probably no longer exists, though attempts have been made to identify it with surviving charts.[5] Fortunately, Fernando gives the text of the letter, which has sufficient detail to provide a general idea of the chart:

From Paolo the Physician, to Fernão Martins, canon of Lisbon, greetings.
I . . . have often spoken of a sea route to the Indies, where the spices grow, shorter than the route which you are seeking by Guinea. You tell me that His Majesty requests some statement or explanation to enable him to understand and take that route . . . I am therefore sending His Majesty a chart drawn by myself, showing the western coast from Ireland down to the end of Guinea, with the islands off that coast, and opposite, directly to the west, the beginning of the Indies and the islands at which you are bound to arrive. It shows how far from the North Pole you are to steer, and the distance in leagues to those places so rich in all spices, jewels and precious stones . . . The vertical straight lines show the distance from east to west, the lines crossing them the distance from north to south.

In short, here was a map of the Atlantic and Pacific oceans conjoined, with lines of latitude and longitude. Toscanelli goes on to describe Cathay, the wealth of the Great Khan, the golden island of Cipango and the glories of the cities of Zaitun and Quinsay. He is probably drawing on Marco Polo, who may well be his source for a reference to oriental ambassadors to the Pope, though Toscanelli also refers to a conversation between himself and a recent envoy. The chart must have shown the island of Antilia, for the letter mentions the ten 250-mile longitudinal spaces between it and Cipango, making up a distance of 2,500 miles of open sea. Toscanelli implies with a landsman's airy confidence that Antilia will serve as a stepping stone, and appears to accept its presence as a fact.

There were probably no countries on the chart which were not on earlier charts of the Atlantic or maps of the world; the great difference was in orientation. Toscanelli's innovation was the shift from the traditional representation of the world as centred on the eastern Mediterranean or the Holy Land; unlike his predecessors, he was able to sever his mind from the old earthbound view of the journey to and from the orient, step after step, river after river, inn after flea-ridden inn. Others had read about Quinsay and Cipango; others knew the earth was round. Toscanelli simply had the extra vision to imagine viewing the supposedly oceanic side of the world from its centrepoint, to place Europe on the right of the chart and Cathay and India on the left.

It was still a wide ocean, according to Toscanelli's lines of longitude: 5,000 nautical miles from Lisbon to China. Columbus welcomed the concept, but not the mileage, which was not in accordance with his own mathematics. He preferred his own, and Alfragan's, calculation of the number of miles in a degree on the Equator, underestimating by a quarter; he also thought that China extended well to the east of its true extent, and overestimated the distance between Japan and mainland Asia.

Columbus wrote again to Toscanelli, evidently stating his intention to sail westward. The reply, again quoted by Fernando, adds little of interest, beyond mentioning Toscanelli's discussions with 'eminent scholars who have come from those places to the Court of Rome and . . . merchants who have traded a long time in those parts'. Columbus was clearly impressed by the Florentine; he preserved a copy of the first letter in his own handwriting at the back of one of his books.[6]

Toscanelli, however, merely added scholarly confirmation to Columbus's existing convictions. According to Fernando his father was quick to seize on any fragment of nautical reminiscence which suggested the accessibility of land to the westward. A hint of scepticism, fostered by hindsight, invades Fernando's normal filial loyalty as he writes of 'these fables and stories . . . As they fell in with his own designs, he committed them carefully to memory. I shall relate them for the interest of those who enjoy such curiosities.'[7]

Most of these seaman's tales were told to Columbus by Atlantic islanders. In the Journal (see the entry for 9 August) he mentions receiving information on regular sightings of land west of the Canaries from the Spaniards of Hierro and Gomera, and from the Portuguese in the Azores. Fernando gives a much fuller list, with names: Martín Vicente, *piloto* of the King of Portugal, who 'found himself' 450 leagues west of Cape St Vincent, and took out of the water a piece of ingeniously carved wood after days of constant westerly winds; Pedro Correa, the Admiral's brother-in-law, who found a similar piece on the island of Porto Santo, and who told him that huge canes, unknown in Europe, were brought ashore by the west wind; people in the Azores who told him that after prolonged westerlies pine trees of an unfamiliar species were cast up on the islands, and that on Flores two corpses with broad, alien faces had been washed up.

Other mariners claimed to have seen islands in the western ocean. A Madeira man, Antonio Leme, said he had seen three, but Columbus was wary of accepting this and other claims, setting them down to sightings of reefs or detached sections of floating rock of the kind described by the ancients, for he knew the men had not sailed very far west. Fernando supports his father's explanation, suggesting that 'the islands [*sic*] of St Brendan were probably of this kind . . . Cases like these possibly explain why people on Hierro, Gomera and the Azores told the Admiral that they sighted islands in the west every year.'

Fernando mentions that another Madeiran asked the King of Portugal for a ship to explore an island which he saw every year in the same position, and that in the time of the Infante Dom Henrique a Portuguese ship, driven off course, found Antilia. Columbus also collected information from seamen of the Spanish mainland: Pedro de Velasco, of Palos, who had been *piloto* on the expedition of the Portuguese Diogo de Teive, told him that west of Ireland, despite strong winds from that quarter, the sea remained calm, and he concluded that they were in the lee of land further west. A one-eyed seaman from Puerto de Santa María and a Galician whom he met in Murcia both told him that they had been on voyages during which land was sighted west of Ireland.

According to Fernando these last sightings were of the same land which a Portuguese called Fernão Dulmo tried to discover: 'I tell this just as I found it in my father's writings, to show how some men will base great enterprises on small things.' This is a reference to an attempt to reach the mythical Antilia in 1487. Dulmo, from the Azores, and a Madeiran called João Estreito set off from Terceira after agreeing with the King of Portugal that the expedition would be at their expense, and that they would be granted whatever they discovered and titles of honour in the event of success. They sailed into historical oblivion.[8]

It has been suggested[9] that the Dulmo–Estreito expedition may have been intended as an economical first stage of the Portuguese Crown's attempt to find a westward route to the orient, and that the stimulus came from Columbus's presentation of his project to King João II in 1484. Fernando states clearly that his father's first attempt to find backing was an approach to João, who gave it serious consideration, but was put off by the explorer's demands for reward and decided to fit out a caravel himself; Las Casas says the same.[10]

Turned down by Portugal, Columbus decided to look elsewhere. His wife had died, and he decided to present himself and his plan at the Court of Spain. To avoid loss of time in the event of a second rejection he sent his brother Bartholomew to England to try to interest Henry VII.[11] Bartholomew was a maker of charts and nautical instruments, and had been living in Lisbon. If we can accept Fernando's account (other evidence is hard to come by) Bartholomew had a stressful time: captured by pirates, robbed, ill and penniless in a foreign land, he was long unsuccessful. He was finally granted interviews with Henry, who accepted the proposal with interest, but too late. Fernando does not mention that Bartholomew also spent time in France, as later French sources state, and again documentary evidence is lacking.

Columbus himself is reputed to have been in a state of disillusion and poverty when he left Portugal, probably in the middle of 1485, and to have crossed the frontier secretly to avoid detention by the King. After the death of Felipa he chose to take his young son Diego with him rather than to leave him with his wife's family. He went first not to the Spanish Court, but to the small seaport of Palos, near Huelva, on the Atlantic coast of southern Spain. The accounts of the next seven years are conflicting and speculative; what emerges from all of them is a picture of frustration and slights, of Court bureaucracy and conservatism, support offered and withdrawn, success glimpsed but elusive.

Why he went to Palos is unclear. He may have had friends in the seafaring community; an acquaintance there, Pedro de Velasco, has already been mentioned, but most available evidence suggests that there was no substantial link between Columbus and the town. His principal reported act on arriving there was to leave young Diego with the friars of the nearby Franciscan monastery of La Rábida. Possibly he had some previous link with the monastery; certainly the Franciscans later helped him considerably in the tortuous attempts to put his case to Ferdinand and Isabella.[12]

Columbus refers more than once in the Journal to the ignorant and prejudiced opposition he faced in trying to bring his scheme to the notice of the King and Queen. Progress depended on the institutionalized *enchufe* (introductions, having access to the right ear) which is still an aspect of modern Spanish society. This foreigner of variegated background, arriving from the capital of a country which Spain had some reason to distrust, must have had a persuasive tongue and a gift for lucid exposition to win what support he did. If he chose to leave Diego at La Rábida by chance, he was fortunate in his choice. One of the friars, Fray Juan Pérez, the head of the community according to Fernando, was or had been a confessor to Queen Isabella. Neither Fernando nor Las Casas mentions Fray Juan as having any role in this part of the story, but both describe his crucial assistance at a later stage.

Another valuable friendship which possibly arose from this visit to La Rábida was with a second Franciscan, Antonio de Marchena, the *custos* or regional supervisor of the sub-province of Seville, who was something of an astronomer, and moreover had the ear of several important members of the aristocracy.

The order of events in the years 1485–92 is disputed. For Columbus himself, in his later years, the sequence of this period must have merged into a weary confusion of journeys, meetings, pleas, appointments and disappointments. Even the early historians have difficulty in unravelling things. Both Las Casas and Fernando say that Columbus went immediately from Palos to the Court of Ferdinand and Isabella in Córdoba and put his case. Las Casas gives the date of his arrival as 20 January 1485; this is the only firm date for any event from 1485–92.[13]

Yet modern research suggests that Las Casas was wrong, that Columbus did not arrive in Córdoba until January 1486, and that he was unable to approach the King and Queen until their return from the north in the spring of the year.[14] In 1485, on the advice of Fray Antonio de Marchena, he applied to a member of the high Spanish aristocracy in Seville, the Duke of Medina Sidonia.[15] Negotiations appear to have gone well initially, but to have been broken off when the Duke lost the royal favour and had to quit Seville.

Columbus's next target was the munificent Duke of Medinaceli,[16] who had shipping interests in Puerto de Santa María and received him very favourably. According to Las Casas[17] the Duke not only promised to pay all the expenses of the voyage, including the construction of three new vessels, but hearing of Columbus's poverty supported him in his day-to-day living. Unfortunately, moved by conscience, vainglory or a desire for insurance, the Duke applied to the King and Queen for their approval, and must have been mortified when Isabella expressed interest in the project but told him in flattering but unequivocal terms to look to his own affairs and leave the sponsoring of world exploration to those whose royal dignity qualified them for it. In the words of Las Casas, 'the Duke was unbelievably distressed by this, for the better he understood the project the more he wanted to go ahead with it and bring it to completion. However, being a wise man, and having no alternative, he accepted the Queen's wish, and being also a good Christian he took it to be the will of God and agreed to bear with it.'

When the Duke offered support, and even more so when Isabella expressed interest, Columbus must have thought his main difficulties were over, but there were still many hurdles in front of him. On 20

January 1486 he arrived in Córdoba, from where Ferdinand and Isabella had been conducting the campaign against the Moors of Granada, and there, in the words of his son, 'by his likeable nature and pleasant conversation won the friendship of men who became his staunchest supporters and were best placed to press his case to the King and Queen'. It may well be that his visit to La Rábida produced an introduction to these men from Fray Juan Pérez, or even that he went to the monastery deliberately to seek such an introduction in the prior knowledge of Pérez's contacts with the Court.

Both Fernando and Las Casas mention the special role of the Aragonese Secretary of the Household, Luis de Santángel; Las Casas also lists among Columbus's supporters Cardinal Pero González de Mendoza, the royal tutor Diego de Deza, later Archbishop of Seville, and Juan Cabrero, the King's Chamberlain. Las Casas mentions later letters in Columbus's own hand in which he describes Deza and Cabrero as his special supporters, but goes on to say that the greatest influence was exerted by Santángel, who had particular access to the ear of the Queen.

Ferdinand and Isabella were away from Córdoba, as we have seen, until the spring of 1486. Before then, or soon afterwards, Columbus's 'likeable nature and pleasant conversation' found another outlet and won him access to the company of Beatriz Enríquez de Harana, a girl of peasant stock whose parents were dead and who was living with relatives of modest shop-keeping status in the town. In 1488 she became the mother of the illegitimate Fernando, who turned out to be so loyal a biographer of his father and a support to his legitimate half-brother Diego in later years. The signs are that this was a love match, though Columbus never married Beatriz, probably because he thought it socially disadvantageous. The stresses of life and voyaging separated them, but she remained in Columbus's mind to the last; he took care to support her financially, and in his will he mentioned his great debt to her and his heavy conscience. He made no specific bequest to her, but asked Diego to look to her welfare. Diego, too, with the blood of Portuguese aristocrats in his veins, mentioned Beatriz in his own will.[18]

When the King and Queen returned a royal commission was set up to examine the project. The chronology of its deliberations is vague; it took its time. Fray Hernando de Talavera, Prior of the monastery of El Prado, near Valladolid, was ordered to assemble a group of 'persons whom he thought most knowledgeable in cosmography'. According to Las Casas he had problems in selecting his men, for 'the depth of ignorance surrounding the subject in Castile in those days was astonishing.'[19]

The members of the commission met many times, first in Córdoba and later in Salamanca; they adjourned many times, and went away on their own business many times, and came back, and said many things which seem laughable now. They were laughable already a few decades later, when Las Casas and Fernando wrote about them. The world was thousands of years old; if there were lands to discover someone would have done it; Ptolemy and the other wise men would have known about them. The world was too large; Seneca said that the ancients thought the Ocean Sea to be infinite and, even if navigable, empty; even if it contained islands, they could not be habitable; even if they were habitable, they could never be found. If a vessel sailed west, it could never return; the world was admittedly round, so if one sailed out of the hemisphere described by Ptolemy one would be going downhill. To return, a ship would have to sail uphill, which was impossible; 'a fine piece of deep thinking,' comments Las Casas, 'and a real sign of mastery of the subject!'[20]

Other evidence brought forward against Columbus included the opinion of the ancients that of the five zones of the world three were uninhabitable, and St Augustine's statement that the Antipodes did not exist. No one, notice, contended that the world was flat, with an edge one could sail over, but Columbus's views failed to impress; 'the more convincing his arguments, the less these ignorant men understood, for when a mathematician grows old, his established misconceptions make him incapable of grasping the truth.'[21]

This chapter of misery continued until the commission presented its report in 1490. Glimpses of Columbus's life in the meantime are scanty. He was given a modest royal retainer; treasurer's records mention payments to him in 1487, 1488 and 1489, in two cases to enable him to comply with summonses to come to the royal campaign headquarters outside besieged Andalusian cities. It is likely that he spent much of his time in Córdoba with Beatriz, his books and, from 1488 onwards, his new son Fernando. (He remembered Córdoba and the surrounding countryside with affection during the voyage. In the Journal, when he needs to convey the calmness of the sea, the balmy weather or the richness of the islands' greenery, he usually makes comparisons with Andalusia, and within it either the Guadalquivir river at Seville or the landscape around Córdoba. Despite the lasting bitterness engendered by the long struggle with his Spanish detractors, he evidently drew temporary comfort from his new homeland.)

The commission's report was predictably unenthusiastic, but Ferdinand and Isabella's response was not totally negative. Las Casas states that they suggested to Columbus that the matter might be raised again at some future date after the war with the Moors had been successfully concluded. Another reason suggested by La Casas for their muted response was the general economic situation, for 'hard times make hard hearts'. He also offers some monkish reflections on the will of God.[22]

There is no information about Columbus's movements between the submission of the report and mid-1491. He may have remained at Court awaiting the pleasure of the King and Queen, though there is no evidence that his retainer was still being paid. In the summer of 1491 he went back to Palos and La Rábida, intending to remove Diego from the monastery, take him to Córdoba (according to Fernando) or Huelva (according to Las Casas), and proceed to France to present his project there. The visit to La Rábida was a crucial point in his life, and the tide appears to have been turned by Fray Juan Pérez, to whom Columbus told his woeful tale and explained the details of the project. A local scholar and astronomer called Garci Hernández was brought into the discussions. He later testified to the court which considered the *pleitos de Colón* (the legal representations in the dispute between the Crown and the Columbus family over the legitimacy of the claims of the explorer and his successors to the rewards from the discoveries, of which more presently), and his testimony has a ring of authenticity in its description of the events which followed:

[The witness said that] the three of them talked the matter over and chose a man from here to take a letter to Queen Isabella, may she rest in holy glory, from Fray Juan Pérez, who was her confessor, and the bearer of the letter was a *piloto* from Lepe called Sebastián Rodríguez. They made Columbus stay in the monastery until Her Majesty's reply arrived and they knew the outcome, and after a fortnight the Queen wrote to Fray Juan Pérez thanking him for his good intentions and ordering him to present himself at Court before Her Majesty, and to leave Christopher Columbus with the hope of a fair outcome until Her Majesty wrote to him. Having read the contents of the letter, the friar left the monastery secretly before midnight, and in obedience to Her Majesty rode to the Court on a mule, and there were consultations about the possibility of giving Columbus three ships to enable him to sail on a voyage of discovery and make good his claims. The Queen then sent twenty thousand *maravedis*, in florins, by the hand of Diego Prieto, a citizen of this town, with a letter to the witness telling him to give them to Columbus to allow him to dress decently, buy himself a mount and go to the Court. Columbus was given the money and appeared before the Queen . . . to discuss the matter.[23]

By all accounts King Ferdinand faded into the background in the later stages of the negotiations, and Isabella's change of heart was enough to enable the revival of the scheme. When Columbus arrived at Court he again had to face interrogation by experts, but the indications are that this time he convinced them, not necessarily that he was right in his estimate of the distance to be sailed, but at least that the odds against success were sufficiently mitigated by the small scale of the proposed investment. He then lost the advantage he had gained, and was again rejected, because of the extent of his demands for personal reward. He requested not only ships, crews and stores, but also elevation to the nobility; appointment as Admiral of the Ocean Sea and as Viceroy and Governor of the lands he might discover; the right to appoint administrators and justices there; control of the selection of justices dealing with oriental trade in the ports of Spain; and a tenth of everything bought, bartered for, or produced in the area of his Admiralty. He also demanded an eighth of everything he brought home, on condition that he would pay one eighth of the expenses of the voyage. It would have been witless to make these huge demands while still seeking to convince Isabella and her experts that the project was viable. Columbus probably brought up the matter of his rewards only after his basic proposal had been accepted. He was turned away again, this time without the hope of reconsideration in the future.

He left Santa Fe for Córdoba at the beginning of January 1492, resolved once more to offer his plan to France. Again he was saved by a supporter close to Isabella. The Aragonese courtier Luis de Santángel went to the Queen on the day Columbus left, and pleaded with her to reconsider. He pointed out in eloquent terms the possible gains and the fact that, though Columbus's demands were high, they were dependent on his discovering somewhere, and whatever he might then gain would be dwarfed by the benefits to the Crown. According to both Fernando and Las Casas Isabella was moved by his appeal, so much so that she proposed to pawn her own jewels to meet the initial costs, a suggestion to which Santángel responded by offering to fulfil his desire to serve her by providing the money himself. An official was sent after Columbus, caught up with him at Puente de Pinos, only a few miles from Granada, and brought him back to the Court. In the ensuing weeks the secretary Juan de Coloma drew up the documents of the agreement, including the *capitulaciones* in which Columbus's rewards are stated, and the conditional granting of his titles. The King and Queen also gave him a general letter of introduction to foreign rulers and a passport. Decrees were issued suspending criminal proceedings against men who signed for the voyage, ordering the towns of Andalusia to afford Columbus every facility and prohibiting the taxing of provisions and stores purchased by him.[24]

There is no evidence that the Queen's grand gesture was called on, or indeed that it was necessary. The Moorish capital had fallen by now, and if Isabella ever did have the idea of pawning her jewels it is unlikely that she would continue to contemplate so theatrical a course after regaining the kingdom of Granada, with its huge potential for both plunder and revenue-raising. Columbus's own contribution to the costs of the voyage was almost certainly made with borrowed money. The total outlay was about two million *maravedis*, and Columbus had to find a quarter of a million, a fair sum. An able seaman's wages on the voyage were a thousand *maravedis* a month, a master's two thousand. Columbus had plenty of aristocratic and commercial contacts who would be interested in the investment, some dating back to his days in Genoa or as an agent in Madeira,[25] some more recent such as the Duke of Medinaceli, or Santángel. In later life he expressed a generalized goodwill towards the Bank of St George in Genoa,[26] but from considerations of time arising from his wish to sail before the end of the summer the likelihood is that he applied to Spanish sources to make up his contribution.

He left Granada on 12 May 1492 and went to Palos. He had several possible reasons for choosing Palos as his point of departure: the link with La Rábida was one; another, according to Las Casas,[27] was that he had acquaintances in the seafaring community there, though this is denied by others. The town was also handily placed for departure for the Canaries, the first stage of his planned route. However, the decisive reason was that the Crown was providing the bulk of the finance,[28] and the town of Palos, for some reason of civic debt or default, owed the Crown the services of two vessels for three months.[29]

Columbus arrived in Palos in the middle of May,[30] and sailed on 3 August – a period of say eleven weeks. This is not a long time in which to assemble, equip and crew a modest fleet. Two of the ships were to be made available by the town, but it is unlikely that they were being held idle in good trading weather in readiness for the Crown's anticipated demands, or that their sails and rigging were in a prime state to sail around the world. The third vessel, the Santa María, was the subject of a separate, commercial negotiation. It is equally unlikely that the able seamen of Palos, even those who eventually went on the voyage, were lined up on the quays awaiting employment. Some of the crew were absent when the advance pay was handed out on 23 July (see Appendix II). Columbus may have done some of the organizing from a distance before arriving in Palos in mid-May, but there is no evidence of it.

Indeed, there is evidence to the contrary, but it is tainted. In the *pleitos* (see Appendix I) some of the questions put by the Procurator Fiscal of the Crown were phrased to present a picture of Columbus arriving in Palos as a stranger, an outsider entering a tightly knit community of families and circles of friends, in which he made no headway for two frustrating months until a rich seafaring family, the Pinzóns, decided to help him with money and influence and to participate in the venture themselves. Witnesses in the *pleitos* testify that it was only through the influence of this family that men were persuaded to sign on.

The Pinzón brothers certainly were experienced sailors; that much is proved by their appointment to officers' posts in the fleet, Martín Alonso and Francisco Martín as captain and master respectively of the Pinta, and Vicente Yáñez as master of the Niña. Several witnesses testified to their wealth, especially that of Martín Alonso. Their role in recruiting crewmen is indisputable; the payroll reveals that when the advance wages were given out Martín Alonso and Vicente Yáñez received the pay of several absent sailors and stood as guarantors for others. At the time of the *pleitos*, wishing to undermine the claims of Diego Columbus, the Crown tried to build a larger role for the Pinzóns, crediting Martín Alonso not only with a literate background and a vision equal to that of Columbus, but also with having done archival research in the Pope's library and possessing ancient quasi-scriptural evidence of a western sea route to the orient. There was also an attempt to make out that Columbus had agreed to cede some of his rewards under the terms of the *capitulaciones* to Martín Alonso in return for financial and general help. Unfortunately for the Crown's credibility, the witnesses supporting its case provided mainly hearsay evidence, with the contradictions which one might expect from middle-aged or elderly men recalling events after over twenty years. The exception, verbose and suspiciously precise, is the person who stood to gain most from the success of the Crown case: Arias Pérez, the son of Martín Alonso Pinzón.

As Las Casas points out, it would have been odd if the Pinzóns had come to any kind of formal agreement about the sharing of rewards so large on the basis of a mere handshake, but there was no reference to legal documentation at the time of the *pleitos* or at any other time. Moreover Las Casas, who is admittedly heartily pro-Columbus and who criticizes Martín Alonso for his disloyalties on the voyage, points out that if an agreement had been made Pinzón's heirs would surely have brought a case against Columbus themselves. Martín Alonso died shortly after the return to Spain, but Las Casas knew Vicente Yáñez, who lived a long and creditable life afterwards and never gave any hint of such an agreement; nor did anyone else until the *pleitos* began.

Still, no doubt Columbus had his difficulties in Palos; there was probably resentment about the obligation to furnish two ships, and a distrust of this foreign incomer who appeared to be the Crown's agent in the requisition. Obviously the Crown would not allow the town to palm off a couple of decaying hulks, and the Niña, certainly, was a well found ship. Whether Columbus had to select the ships, or whether they were chosen by some internal civic debate, there was bound to be resentment in some quarters. In his early entries in the Journal he mentions difficulties with the fitting out of the ships, and

blames the Pinta's faulty rudder on disgruntled shipwrights in Palos.
We cannot tell whether the owners of the Pinta and the Niña thought
they had drawn the long or the short straw; whether Cristóbal
Quintero and Juan Niño sailed on their own vessels as enthusiastic
participants in a great enterprise, or because they thought that if the
basis of their livelihood was to sail away towards the setting sun on
this mad royal mission they might as well be aboard, where they could
at least exert some moderating influence. Columbus had differences
with Quintero in the fitting out period, and saw him as an unwilling
and even treacherous participant (see the entry for 6 August).

The Pinzóns were an experienced, prosperous family with considerable local status and power of maritime patronage; exactly the
kind of men whom anyone in Columbus's situation would approach
at the earliest opportunity if he had any sense. Columbus had plenty
of sense, and whatever the rights and wrongs of Martín Alonso's
behaviour in the Caribbean and the later claims about the inspiration
and financing of the voyage, the Pinzóns' role in the summer of 1492
was crucially helpful.[31]

Vessels Well Suited

I left the city of Granada on Saturday, 12 May 1492, and travelled to the port of Palos, where I prepared three vessels well suited for such an enterprise. I left that port, amply furnished with provisions and well crewed with seafaring men, on Friday, 3 August, sailing for Your Majesties' Canary Islands in the Ocean Sea, intending to set my course from there and to sail until I reach the Indies.

The many paintings, reconstructions and models of Columbus's ships are as speculative as the portraits of the man. There are no authentic contemporary plans or paintings of them, and neither Columbus nor anyone else goes into any detail about their size and tonnage. The bases for our speculation include the remains of mediaeval vessels revealed by archaeology; altarpieces depicting saints whose miracles or martyrdom took place in a maritime environment; manuscript miniatures, some by artists who were masters of their delicate medium but had scant knowledge of hull construction and rigging; and early woodcuts. The technical limitations of the woodcut cause the artists to simplify, so that details of rigging are often omitted. There is dispute, for example, as to whether vessels of the period had ratlines (the cross-ropes on the shrouds which provided a kind of fixed rope-ladder to allow the crew to climb the mast). They are often omitted from woodcuts, some of which nevertheless show sailors in postures which are only explicable if they had ratlines.

The models hung in churches as votive offerings are another source of information. These, though rare and usually incomplete, provide authentic constructional details. By putting all these together, with a dash of cautiously applied sixteenth-century material, one can reach reasonably firm opinions on fifteenth-century hull structure and rigging. Columbus often mentions the setting or taking in of specific sails on the Santa María and the Niña, and at one point, having told us that he set all his available canvas, gives us a list of the individual sails.

As for hull dimensions, his references to the size of his vessels are not very helpful, but our knowledge of the crew numbers and their rough disposition in the three ships assists us towards educated guesses as to their tonnage. Our wonder at the enterprise and bravery of the era increases when the probability emerges that the largest of the three was probably no bigger than a middle-sized modern fishing vessel.

Columbus's statement about the suitability of his ships was written early in the voyage, in generally favourable wind and weather, and familiar waters. He later came to dislike the most famous of them, the Santa María, for her larger size and general unhandiness, and to love the smaller but sweetly handling Niña. Some writers allude to Columbus's three caravels, failing to observe a distinction made clear by the Admiral himself between the two *carabelas*, the Pinta and the Niña, and the *nao*, which is his only way of referring to the Santa María. He never mentions her name in the Journal, obviously feeling that *la nao* is sufficient indication. (After he has transferred to the Niña he refers to her similarly as *la carabela*, rather than by her name.)

The difference between the *nao* and the *carabela* is partly of hull form and partly of rig.[1] *Nao* is a variation of *nave*, 'ship', and was probably used earlier in the Middle Ages in the same general sense of a sailing vessel larger than a boat, but in the fifteenth century it acquired the more specific meaning of a fair-sized cargo-carrying vessel of a certain shape and rig. The *nao* was constructed according to the dimensions summarized in the Spanish phrase *as, dos, tres*, 'ace, two and three'. The ace was the breadth of the vessel, the keel length was twice the breadth, and the length overall was half as much again. This produced a stout vessel of large carrying capacity, with no great pretensions to speed. Her manoeuvrability was reduced and her progress retarded by high fore- and sterncastles, which caught the wind when it was on the beam or when the ship was close-hauled, so that she was always struggling to recover the leeway, or downwind movement, which this produced.

In the late fifteenth century the tonnage of a *nao* was probably from about 100 to 600 tons. The evolution of the carrack, a generally larger vessel, is difficult to disentangle from that of the *nao*. Some writers allude to differences in stern construction as the distinguishing feature, but the factor of size and national semantic variation are possibly more important. Columbus evidently thinks of the carrack as larger than the *nao*: when he wishes to illustrate the depth of an anchorage, he tells us that a carrack could lie there; when he needs an image to show the breadth of a harbour he tells us that carracks could tack about in it. The *nao* was a vessel of intermediate size, probably fulfilling the kind of unpretentious, workaday role played by the brig and the barquentine in the nineteenth century.[2]

By the fourteenth century, from a single mast amidships, bearing a single square sail, the rig of the *nao* had been developed by the addition of a mizzenmast with a lateen yard carrying a large triangular sail. The lateen, characteristic even now of Mediterranean and Middle Eastern vessels, must have improved the ship's handling characteristics considerably. Fourteenth-century depictions also show the rudder developed into its modern form, a great advance on the earlier steering oar, and a bowsprit, employed initially as a point of rigging only. In the fifteenth century we see further additions to the *nao*: a foremast with a square foresail; a sail set under the bowsprit, which must have further improved manoeuvrability; and eventually a rudimentary topsail set above the crow's nest on the mainmast. The topsail, which began as a small triangle tapering to its foot, soon became a square sail with its bottom corners spread towards the ends of the mainyard, before finally being divided horizontally into two as one of the most useful assets of the large nineteenth-century sailing ship.

Columbus lists his full suit of sails as follows:

On the mainmast, the *papahigo* or maincourse, to the bottom of which could be laced either one or two *bonetas* or bonnets. Adding a bonnet was the old equivalent of shaking out a reef; in storm conditions one removed the bonnets to shorten sail.

On the main topmast (probably not yet a separate spar), the *gavia* or topsail.

On the foremast, the square *trinquete* or forecourse.

Below the bowsprit, the *cebadera* or spritsail. The spanish name means 'nosebag', which gives an idea of the sail's position below the bowsprit and the jut of the forecastle.

On the mizzenmast, the *mesana*, a triangular lateen sail on a sloping yard.

In favourable winds the sail of the ship's boat might also be set on the sterncastle.

The *carabela* probably evolved later than the *nao*, though its origins are obscure.[3] The earliest reliable instance of the use of the word in Spanish is a 1434 document. There is a mention in a Portuguese legal manuscript as early as 1255, but this appears to be a reference to a small fishing boat. In 1587 García de Palacio describes the *carabela* as 'a long, narrow vessel with lateen sails', a definition probably already generally applicable at the time of Columbus. The authorities vary in estimating the size, from below 50 up to 200 tons, with a range of tonnage generally smaller than that of the *nao*, but overlapping with it.

It was narrower and lighter than the *nao*, with no forecastle and normally no bowsprit. It was usually lateen-rigged, and contemporary drawings and paintings show vessels of similar hull form with one, two or three masts.

The lateen rig enabled the caravel to sail much closer to the wind than the square-rigged *nao*. A spur to the development of the caravel was the Portuguese exploration of the Atlantic coast of Africa, and at some time before Columbus the lateen rig had been replaced in some caravels by a hybrid rig with a square sail on the foremast which gave them more speed in following winds. The caravel, in fact, was a versatile vessel whose rig could be altered to meet the demands of prevailing winds and specific voyages. The Niña was lateen-rigged when she left Palos, but with the steady following weather in the northeast trade winds Columbus saw that she would be improved by a square rig, and during the delay in the Canaries while the Pinta's faulty rudder was being repaired he took advantage of the opportunity to re-rig the Niña. 'We made her *redonda*,' he wrote – literally, 'we made her round', although *redonda*, 'round', actually means 'square-rigged' in a nautical context. Since the same operation was not necessary for the Pinta, the presumption is that she was already carrying square sails when she left Palos. We see the *disadvantage* of square-rigging a caravel on the homeward journey, when the Pinta has difficulties against the head winds (though the blame for this is ascribed by Columbus partially to Pinzón's failure to replace her faulty mizzenmast in the Indies).[4]

We have no exact information on the number of masts of the two caravels; the likelihood is that the Pinta, initially, and the Niña, after re-rigging, had three masts: the mizzen carrying a lateen sail, the foremast a square sail, and the mainmast probably a square sail or possibly another, larger lateen sail. The Niña certainly had a square mainsail as well as a square foresail on the homeward journey, for in his entry for 14 February Columbus writes of sailing with only the foresail set after taking in the mainsail, and on the following day he mentions putting a bonnet on the mainsail.

It has been generally supposed that the Niña was smaller than the Pinta. Evidence for this is that she is normally listed after the Santa María and the Pinta by early historians, and that Martín Alonso Pinzón, captain of the Pinta, was senior to his brother Vicente Yáñez, who captained the Niña. Her name, which means 'little girl', has probably reinforced the idea that she was the smallest of the three vessels. The most convincing evidence is that she had the smallest crew, though the crew lists are for the start of the voyage; it is conceivable that she needed fewer crew initially because of her lateen rig, and that crew numbers were adjusted between the three vessels in the Canaries when she was converted. She is the only one of the three of which any indication of tonnage survives. Michele de Cuneo, who sailed in her on a later voyage (she was a very durable ship), said that she was around sixty tons, and she is known to have carried a cargo of fifty-one tons on a different voyage.[5]

The Niña's name is in fact irrelevant to her size, being only her nickname. Although it probably acquired an affectionate connotation, it was based on the name of the owner, Juan Niño. It was a common practice at the time for a ship to have two names, her 'registry' name, often that of a saint, and a nickname. The Garza, 'Heron', was named after her owner and master Francisco García; the Gorda, 'Fat Woman', after her owner Andrés Martín de la Gorda; and the Bachillera, 'Blue stocking', after her owner Gonzalo Bachiller.[6] The Niña's 'registry' name was Santa Clara, after the local patron of sailors, Santa Clara de Moguer, to whom her crew vowed a pilgrimage during the worst storm of the voyage.

Pinta, too, rings like a nickname. It is a feminine adjective meaning 'spotted' or 'piebald', but she may well have been owned previously by the Pinto family of Palos, although her owner at the time of the voyage was Cristóbal Quintero. We do not know her official name. The Santa María was officially so named after being chosen for the voyage; she had previously been known as the Gallega, 'Galician'.[7] This has given rise to the natural conclusion that she was built in Galicia, in northwestern Spain; Galicians, in particular, like this idea. It is quite possible, however, that she had been owned by a family called Gallego, which is a common enough surname in mediaeval Spain; there is a Rodrigo Gallego in her crew list. At the time of chartering she was owned by Juan de la Cosa, who sailed on her as second in command. Her old nickname probably continued to be used during the voyage, since the Basque contingent aboard her had probably been part of her former crew.

Running free in the trade winds on the outward voyage, the Santa María presented no handling problems, though even then Columbus mentions the superior speed of the smaller caravels. Her unsuitability for the voyage was brought home to him as soon as he began the exploration of the islands. The larger vessel, with her deeper draught and generally heavier handling, was less suited than the caravels to picking her way through waters full of reefs and shoals, and the caravels, with their simpler sail plan and ability to sail closer to the wind, were much better able to cope with the many changes of wind and course involved in probing the coasts and inlets of the uncharted islands. Columbus criticizes Martín Alonso for his greed and insubordination in going off on his own in the Pinta, but a contributory factor may well have been Pinzón's exasperation at constantly having to shorten sail or heave-to to enable the Santa María to catch up with the sprightlier caravels.

Columbus does complain about the deficiencies of the flagship, blaming the town of Palos for supplying an unsuitable vessel, but the criticism comes late in the voyage, after she has grounded and been lost through negligence for which the ultimate responsibility was his own. There is no way of knowing if a smaller vessel would have cleared the bank on which she grounded, but her loss had nothing to do with her handling qualities. The very fact that the helm had been handed over to one of the apprentice seamen suggests that she was a kindly enough vessel. When Columbus set sail from Palos, hoping to return laden with the rich offerings of the east, he was probably happy enough to have the broader hold of the Santa María beneath his feet, and to have his superior position as Admiral in command of the Pinzón brothers confirmed by the dignity of the largest vessel.

The contrasting qualities of the three ships provided as good a little fleet as one might hope for to meet the demands of a voyage combining a long ocean passage with island exploration. One can suggest ways in which they could have been deployed more flexibly after the arrival in the Indies, perhaps using the Santa María as a base vessel and repository for stores, trading goods and things acquired, and the nimbler caravels, with their smaller draught, for exploring the coasts and harbours. Columbus's ability to reorganize on this basis was constrained by growing mistrust, the position of the Pinzóns as captains of vessels crewed largely by their fellow townsmen, and by the simple need for a small body of men in alien surroundings to stick together. His complaints about the Santa María ring very much like an attempt to shift some of the blame for her loss.

The crew list for the expedition has been compiled from an incomplete payroll, supplemented from allusions to individuals in the Journal and other documentary sources. The most important of these are the records of the *pleitos*; the witnesses include members of the crews, who sometimes mention shipmates in their testimonies (see Appendix I). Both Fernando Columbus and Las Casas say that the fleet had ninety men. Modern research, especially that of Alice Gould in the 1920s and 30s,[8] suggests that the eighty-seven who have been identified were distributed, at least on departure, as follows:

Santa María

Admiral:	Christopher Columbus
Master:	Juan de la Cosa (owner)
Piloto:	Peralonso Niño
Marshal:	Diego de Arana (or Harana)
Secretary:	Rodrigo de Escobedo

Purser:	Rodrigo Sánchez de Segovia
Surgeon:	*Maestre* Juan Sánchez
Boatswain:	Chachu
Boatswain's mate:	Domingo de Lequeitio
Carpenter:	Antonio de Cuéllar
Able seamen:	Domingo Vizcaíno (cooper)
	Lope (caulker)
	Juan de Medina (tailor)
	Diego Pérez (painter)
	Alonso Clavijo
	Gonzalo Franco
	Pedro Izquierdo de Lepe
	Juan de Jerez
	Rodrigo de Jerez
	Juan Martínez de Azoque
	Juan de Moguer
	Juan de la Plaza
	Juan Ruiz de la Peña
	Bartolomé de Torres
	Luis de Torres (interpreter)
	Bartolomé Vives
Grumetes:	Cristóbal Caro (silversmith)
	Diego Bermúdez
	Alonso Chocero
	Rodrigo Gallego
	Diego Leal
	Pedro de Lepe
	Jacomo el Rico (Genoese)
	Martín de Urtubia
	Andrés de Yevenes
	Juan
Admiral's steward:	Pedro de Terreros
Admiral's page:	Pedro de Salcedo
Royal observer:	Pedro Gutiérrez, Butler of the King's Table

Pinta

Captain:	Martín Alonso Pinzón
Master:	Francisco Martín Pinzón
Piloto:	Cristóbal García Sarmiento
Marshal:	Juan Reynal
Surgeon:	*Maestre* Diego
Boatswain:	Juan Quintero de Algruta

Able seamen:	Antón Calabrés
	Francisco García Vallejo
	Alvaro Pérez
	Gil Pérez
	Diego Martín Pinzón
	Cristóbal Quintero (owner)
	Sancho de Rama
	Gómez Rascón
	Juan Rodríguez Bermejo
	(possibly also called Rodrigo de Triana)
	Juan Verde de Triana
	Juan Vezano
Grumetes:	Pedro de Arcos
	Juan Arias
	Juan Cuadrado
	Fernando Medel
	Francisco Medel
	Alonso de Palos
	Pedro Tegero
Steward:	García Fernández
Captain's page:	Bernal

Niña

Captain:	Vicente Yáñez Pinzón
Master:	Juan Niño (owner)
Piloto:	Sancho Ruiz de Gama
Marshal:	Diego Lorenzo
Surgeon:	*Maestre* Alonso
Boatswain:	Bartolomé García
Carpenter:	Alonso de Morales
Able seamen:	Juan Arraez
	Pedro Arraez
	Ruy García
	Rodrigo Monge
	Bartolomé Roldán
	Juan Romero
	Pedro Sánchez de Montilla
	Pedro de Villa

Grumetes:	García Alonso
	Andrés de Huelva
	Francisco de Huelva
	Francisco Niño
	Pedro de Soria
	Fernando de Triana
Captain's page:	Miguel de Soria

The word *grumete* is sometimes translated as 'ship's boy', but 'apprentice seaman' is probably nearer the mark. The proportion of able seamen to *grumetes* conforms closely, and in the Santa María's case exactly, to that recommended by García de Palacio in his sixteenth-century *Instrucción náutica*.[9] He recommends a greater number of pages, however, equal to one-tenth of the number of the seamen, in addition to those serving the officers. 'Page' suggests duties rather grander than those specified by García de Palacio: 'Leaving aside those pages who serve the captain, master and *piloto* aft, who do whatever they are ordered, the others sweep the ship, set the table, serve the meals . . . make spunyarn . . . say the service at nightfall and give the morning greeting, and perform other manual work, to leave the seamen and *grumetes* free to concentrate on working the ship.'[10]

Apart from the odd foreigner (Juan Arias, from Tavira in Portugal; one Genoese; perhaps a Calabrian, Antón Calabrés; just possibly a Venetian, Juan Vezano), the crews were Spanish. Most were Andalusians, some from inland towns some distance away, such as Jerez, Montilla and Seville, but many from Palos or nearby places such as Huelva, Moguer and Lepe. There was a group of northerners, and specifically Basques, who had probably been part of the Santa María's crew when she arrived in Palos, but a high proportion of the rest had probably been known to each other as shipmates or neighbours for a long time. Close relatives among the seamen were not split up: the two Medel brothers both sailed on the Pinta, as did Gil Pérez and his nephew Alvaro, and the two Quinteros; Juan Arraez went with his father on the Niña.

At least one group of friends stuck together. Bartolomé de Torres, in gaol for murder, had been rescued by his friends Alonso Clavijo, Pedro Izquierdo and Juan de Moguer. They were all pardoned under the terms of the Crown amnesty offered to anyone who signed on for the voyage, and all sailed together on the Santa María. They must have been old shipmates; all four were paid as able seamen, and at least two of them sailed on one of Columbus's later voyages.[11]

At officer level, however, families were divided. In the great storm which separated the two caravels for good on the homeward passage, when the lanterns which were the last link between them had flickered and vanished in the howling night, only the Pinzóns had their own fear worsened by ignorance of the fate of a brother. Even in the euphoria which followed the Niña's safe arrival in the Tagus, Vicente Yáñez's heart must have been heavy after watching the Pinta vanish with not only his two brothers but an older cousin, Diego Martín Pinzón, aboard. The Niño brothers were split up initially, Peralonso as *piloto* of the Santa María and his brothers sailing on the Niña, Juan as master and Francisco as *grumete*, but after the loss of the flagship Peralonso transferred, with Columbus, to the Niña.[12]

Those were the close relationships, but there may well have been cousins, brothers-in-law, and so on, especially among the men recruited in Palos with the help of the Pinzóns and the Niños. Pedro de Arcos, acting as a witness in the *pleitos*, said that 'Martín Alonso determined to go . . . and he took many relatives with him, for this witness saw them go.'[13]

Considering the small dimensions of the vessels, and their simple rigs, one is struck by the size of the crews. The Santa María set five sails as a maximum; the Pinta probably only three; the Niña three, and originally possibly only two. A large Indian Ocean dhow for long-distance passages in the twentieth century, with a size and rig something like the Niña's, carries about a dozen men, sometimes fewer.[14] A mid-nineteenth-century three-masted sailing ship, before the invention of donkey engines and brace winches, carried a crew of only about fifty, in times of cheap labour, to handle her two dozen sails. The Challenge, completed in New York in 1851, the largest clipper ship built up to that date, had a mainmast 230 feet high and would have dwarfed the Santa María if set alongside her. She had fifty-six seamen and eight boys when she sailed on her maiden voyage.[15]

The largest full-rigged sailing vessel ever built, the Preussen, 433 feet long, had five masts over 200 feet high, and a full spread of canvas totalling some 60,000 square feet, divided into over forty-five sails. Always hard driven, she sailed repeatedly from Hamburg around Cape Horn to Iquique in the early years of this century, returning with 8,000 tons of nitrate. In the most demanding waters on earth, she needed a full complement of only forty-seven officers and men. Her sister ship, the slightly smaller Potosí, had only twenty able seamen and a total complement of forty-one.[16] The Pinta or the Niña could have sheltered from the rain under the Preussen's or Potosí's mainsail, yet they had crews of at least twenty-six and twenty-two.

Even allowing for division into watches, the crewing of Columbus's expedition seems generous. It may have been an insurance against sickness or disaster. The Admiral comments on the good health of the crew in the Indies, which may indicate that losses due to sickness were normally to be expected. When he has to work the ship with only half a crew, however, after the rest have been detained in the Azores by the Portuguese, he complains that he has only three men left who know anything about sailing. This may indicate that, despite his initial blithe statement on leaving Palos that his ships are crewed by experienced seafarers, some of the men were enlisted with a view to other purposes such as defence or, eventually, portering and labouring, and were listed as *grumetes* because they were on the same wages as the apprentice seamen.

There are other puzzles; he mentions leaving behind in the fort of Navidad with the men who formed the first settlement[17] a lombardier cum engineer, but no such function is mentioned in the crew list. Were the seamen who are listed as having another trade such as tailor, painter or cooper really sailors at all, or simply landsmen on able seamen's pay rates? It seems likely, certainly, that the *grumete* Cristóbal Caro, a silversmith, was enlisted specially for his skills in assessing and working the precious metals which Columbus expected to find, and that he was rated with the apprentice seamen for purposes of pay.

In his *Instrucción náutica* García de Palacio stipulates that a ship of five hundred to seven hundred tons needs fifty able seamen, one of three to five hundred needs thirty-five, and one of one to three hundred needs twenty (these figures do not include the *grumetes*, who should number two-thirds of the figure for the able seamen). By these standards, Columbus's vessels were not over-crewed, although by García de Palacio's time rigging had grown somewhat more complex. In the payroll for the fourth voyage, in 1502, a greater range of specific trades is mentioned: as well as the able seamen and *grumetes* Columbus's flagship had a lombardier, two trumpeters and four *escuderos* (roughly equivalent to marines), all paid the same wages as the able seamen; a caulker, paid 50 per cent more; and a carpenter, whose pay was in between the two rates.[18]

The three surgeons named in the crew lists, unlike those of modern naval vessels, were not really of officer status. They had an easy time of it during the voyage, if we can take literally Columbus's statement that no member of the crews suffered a day's illness except one old man with the stone. Unfortunately only two of them came home, and *maestre* Juan Sánchez, who was left in the Indies, may well have had to perform some stern work with small resources before he, like the rest of the tiny garrison, succumbed to the clubs and arrows of the Indians.

To understand the responsibilities of the various officers we may turn again to García de Palacio. The *Instrucción náutica* was written when the demands of long ocean voyages had brought about a few technical advances. However, the author's detailed definitions of the roles of the various officers not only have every appearance of being rooted in tradition, but also reproduce the terminology of rank used by Columbus, and are probably valid for the period of the voyage.

For us, 'master' and 'captain' are synonymous. The Pinzón brothers, Martín Alonso and Vicente Yáñez, are captains, *capitanes*, of the Pinta and the Niña respectively. Yet each ship also has a master, *maestro*: Juan Niño, the Niña's owner, is her master, and the third Pinzón brother, Francisco Martín, is master of the Pinta, despite the presence on board of the ship's owner, Cristóbal Quintero. The Santa María has no captain, since Columbus, as Admiral, exercises the duties of captain, but she too has a master, Juan de la Cosa, who is also her owner. García de Palacio makes a clear distinction between the captain and the master, describing their roles in different chapters.

He describes the captain in rather vague terms, stressing the importance of moral and religious leadership, the management of men and the fair dispensing of justice and punishment. His most specific statement concerning the captain, that he should leave all navigational matters to subordinates, is not in accord with Columbus's own practice. The master, according to García de Palacio, should be able in business and knowledgeable about goods, take responsibility for the stowing and unloading of cargo and the purchase of stores, and keep good accounts. He should also be an experienced seafarer, a qualification apparently not essential in a captain.

Each vessel also carries a *piloto*; not a pilot, in the modern sense, but a watch-keeping officer with special responsibility for navigation, attached to a single ship. In modern Spanish, *piloto* can mean 'mate'. García de Palacio places this officer third in the hierarchy of command, but he goes into much more detail on his role, stressing the importance of a craft on which the whole enterprise and safety of the vessel depend, and criticizing the low standards of some navigators. He includes in the list of the *piloto*'s necessities a chart, dividers, a twelve-pound astrolabe, a wooden quadrant, compasses, Venetian hourglasses, a lantern with cotton wicks, and a 100-fathom lead line.

Ideally the *piloto* should know astronomy, mathematics and cosmography, but failing this he must certainly be able to take sights with the astrolabe and quadrant. He should know about tides and the phases of the moon, be skilled in taking soundings, be experienced in the use of charts, and so on. Despite the specialized nature of the art, García de Palacio recommends that the *piloto* seek the opinions of his master and captain (so contradicting what he has written earlier) and even of the senior seamen. A mid-sixteenth-century passenger describes this consultational method of navigation with the distressed incredulity of a landsman used to signposts, milestones, a solid road under his feet and an inn around the bend:

What a display of God's omnipotence, to place this subtle and crucial art of seafaring in the clumsy brains and hands of these navigators! You should see them consulting each other: 'How many degrees do you make it?' 'Sixteen,' says one. 'Thirteen and a half,' says another. Then, 'How far do you make it to land?' 'Forty leagues,' says one. 'A hundred and fifty,' says another. 'I made it ninety-two this morning,' says a third. If they were three or three hundred, no two of them would agree with each other.[19]

This consensus policy was apparently normal on Columbus's ships. As well as navigating himself, the Admiral often mentions consultations with the *pilotos*, and evidently the more experienced seamen were allowed to contribute to these. Bartolomé Roldán, in particular, though a mere able seaman on the Niña, marked off the course on his own chart, and Columbus gives Roldán's reckoning equal importance with those of his superiors.

A major puzzle is how Columbus could expect to deceive such an experienced and able group of mariners about the daily distance run by the ships. That he did so at least partially is evident from his accounts of the different conclusions about the ships' position reached by the various navigators, and his statement that the discrepancy was due to his practice of giving them a reduced figure for the daily run in order to avoid discontent among the crews about their distance from home. It is not as if he alone were in possession of a mechanical device for recording speed; the ship's log had not yet been invented, and assessing speed was a matter of 'feel' and perhaps observing the rate at which the ship passed a piece of timber thrown from the bows. Columbus had great experience, but then so had the Pinzóns and Juan de la Cosa, and some of the senior seamen had probably been at sea longer than any of the officers. It is hard to believe that none of them smelled a rat; if they did, Columbus's attempt to reassure by deception was probably self-defeating, contributing to the mutinous feelings and to the evident alienation of the Pinzóns.

Shipboard Life and Sailing

Despite their low status and wages, the pages mentioned in the previous chapter played a crucial part in the most fundamental aspect of the ship's routine and progress: timekeeping. In a Spanish vessel the day began with a page's voice chanting a conventional rhymed benediction:

Bendita sea la luz	Blessed be the light
y la Santa Cruz;	and the Holy Cross;
y el Señor de la Verdad	Blessed be the Lord of Truth
y la Santa Trinidad;	and the Holy Trinity;
Bendita sea el alma	Blessed be the soul
y el Señor que nos la manda;	and the Lord who tends it;
Bendito sea el día	Blessed be this day,
y el Señor que nos la envía.	and the Lord who sends it.

These are the lines which woke Eugenio de Salazar, who wrote a pained but witty description of life as a passenger on a vessel sailing from Tenerife to Hispaniola in the middle of the sixteenth century.[1] They set the tone for a routine pervaded by naïve religious observance, and were followed by the Lord's Prayer, the *Ave Maria* and a more specifically nautical blessing: 'May God give us a fair day and a good voyage; may the vessel make a swift passage, with her captain, master and fine ship's company. God give her a good voyage, and God give you a good day, gentlemen, from stem to stern.'

The pages not only got the daily routine underway at the change of the watch; they were responsible for turning the *ampolletas*, the sandglasses which were the principal means of timekeeping, and on cloudy days and nights, the only means. The sand ran for half an hour;

eight glasses made up a four-hour watch. The glass was also a basic tool of the navigator; Columbus refers repeatedly to the distance run in a specific number of glasses, or the number of glasses throughout which the ship maintained a particular speed.

At nightfall a page was the protagonist in another little piece of religious theatre: bringing the light to the compass binnacle, he chanted: 'Amen, and God give us a fair night. May the ship make a swift passage and a good voyage, captain and master and good ship's company.' In Salazar's ship two pages then recited the Lord's Prayer, the *Ave Maria*, the Creed and the *Salve Regina*, and went off to watch the sandglass through the dark hours, starting the night with yet another blessing:

Bendita la hora en que Dios nació,	Blessed be the hour of God's birth.
Santa María que le parió,	Blessed be the Virgin who bore him.
San Juan que le bautizó.	Blessed be St John who baptized him.
La guarda es tomada;	The watch is changed;
la ampolleta muele.	The glass is running.
Buen viaje haremos	We will have a fair voyage
si Dios quisiere.	By the grace of God.

The nightfall ceremony may have been less elaborate than this on Columbus's ships, but it certainly took place. He calls it simply the *Salve* ('which all sailors sing or say'). It may therefore have consisted solely of the *Salve Regina*, although the single word may have come to embrace the whole, extended ceremony. Practice probably varied from ship to ship, depending on the piety of the captain, and from day to day, depending on the weather. Salazar describes a much more elaborate service, with a sung litany, an altar, candles and images, conducted by the master every Saturday evening, with the pages acting as altar boys.

In a small vessel one had to be a sound sleeper; as well as the absence of anything approximating to a bed, the off-duty watch had to contend with another ditty from the page every half-hour. The main aim of this was to check that the for'ard lookout was awake. When the first glass ran out, for instance, the page sang out:

Buena es la que va,	A good one gone,
mejor es la que viene;	a better to come;
una es pasada	The first is over,
y en dos muele.	the second to run.
Más molerá,	More to follow
si Dios quisiere.	if God is willing.
Cuenta y pasa,	It counts and it's done;
que buen viaje faza.	may she make a good run.
Ah de proa, alerta,	Bows, there! Wide awake!
buena guardia!	Keep your eyes peeled!

At midnight the page had to wake the new watch, shouting 'Watch! Watch! You gentlemen sailors of the *piloto's* watch; now is the time; rouse yourselves, rouse!'

Being woken at midnight was only one source of distress for Eugenio de Salazar, whose letter depicts the Atlantic crossing as multifaceted and rarely abating misery: seasickness; the monotony of empty horizons; the discomfort of confined quarters; the stench of vomit and bilge water; the incessant noise of the pumps; cockroaches like flocks of poultry; mice as big as wild boar; lice which vomited undigested lumps of cabin boy; the ship black on the outside and blacker within; dirt on every surface; black walls, black decks, unwashed officers and filthy crew.

The food is another target of his complaints: dirty tablecloths, on which the pages piled heaps of broken biscuit 'so white and clean that cloth and biscuit together look like a wheatfield with piles of dung on it'; boiled ox bones with a few shreds of meat adhering; on Fridays and feast days, boiled beans; bad water, doled out by the ounce, like medicine. There is another piece of polite ceremonial from the pages:

Tabla, tabla,	Table, table,
señor capitán y maestre	captain, master
y buena compaña.	and good men of the crew.
Tabla puesta,	Table is set;
vianda presta.	food is ready.
. . . Viva, viva	Long life and health
el Rey de Castilla!	to the King of Spain!
Por mar y por tierra,	On land and sea,
quien le diere guerra	whoever fights him,
que le corten la cabeza!	may he lose his head!
Quien no dijere Amén,	If you won't say Amen,
que no le den a beber.	you'll go without drink.
Tabla en buena hora;	Welcome to table;
quien no viniere que no coma.	Come, or do without.

Then the crew fell on the food like dogs, with farting, belching and puking on all sides. For the relief of the bowels there was a seat suspended over the side of a lurching ship. Sailing, concludes Salazar, is as evil a necessity as women. The land was made for men; the sea for the fish.

It is to be hoped that the provisioning of Columbus's ships approached the more liberal scale proposed by García de Palacio:

A master should provide stores of food in excess of what is normally necessary for the voyage facing him, but if we must specify exact quantities he should provide one and two-thirds pounds of bread, three-quarters of a litre of wine, and a litre of water per person per day. For every thirty men there should be half a bushel of chickpeas or beans. As for meat, fish, oil, vinegar and other items, the more and the higher the quality the better, for if a master treats his crew well they will be strong, fit and merry, and will take pains to respond with due service and hard work.[2]

Salazar was travelling on a fair-sized, passenger-carrying vessel. The amenities must have been even fewer on Columbus's little ships. Apart from some minimal privacy enjoyed by the officers, the ships' companies must have had a comfortless, cheek-by-jowl existence in which discontent and distrust arose and simmered easily, and which made the scent of land, the spacious woods and the water and fresh food of the Indies seem even more delicious.

Salazar's misgivings about the efficiency of navigators would have found little relief if he had sailed with Columbus. The Admiral's technical aids were few, and the most sophisticated among them turned out to be largely useless and in one or two cases grossly misleading. Fifteenth-century sailors had at their disposal charts of varying reliability, necessarily speculative in their representation of distant waters; the sandglass for time-keeping, subject to inaccuracies due to careless or dozing pages who missed the moment at which it ran out; the mariner's compass, though precise details of the relationship between the needle, true north, magnetic north and the Pole Star were beyond the average navigator; some knowledge of the celestial bodies, especially of the stars known as the Guards and their rotation around the Pole Star; and two instruments capable of taking an accurate reading of the altitude of a star or the sun: the quadrant, usually of wood, and the heavy brass astrolabe.

Columbus probably had reasonably reliable small-scale charts of the coasts of the Iberian peninsula, the Canaries and the Azores. He and his brother Bartholomew had probably produced and sold such charts themselves. We know that he had a speculative chart extending into the west Atlantic, possibly that supplied by Toscanelli, or based on it, and possibly reaching as far as Japan and the Chinese mainland. A fifteenth-century chart was a picturesque affair, often including not only depictions of vessels in full sail, sea monsters and distant potentates, but also, more practically, finely executed wind roses similar to modern compass cards. From the points of these emerged rhumb lines, so that the chart was criss-crossed by a network of lines representing the basic range of courses, or compass bearings, and making it simple to work out the course from one known point to another.

The quadrant and astrolabe were both used for finding latitude by measuring the elevation of the sun or the Pole Star above the horizon. If the Pole Star was used the procedure was simple; if the sun, being apparently mobile, was used a mathematical formula was involved.

Introduction

The quadrant was a primitive device in the form of a quarter-circle with two sights along one of the straight edges, a weighted cord suspended from the right angle and a graduated scale of degrees around the arc. The navigator aligned the sights on the celestial body, nipped the cord against the face of the scale and read off the number of degrees, or, in early examples, the name of a port on a specific latitude.

The astrolabe was a heavy brass dial hanging from a metal ring. It had a scale of degrees near its circumference, and an arm with a sight-hole at each end was pivoted in the centre of the face. One aligned the two holes on the star or the sun, either by looking through them or by letting the sunlight pass through the upper hole and adjusting the arm so that the beam continued through the lower one, and read off the degrees indicated by a pointer on the arm. Both instruments were easy to use on *terra firma*, but on a heaving deck it was difficult to take a reliable reading with either, and both needed a clear sky.

That unhappy voyager, Eugenio de Salazar, gives a disturbing description of the difficulties undergone by the navigators to whom he has entrusted his life and family:

You should see the *piloto* . . . taking up his astrolabe at midday, looking up at the sun and trying to make it shine through the holes in his instrument, and failing, and trying to adjust it. He finally pronounces judgement on the altitude of the sun; sometimes he has it 1,000 degrees too high, sometimes he is so far below it that it would take him 1,000 years to reach it. The most tiresome thing was their secrecy with the passengers about the readings and about the distance run by the ship, though later I understood the reason: they know that they never get it right. I kept my patience, for I realized they did well not to display the results of their inaccuracy; they take the altitude with a degree of give and take, and the width of a pinhead on their instrument will put you 500 miles out in your reckoning.[3]

Columbus has no great skill with either of these instruments. He produces some wildly erroneous readings of latitude, sometimes acknowledging their improbability, and finally says that he is hanging up his quadrant until he reaches port again and can have it seen to. It is difficult to see what could go amiss with a quadrant, other than a broken cord; if it was made right it stayed right. It is hard to believe that such an experienced sailor could have taken a sight on the wrong star, but this seems to be the only possible explanation of his reading on 21 November. His sighting of the star gave a latitude of 42°N, which, as Las Casas points out, would suggest that the ships were in the latitude of the Florida coast.

In Columbus's day a knowledge of astronomy was useful for more than direction-finding and calculation of latitude. At night, given a clear sky, one could tell the time by the position of the stars known as the Guards in their anti-clockwise rotation around the Pole Star. This position is expressed in terms of an imaginary human figure with the Pole Star at his navel and his forearms extended sideways, giving four positions, and diagonal lines giving four intermediate positions. The Guards could be, for instance, at the arm on the west, or at the foot, or at the line below the arm on the east. Each eighth of a circle represented three hours. The Journal entry for 30 September reads: 'At nightfall the stars called the Guards are close to the arm on the west side, and at dawn they are on the line below the northeastern arm, so it appears that in the whole night they move only three lines, or nine hours. This is so every night.'

Longitude was calculated by dead reckoning, which accounts for the discrepancies between the positions calculated by the different navigators. Dead reckoning involves putting together the figures for the known course or courses and estimated speed or speeds over a given period of time, and so working out a position in relation to the previous point calculated and pricked off on the chart. *Hacer punto*, 'making a point', is Columbus's phrase. On a long voyage the possibility for cumulative error on the part of a man not skilled in estimating speed and leeway was considerable, even when his superior was not deliberately supplying false information. Unknown currents in strange waters were another factor contributing to inaccurate reckonings. All in all, the lookout in the bows and the page who kept him awake bore a heavy weight of responsibility, even when the landfall sought was on a familiar coast.

On days when he made many changes of course Columbus may well have simplified his calculations by using an old device called a traverse board, which had a face like a wind rose with lines of holes radiating along each point. A peg was put in the relevant point with each turn of the sandglass, and at the end of the day, by relating the ship's speed and the number and distribution of the pegs to a table, one achieved a new reading of miles of latitude and longitude which enabled one to mark a new position on the chart.

Columbus gives distances in *millas* and *leguas*, miles and leagues, and speeds in miles per hour. It has generally been supposed that for him *milla* means the old Roman mile of 4,850 feet, 4 such miles making up a league. A modern nautical mile is 6,080 feet, and there is no such thing as a modern league. On this basis Columbus's league equals 3.18 nautical miles. In my translation I have converted his distances in *millas* to nautical miles, expressed leagues as equal to 3 nautical miles, rounding off to the nearest quarter or third, and given speeds in knots to avoid the landlubberly 'miles per hour'. A knot is a unit of speed, not distance; a vessel sailing at 5 knots runs 5 nautical miles in one hour.

It has lately been argued[4] that Columbus's mile was equal to only about five-sixths of the Roman mile, and that his league was therefore a shorter one than that used by Iberian sailors. This, it is claimed, explains the two different figures given by Columbus for each day's run, the higher being his own, the lower being a conversion to the Spanish measure for the mainly Spanish crew, and not, as has generally been supposed, a false figure given to the crew to assuage discontent. I find this unconvincing; Columbus's seafaring had been largely in Portuguese vessels, and it is hard to see why he should use Italian units in a Spanish ship and in an account written explicitly for the information of the Spanish Crown. A strong counter-argument is the simple fact that the reduction is not always in the same ratio: fourteen leagues reduced to eleven; fourteen reduced to thirteen; twenty-four reduced to twenty-one; twenty-five reduced to twenty; thirty-nine reduced to thirty; forty reduced to thirty-three; forty-seven reduced to forty; fifty-nine reduced to forty-four. These do not seem to be mathematically calculated conversions, but rather figures which Columbus thought he could get away with. Both Las Casas and Fernando state clearly that Columbus used the double reckoning as a way of maintaining the morale of the crew.

The ships achieved highly creditable speeds in favourable conditions, the Pinta and the Niña being faster and handier than the Santa María. Vessels of the period could run cheerfully at six to eight knots, and on occasion at much higher speeds. Pedro de Medina wrote in 1545 that the maximum speed of a sailing vessel was four leagues an hour, by which he probably meant twelve knots, and that two leagues an hour (six knots) was normal. Columbus's entries for the first week in October record some outstanding sailing, including a full day's run at an average of almost eight knots, and speeds of almost twelve knots at times during the night of 8 October. This last figure caused Las Casas to question the handwriting. Such a speed was rare even among the much more highly developed sailing ships of the nineteenth century, except in the tea and wool clippers and the great American vessels built for the San Francisco trade, whose design deliberately sacrificed carrying capacity for speed, and the fastest of which were liberally crewed to take advantage of their huge sail areas.

Columbus chose to set sail west from the Canaries, but to return by a more northerly course. It is unlikely that this was a fortuitous decision; it was certainly the right one. His reasons for going via the Canaries may have included a wish to water and victual his ships at the last possible moment before leaving the known world, and a prudent thought for the possible need to set right unforeseen problems such as the Pinta's faulty rudder, but his main reason was probably his awareness of the prevailing winds. His voyages in the Guinea, Madeira and Iceland trades, and his conversations with the seafaring men of the Azores and the Canaries, had clarified the basic factors in northern hemisphere sailing: the steady northeast trade winds which would take him westward from the latitude of the Canaries, and the stormier but generally reliable westerlies of the north Atlantic for his passage home.

Restoring and
Translating the Journal

The shipboard Journal written by Christopher Columbus has long been
lost. Parts of it, however, have survived, in Bartolomé de las Casas's
early sixteenth-century copy of the original.[1] Las Casas made rather a
mess of it. Normally a polished if rather orotund writer, he turned the
Journal into a syntactical hotch-potch, and it is unlikely that he thought
of his version as a finished piece of work. Long passages, including the
Prologue, the entries from 11–24 October, and considerable parts of
other entries, reproduce Columbus's original prose verbatim and
probably without substantial omissions. Elsewhere Las Casas alters
Columbus's first-person entries ('We sailed . . . I reckoned . . .') to
third-person narrative ('They sailed . . . He reckoned . . .').

Las Casas probably looked on his version of the Journal as a
working document to help him in the composition of his *Historia de las
Indias*. He was following a practice hallowed by time in mediaeval
Spanish historiography, which habitually incorporated textual
material, often originally from popular sources, in a way intended to
imply omniscience while masking the fact that the historian was
making life easy for himself. The result in the case of the Journal is a
most uneasy amalgam, which has nevertheless been accepted as the
best material available and translated straightforwardly by the authors
of previous versions in English. The present translation is an attempt
to come closer to the content of Columbus's original.

The variation from first-person to third-person narrative is a jarring
technique in itself, but the situation is not simply that some entries are
in one and some in the other; the switch of mode often occurs within
an entry, sometimes even within a sentence. Consider the following
examples, literal translations from the Las Casas text:

The Admiral [i.e., Columbus] did not want to leave the river. Instead he gave orders to row to where the Indians were and there were many of them all dyed red and naked as they were born and some had plumes on their head and others feathers. They all had handfuls of assegais. I [i.e., Columbus] approached them and gave them a few mouthfuls of bread and I asked them for the assegais in exchange for a hawk bell or a little brass ring. (3 December)

All this the Admiral understood with difficulty, but he was still sure that there was a great quantity of it in those parts, and that if he could find the source there was a great deal of it to be obtained and as he imagined for almost nothing. And he says again that there must be a lot, for in the three days that he had been in that harbour he had had good pieces of gold and he cannot believe that they bring it there from another land. May Our Lord in whose hands are all things see fit to guide me and give me whatever may serve Him. (23 December)

It is evident that Las Casas's procedure, in some entries at least, involved little more than changing the verbs and pronouns to produce a third-person narrative. Sometimes it is almost as if we are looking over his shoulder: he copies a verb in the present tense, realizes his mistake, crosses it out, and rewrites it in the past tense. Sometimes his lapse is more prolonged and he simply goes on copying the first-person original verbatim, then becomes aware of the lapse and tries to retrieve the syntactical situation with an interpolation:

And he says that he hopes in God that when he returns, as he intends [altered to 'intended'] from Spain he will [altered to 'he would'] find a barrel of gold which those he was going to leave behind would have obtained and they would have found the gold mine and the spices and everything in such quantity that the King and Queen within three years would undertake and organize themselves to go to conquer the Holy Sepulchre, for so (he says) I requested Your Majesties that all the wealth gained in this my enterprise should be spent on the conquest of Jerusalem and Your Majesties laughed and said that you agreed and that such was your intention in any case. These are the Admiral's words. (26 December)

He said that on the previous Sunday, 11 November, he had thought it a good idea to seize some of the people from that river to take to the King and Queen, so that they might learn our language and tell us about their land and so that on their return they may be interpreters for the Christians and may adopt our customs and the matters of the Faith, for I saw and recognize (says the Admiral) that these people have no religion. (12 November)

The impression that Las Casas is following Columbus's original closely, altering syntax rather than abbreviating, is reinforced by his frequent interpolation of *dize*, 'he says', in passages such as the following (notice again the anarchy of tense and the failure to alter *ayer*, 'yesterday'):

He sailed three hours before dawn from the bay called the Golfo de las Flechas with a land breeze, then with a west wind he headed E by N, intending, he says, to go to the island of Carib where live the people whom all those islands and lands fear [altered to 'feared'] so much because, he says, they went about all those waters with innumerable canoes and he says that they ate the men they can catch. He had been informed of the course, he says, by some of those four Indians whom he captured yesterday. (16 January)

There have been suggestions that in the third-person parts of his version Las Casas was summarizing. Various factors may be set against this. First, there is the evidence of word-for-word transfer in the above examples. Secondly, if one compares the length of the daily entries in the first-person and third-person narratives, there is no obvious discrepancy suggesting abbreviation in the latter mode. Some of the third-person entries for the outward voyage are admittedly short, but then there was nothing to record except course, weather, distance run and the occasional bird or floating object. We see a similar brevity in the first-person entries too, when Columbus has spent a whole day simply sailing; the entry for 18 October consists of a single sentence.

Thirdly, we have the evidence of Fernando Columbus's biography of his father. This was published in an Italian translation,[2] but even so it provides invaluable evidence, not only of the content of the original Journal, but also of the changes made by Las Casas. At certain points where the Las Casas version is in the third person, Fernando quotes the first-person narrative of his father's original. Compare the two in their accounts of the events of 18 December. Fernando is quoting directly from the original Journal. The corresponding Las Casas passage is turned into third-person narrative. It is evident that neither Las Casas's procedure nor that of the intervening scribe has involved notable abbreviation, either in the direct transcription in the first person or in the conversion to third-person narrative. One sentence has been moved forward in the Las Casas account, probably by carelessness; Fernando's order at this point is more logical. Having written the sentence in question (italicized), Las Casas realizes that he has skipped two sentences and includes them. For the purposes of this comparison I have made no attempt at beauty of style, but have adhered as far as possible to the sentence structure of the originals.

Fernando	*Las Casas*
Without doubt it would be a great pleasure to Your Majesties to see his dignity and the respect which his people have for him, although they all go naked. He, as soon as he	And the Admiral says to the King and Queen, 'Your Majesties would doubtless have been pleased by his dignity and the reverence in which they all hold him, although they all

came into the ship and found that I was under the sterncastle where I was eating, came quickly to sit down beside me, without giving me time to go to meet him, or to rise from the table. And when he came in under the sterncastle he signalled to them all to stay outside, and so they did, with great alacrity and respect, all sitting down on the deck except two men of mature age, whom I judged to be his counsellors, who sat down at his feet. It was indicated that this was the cacique, and *I, thinking that he should eat, ordered that food should be brought to him, what I had been eating myself,* and so he took some of everything, just the amount one takes to sample. He sent the rest to his people, who all ate of it. The same thing happened with the drink; he only took it to his lips and then gave it to the others. And he did everything with a wonderful dignity, and said few words, and those which he said, as far as I could understand, were very weighty and serious. The two men watched the mouth of this king, and spoke for him, and with him.

With great respect, when he had eaten, one of his gentlemen brought him a belt like those of Castile in its form, but of different craftsmanship, which he took in his hand and gave to me, with two pieces of gold, skilfully worked. Of this gold I think that they find little here, though I believe that this place is close to the one where it is found [*dove nasce,* literally 'where it is born'], and there there is much of it.

And, thinking that he would be pleased by a coverlet which was on my bed, I gave it to him, with a necklace of very beautiful amber

go about naked. As soon as he came aboard he found me eating at table under the sterncastle, and he came quickly to sit beside me, not allowing me to go to meet him or rise from table, but wanting me to go on eating. *I thought he would like to eat some of our food, and ordered him to be brought things to eat.* And when he came in under the sterncastle he gave a sign with his hand to tell all his people to stay outside, and so they did with the greatest alacrity and respect in the world, and they all sat down on the deck, except two men of mature age who I thought must be his counsellors and tutor, who came and sat down at his feet. And of the foods which I put before him he took of each just the amount one takes to sample, and then he sent the rest to his people and they all ate of it, and he did the same with the drink; he just took it to his lips and then gave it to the others, all with a wonderful dignity and very few words, and those which he did say, as far as I could understand, were very intelligent and sensible, and those two men watched his mouth and spoke for him and with him and with great respect.

When he had eaten a squire brought a belt which is made like those of Castile, but of a different workmanship, and he took it and gave it to me; also two pieces of worked gold, which were very thin, for I believe that here they get little of it, although I believe they are very near to where it is born [*nace*] and there is a lot of it. I saw that he was pleased by a coverlet which I had on my bed; I gave it to him, with some very fine amber beads which I had round my neck, and some red shoes, and a flask of beads which I was wearing round my neck, and a pair of red shoes and a bottle of orange blossom water, at which he was so pleased that it was amazing. And he and his counsellors showed great sorrow because they did not understand me, nor I them. However, I understood that they told me that, if I had need of anything, the whole island was at my command.

Then I ordered to be brought a letter case of mine, on which as a token there is a gold medal of the weight of four ducats, on which are sculpted the images of Your Majesties, and I showed it to him, saying again that Your Majesties ruled the greater part of the world, and that you were very great princes. And I showed him the royal banners, and the one with the cross, which were greatly admired by him. Turning to his counsellors he said that without doubt Your Majesties were great rulers, because from so far away as the sky you had sent me here without fear. Many others things happened which I did not understand, although I could see that he showed great wonder at everything. But as it was now late and he wished to leave, I sent him ashore in the boat with great ceremony, having many lombard shots fired, and as soon as he landed he went off in his litter with more than two hundred men, and one of his sons was carried on the back of a distinguished man, and to all the sailors and people from the ships whom he met on the land he ordered food to be given, and commanded that great courtesy be paid them.

Later a sailor who met them on the road told me that each of the things which I had given him were

orange flower water, which pleased him so much that it was wonderful. He and his tutor and counsellors are very sad because they did not understand me, nor I them. However, I understood that he told me that if I need anything here all the island is mine to command.

I sent for some beads[3] of mine on which as a token I have a gold *excelente* on which is engraved Your Majesties' portrait and I showed it to him, and told him again, as I did yesterday, that Your Majesties commanded and ruled the best part of the world and that there were no princes so great, and I showed him the royal banners and the others with the cross, which impressed him very much, and what great rulers Your Majesties must be, he said to his counsellors, since from so far away, from the sky, you had sent me here without fear, and many other things happened which I did not understand, except that I could see he was amazed by everything.

When it grew late and he wanted to leave the Admiral sent him ashore in the boat with great ceremony, firing the lombards repeatedly. When he reached the shore he got into his litter and went off with all his men, over two hundred. His son was carried behind him on the shoulders of a distinguished Indian. Whenever he met sailors or others from the ships he ordered them to be given food and treated with honour. A sailor said that he saw him go past on the road and that all the things which the Admiral had given him were being carried ahead of him by one of his most important men. The son was some way behind the king, accompanied by just as many being carried ahead of him by a very distinguished man, and that on the way his son did not travel with him, but some way behind, with just as many people following him, and with almost as many a brother of his was going on foot, held by two distinguished men under his arms; to him also I had given a few little things when he came to the ship after his brother.[4]

people, and one of the king's brothers was some way back again, but he was on foot, supported by the arm by a distinguished Indian on either side. This brother came to the ship some time after the king, and the Admiral gave him some of the barter goods.[5]

Compare also the two accounts of the shipwreck of the Santa María. Again, Fernando reproduces the content and syntax of his father's original text. Las Casas begins by converting it into third-person narrative, omitting virtually nothing, but towards the end his technique breaks down, he finds himself reproducing the original verbatim, and he belatedly retrieves the syntactical situation with an interpolation. Here again there is a slight difference of order: either Fernando missed the reference to the boat being turned away by the caravel (italicized) and introduced it when he realized the fact, or Las Casas included it too soon, realized the fact, and returned to the portion which he had skipped.

Fernando
And it pleased Our Lord that at midnight, seeing that I had lain down in bed, and as we were in a dead calm, and the sea as flat as in a dish, everyone went to lie down, leaving the helm in the hands of a boy. Then it happened that the waters which were running carried the ship very gently on to one of those banks which, although it was night, were making a noise so that they could be seen and heard from a good league away. Then the boy, who felt the rudder ground and heard the noise, began to cry out loudly; and hearing him I got up so quickly that nobody had yet realized that we had grounded in that place, and soon the master of the ship, whose watch it was, came out; and I told him and the other sailors that, having got into the boat which was being towed

Las Casas
It pleased Our Lord that at midnight, having seen the Admiral lie down to rest, and that there was a dead calm, with the sea like water in a bowl, everyone lay down to sleep and the helm was left to the boy, and the current took the ship onto one of the banks, which even though it was night could be heard and seen from a good league away, and the ship grounded so gently that it was hardly noticeable. The boy, feeling the rudder ground and hearing the noise, shouted, and the Admiral heard him and came out so quickly that no one else had yet realized they were aground. Then the master, whose watch it was, came out, and the Admiral told him and the others to haul in the boat which they were towing astern and take an anchor and throw it out astern, and he and

behind the ship, and taking an anchor, they should drop it astern. So then they and many others got into the boat, I thinking that they were going to do what I had told them, and they went off in the boat to the caravel, which was lying half a league away.

Seeing that they were fleeing in the boat, that the tide was ebbing, and that the ship was in danger, I immediately had the mast cut down, and the ship lightened as far as possible, to see if she could be got off. But with the tide still ebbing there was no hope for her, because she took a list, the seams opened, and she filled completely from below the waterline. *Then the caravel's boat arrived to give me help, for when her crew saw the boat fleeing they turned it away, and for that reason it was forced to return to the ship.*

Seeing no other way to save her, I went to the caravel in order to save the crew, and because there was a land breeze, and much of the night was passed, and not knowing for certain the way out of those banks, I jogged off and on in the caravel until daybreak, and then came promptly to the ship along the inside of the bank, having first sent the boat ashore with Diego de Arana of Córdoba, the Marshal of the Fleet, and Pedro Gutiérrez, Your Majesties' Butler, to let the king know what had happened, telling him that, wishing to go to visit him in his harbour, as he had asked me to do last Saturday, I had lost the ship near his village, a league and a half away, on a bank which was there.

When he heard this he showed, by his tears, considerable sorrow at our misfortune, and immediately sent all the people of the village to

many others jumped in the boat, and the Admiral thought they were obeying the order. They had no thought but to escape to the caravel which was half a league to windward. *The caravel, to its credit, refused to take them aboard, so they returned to the ship, but the caravel's boat got there first.*

When the Admiral saw that his people were fleeing and the tide was ebbing, and that the ship was beam-on to the sea, having no other recourse, he ordered the mast to be cut down and the ship lightened as far as possible to see if they could get her off. As the tide was still ebbing there was no help for her and she took a list towards the beam sea, though there was no great swell, then the seams opened, though she held together.[6] The Admiral transferred to the caravel to get the crew to safety, and as there was a land breeze and much of the night was left, and they did not know the extent of the banks, he sailed off and on until daybreak, and then he went to the ship inside the reef on the bank. He had previously sent the boat ashore with Diego de Arana of Córdoba, Marshal of the Fleet, and Pedro Gutiérrez, the Butler of the Royal Household, to inform the king who had sent the message of invitation on the Saturday and asked them to go to his harbour with the ships, and whose village was about a league and a half away from the bank.

When he heard the news they say that he wept and sent all his people, with many large canoes, to unload everything from the ship, and this the ship with many large canoes; and so they and we began to unload, and we cleared the whole deck very quickly, so great was the help given by this king. Later he in person and his brothers and relatives were very diligent, both on the ship and ashore, in ensuring that everything was done properly, and from time to time he sent one of his relatives weeping to beg me not to be downcast, for he would give me whatever he had.

And I state to Your Majesties as certain that nowhere in Castile could one have found such good attention to our things, of which not a lace point was missing, for he had all our things put together beside his palace, where he kept them until the houses which he wished to give us to store them were emptied. He posted armed men around them, and made them stay there all night, and he and all the people of the land were weeping, as if our loss mattered very much to them; the people are so kindly, and generous, and tractable and peaceful that I swear to Your Majesties that there are no better people in the world, and no better land.

They love their neighbour as themselves, and their speech is the gentlest and sweetest in the world, happy and always accompanied by laughter. It is true that they go about naked, men and women alike, but I assure Your Majesties that their customs are very praiseworthy, and the king is held in great majesty, and he is so dignified that it is a delight to see him; and they have excellent memories, and a wish to know about everything which makes

was done, and everything from the decks was taken off quickly, such was the king's concern and diligence, and he and his relatives were supervising, both on the ship and in guarding the things ashore, so that everything would be safe. From time to time he sent one of his relatives to the Admiral, weeping, to tell him not to be downhearted or angry, for he would give him everything he had.

The Admiral assures the King and Queen that nowhere in Castile could such care have been taken with everything, without the loss of so much as a lace point. He had it all put together near the houses while some were being cleared which he wished to give him to store and guard everything, and he set armed guards around to watch all night, and he and all his people kept weeping, they are, says the Admiral, such loving people, so unselfish and willing in everything, for I assure Your Majesties that I believe there are no better people, nor a better land, in all the world.

They love their neighbours as themselves, and their speech is the sweetest in the whole world, gentle and always with a smile. Men and women go about as naked as they were born, but I assure Your Majesties that their habits among themselves are very good, and the king has a marvellous dignity, with a restrained bearing, which is a delight to see, and the memory he has, and he wants to see and enquire about everything, what it is and what it is for. All this is the

them enquire about this and that,   word of the Admiral.[8]
and want to know the cause and
effect of everything.[7]

These similarities do not mean that Las Casas never omits anything. In
other areas Fernando's version supplies material missing from the Las
Casas version. Very occasionally a different account of the voyage by
Las Casas, included in his *Historia de las Indias*, similarly supplies detail
probably taken from the original but omitted from his version of the
Journal (though generally the reverse is true). The *Historia* is also
useful because its more carefully chiselled syntax shows up incon-
sistencies in the Journal which, again, are due to Las Casas's partial and
loose technique of alteration. Compare the accounts of the events of 4
December; the Journal is syntactically anarchic, especially in tense, but
more complete in content; the *Historia* is linguistically improved, but
omits material.

Journal
He set sail with little wind and left that harbour which he called Puerto Santo,
after two leagues he saw a good river of which he spoke yesterday. He went
along the coast and sailed all up the coast beyond the said cape from ESE to
WNW as far as Cabo Lindo which is at the end of the mountain to the ESE and
it is five leagues from one to the other. A league and a half from the end of the
mountain there is a large river, rather narrow, it seemed that it had a good
entrance and was very deep and from there three-quarters of a league on he
saw another very large river and it must come from a long way away it was a
good hundred paces across at the mouth and no bank in it and eight fathoms
at the mouth and a good entrance because he sent men to look and take
soundings in the boat and the water is fresh right into the sea and it is one of
the largest ones ł he had found, and there must be large villages on it.[9]

Historia
He left that harbour which he called Santo in a direction ESE to WNW, because
in this way one could sail the length of the coast, and after two leagues he
found a good river, and a cape which he called Lindo. Then he found another
large river, and three or four leagues further on he found another very large
river which must have come from very far away; it was a hundred paces
across at the mouth, without a bank, and it was eight fathoms deep, with a
good entrance, and the fresh water ran right out into the sea, and it was one of
the largest he had seen; and there must have been, as the Admiral says, large
villages near it.[10]

The English version of the Journal which follows has been reached
by the following processes:

1 The translation of all first-person passages in the Las Casas
manuscript.
2 The restoration into the first person of passages converted, or
partially converted, by Las Casas to the third person, and their
translation.

3 The adoption and translation from the Italian of passages quoted in the first person in the Fernando Columbus version, in preference to corresponding third-person passages in the Las Casas version. Such passages are indicated by oblique strokes, and their origin noted.

4 The occasional insertion and translation of material from the Las Casas *Historia* account or from Fernando's version which one may assume with reasonable certainty to have figured in the original Journal. Again, this material is placed between oblique strokes, with a note on its provenance.

5 The omission, with a note, of comments obviously inserted by Las Casas.

I hope by these means to have produced a version closer to the content and phrasing of Columbus's own account than any published previously. It would be extremely rash to claim that nothing is missing. Las Casas almost certainly omitted material which cannot be retrieved from other sources; sometimes his version ends a sentence with 'etc.', which could be Columbus's own, but probably more often indicates abbreviation by Las Casas, in some cases by the suppression of rhapsodic but repetitive description. Such cases are mentioned in my notes.

My version, therefore, is not Columbus's original, but then neither is Fernando's, nor the Las Casas manuscript, nor any of the myriad translations which have slavishly followed the slapdash Las Casas text. What follows is, I hope, a version corresponding as closely in content to the original as it is possible to produce while that original remains lost. In my choice of language I have tried to avoid making Columbus sound like either Chaucer's shipman or the commodore of a yacht club. My aim has been to convey in an enjoyable form the idiom of a plain-speaking, occasionally pretentious, but devout and literate sea captain in an era when the ocean still had wonders to disclose.

If I have achieved this, I have done so by deliberately avoiding any attempts to convey two aspects of the original. The first is Columbus's unreadable style. He is at his worst when he is trying hardest. The Prologue to the King and Queen contains some of the most impenetrable and unwieldy sentences ever written in Spanish, and even in the more down-to-earth entries his prose is often ravelled and labyrinthine. I wanted the reader to enjoy the Journal, and I have remodelled and punctuated accordingly.

The second feature is Columbus's foreignness. Studies of the language of the Journal suggest that to a contemporary Spaniard it would not have read like the work of a fellow countryman. This is hardly surprising; Columbus had been in Spain only a few years. His

Spanish is astonishingly good in the circumstances, but it does reveal the influence of his youth in Italy, his time in Madeira and Lisbon, and his marriage to Felipa.[11] Any attempt on my part to reflect Genoese vocabulary or Portuguese syntax in an English translation would clearly have been fraught with risk. What matters is what was in his mind, not the faults which emerged from his pen.

THE JOURNAL

Prologue

In Nomine Domini Nostri Jesu Christi

My Lord and Lady, most Christian, most exalted, most excellent and powerful sovereigns, King and Queen of Spain and of the maritime islands.

In this year of 1492 Your Majesties brought to an end the war against the remaining Moorish kingdom on European soil, terminating the campaign in the great city of Granada, where on 2 January this year I witnessed Your Majesties' royal standards raised by force of arms on the Alhambra, the fortress of that city, and the Moorish king emerge from the gates to kiss Your Majesties' hands and those of My Lord the Prince.

In that same month, on the information which I had given Your Majesties about the lands of India and a ruler known as the Great Khan (which means in Spanish 'King of Kings'), of whom I told you that he, like his predecessors, had many times appealed to Rome for men learned in our Holy Faith to instruct him, an appeal to which the Holy Father had not responded, and about the many peoples who were being lost through belief in idolatries and the acceptance of religions of damnation, Your Majesties, being Catholic Christians and rulers devoted to the Holy Christian Faith and dedicated to its expansion and to combating the religion of Mahomet and all idolatries and heresies, decided to send me, Christopher Columbus, to those lands of India to meet their rulers and to see the towns and lands and their distribution, and all other things, and to find out in what manner they might be converted to our Holy Faith; and you ordered me not to go eastward by land, as is customary, but to take my course westward, where, so far as we know, no man has travelled before today.

After expelling all the Jews from your kingdoms and territories, in the same month of January Your Majesties commanded me to sail to those regions of India with a suitable fleet; and for this purpose you granted me great concessions and ennobled me, allowing me to call myself *Don* from then onwards, with the title of Grand Admiral of the Ocean Sea, and Viceroy and Governor in perpetuity of all the islands and mainland that I might discover and win, or which may be henceforth discovered and won in the Ocean Sea, and you ordained moreover that my eldest son should succeed me in this, and so on through future generations forever.

I left the city of Granada on Saturday, 12 May 1492, and travelled to the port of Palos, where I prepared three vessels well suited for such an enterprise. I left that port, amply furnished with provisions and well crewed with seafaring men, on Friday, 3 August, sailing for Your Majesties' Canary Islands in the Ocean Sea, intending to set my course from there and to sail until I reach the Indies, where I will convey Your Majesties' embassy to those rulers and so carry out my orders.

With this end in mind I have resolved to set down each day full details of everything I do and see and experience on this voyage, as will later appear. Moreover, My Sovereign Lord and Lady, as well as describing every night the events of the day, and recording each day the distance run in the night, I intend to make a new chart in which I will set out the whole of the Ocean Sea, with sea and land properly laid out with true positions and courses. I also intend to compose a book including a true depiction of everything, giving its latitude from the Equator and its western longitude.

Above all, I must have no regard for sleep, but must concentrate on the demands of navigation; all of which will be no small task.

The Journal

Friday, 3 August
We set sail on Friday, 3 August 1492, crossing the bar of the Saltés at eight o'clock. Sailed s with a strong, veering wind[1] until sunset, making forty-eight miles, or sixteen leagues; then sw and s by w, on course for the Canaries.

¶ Demonstracion de los vientos.

3 August   Wind rose

83

Saturday, 4 August
Course sw by s.

Sunday, 5 August
Continued on course, running more than forty-two leagues in the twenty-four hours.

Monday, 6 August
The rudder of the caravel Pinta, commanded by Martín Alonso Pinzón, came off its pintles. I suspect one Gómez Rascón and Cristóbal Quintero, the owner of the vessel, who was unwilling to make the voyage. I discovered these two up to various mischiefs before we left port. I was very worried at not being able to help the Pinta without endangering my own vessel, though my concern was reduced because I knew Martín Alonso Pinzón to be a determined and resourceful man. We sailed thirty-one leagues in the twenty-four hours.

Tuesday, 7 August
The Pinta's rudder came loose again. It was fixed, and we continued towards Lanzarote, in the Canaries. Sailed twenty-six leagues in the twenty-four hours.

Wednesday, 8 August
The *pilotos* of my three vessels could not agree on our position. My own reckoning was the best. I was hoping to go to Gran Canaria to leave the Pinta, which is leaking and is sailing poorly because of her rudder, and to find another caravel to replace her, but we were unable to make Gran Canaria.

Thursday, 9 August
. . .[1]

. . . Many honourable Spaniards who are on La Gomera with Doña Inés Peraza, but whose home is on the island of Hierro, have sworn to me that every year they sight land to the west of the Canaries; other people on La Gomera have told me the same. I remember that in Portugal in 1484 a man from the island of Madeira came to ask the king for a caravel to go to that land, which he swore he saw every year, always looking the same. I remember them saying the same thing in the Azores, and all these people described the same course and the same appearance and size.

Having taken on water, wood, meat and the rest of what had been left with the men who stayed on La Gomera when I went to Gran Canaria to repair the Pinta, I finally set sail from La Gomera with my three vessels on Thursday, 6 September.

1 The Ptolemaic universe: the world as a sphere, with the planets rotating around it.

2 The Ocean Sea on the globe of Martin Behaim.

3 The pre-Columbian world: the map of Henricus Martellus, showing the Portuguese exploration of the African coast. At the top right is Cathay, with the cities of the Great Khan.

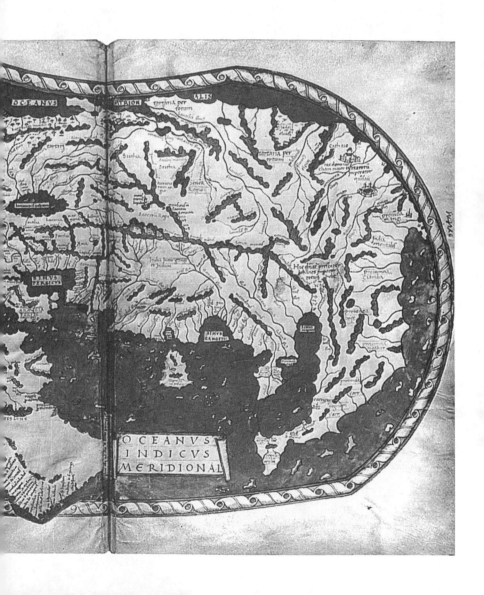

4 Oriental merchants.

5 The pepper harvest.

6 Islands of men and women.

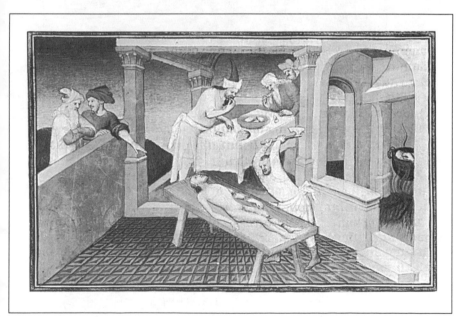

7 Cannibals.

8 The Great Khan and his tablet of gold.

9a and 9b Late fifteenth-century ships.

9a

9b

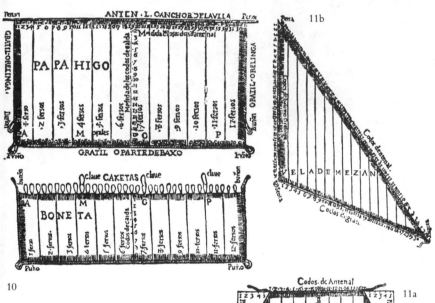

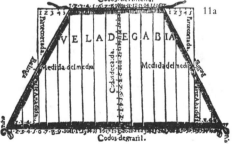

10

10 Mainsail and bonnet of a *nao*.

11a Topsail and 11b lateen mizzensail.

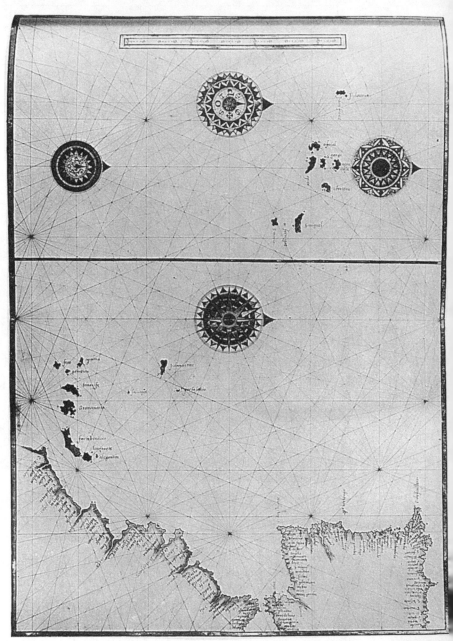

12 Wind roses and rhumb lines on a Portuguese sixteenth-century chart of the Azores and Canaries.

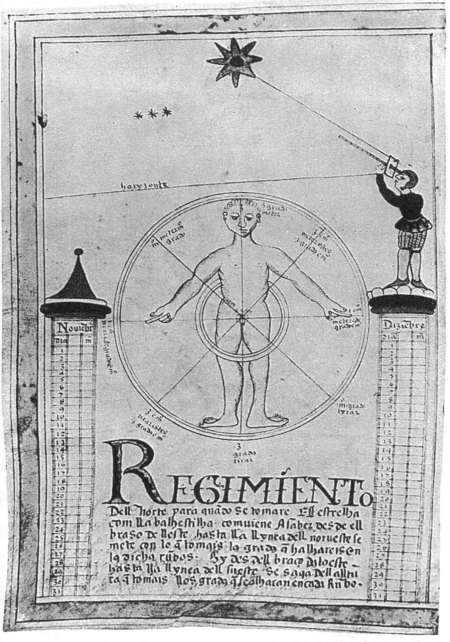

13 The man in the sky. A sixteenth-century Portuguese depiction of the imaginary figure centred on the Pole Star. The small figure at the top is using a *ballestilla* or cross-staff, an instrument not available to Columbus.

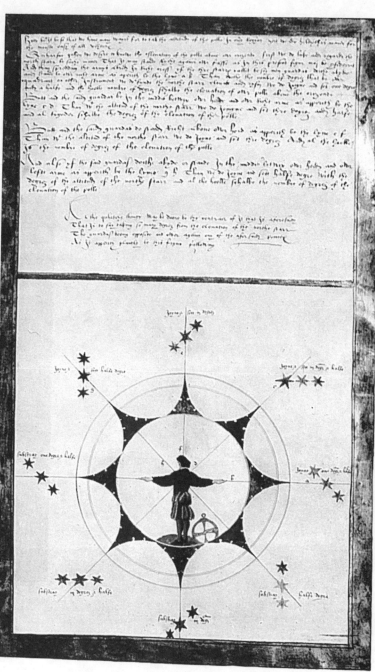

14 The Guards in their rotation around the Pole.

16 A *duho* from Santo Domingo.

15 An early watercolour of
Caribbean Indians fishing.

17

NAÏVE EARLY WOODCUTS OF THE DISCOVERIES

17 Columbus's ships, directed by King Ferdinand, discover the Indies.

18 Columbus and his newly named islands.

19 The building of Navidad.

19

18

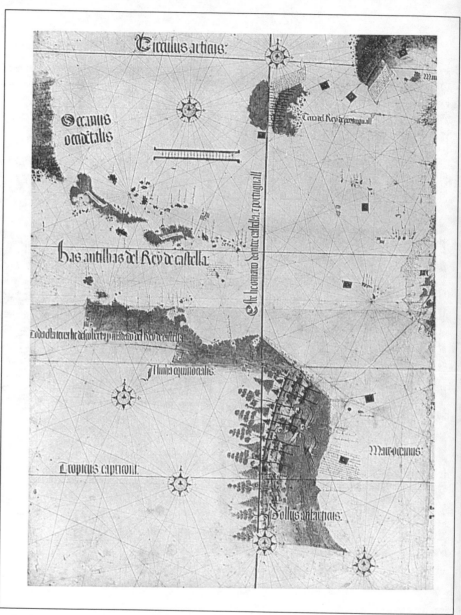

Circulus articus.

Occanus occidentalis

Canael Rey de portugual.

Oat hcomato cortae castella z portugual

has antilhas del Rey de castella.

Coredata ra be delcobra p miado del Rey de castella

Jlinta equinocialis.

Maroccanus.

Cropicus capricorni.

Pollus antarticus.

20 The Indies on the Cantino map of the world, 1502, showing the extension of the discoveries to the mainland of North and South America. The vertical line is the Papally approved division between the areas to be explored by Spain and Portugal. The curious 'Land of the King of Portugal' to the north is Newfoundland.

21 St Christopher as patron.

22 Columbus's signature. The closing cypher is preceded by four lines of his titles, including 'Admiral of the Ocean Sea, Viceroy and General Governor of the Islands and Mainland of Asia and the Indies'.

Thursday, 6 September
I sailed from the harbour of La Gomera and set my course to continue the voyage. I spoke a caravel coming from the island of Hierro; they told me that three Portuguese caravels are sailing around off the island to seize me. It must be because of the king's rancour towards me because I left Portugal for Spain. Calm all day and night. In the morning we were between La Gomera and Tenerife.

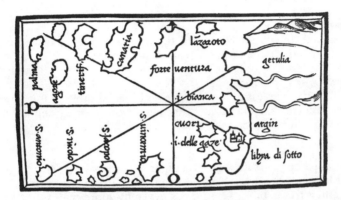

6 September   Map of the Canaries

Friday, 7 September
Calm all day Friday and on through the night until three o'clock on Saturday morning.

Saturday, 8 September
At three in the morning it began to blow from the northeast, and I set a course w. A strong head sea slowed us down; ran about nine and a half leagues, day and night together.

Sunday, 9 September
We sailed sixteen and a half leagues. I have decided to log less than our true run, so that if the voyage is long the crew will not be afraid and lose heart. In the night we sailed ninety-five miles at eight knots, making thirty-two leagues. The helmsmen steered badly, letting the ship fall off a point to w by N, and sometimes even to WNW; I had to reprimand them many times.

Monday, 10 September
Day and night together, we ran sixty-three and a half leagues at close

on eight knots, or over two and a half leagues per hour. I logged only fifty-one leagues, so as not to alarm the crew if the voyage is long.

Tuesday, 11 September
We continued on course w, over twenty leagues. We saw a large piece of the mast of a 120-ton ship, but could not pick it up. Sailed about twenty-one leagues in the night, and logged only seventeen for the same reason as before.

Wednesday, 12 September
Continued on course. We sailed thirty-five leagues, day and night together, and I logged fewer for the same reason.

Thursday, 13 September
Sailed thirty-five leagues, on course w; I logged three or four fewer. Adverse currents. At nightfall the needles were declining slightly NW, and in the morning they were declining slightly NE.

Friday, 14 September
Continued on course w, day and night. We ran twenty-one leagues, and I logged a few less. The people on the Niña said they had seen a tern and a tropic bird. These birds never fly more than twenty-five leagues from land.

Saturday, 15 September
We maintained our course w, something over twenty-eight and a half leagues. Early in the night we saw a marvellous bolt of fire fall from the sky into the sea about four or five leagues away. /These various things are disturbing and depressing the men, who are interpreting them as signs that we have taken a dangerous course./[1]

Sunday, 16 September
We continued on course w. Ran about forty-one leagues; I logged only thirty-eight. Some cloud and drizzle. Today[1] we had temperate breezes, and it was a joy to taste the morning air; all that was lacking was the song of the nightingales, and the weather was like April in Andalusia. We began to see patches of bright green weed, not long detached, it appeared, from the land. /The voyage is growing long, and we are far from home, and the men are beginning to complain about the length of the journey and about me for involving them in it. When they saw these great rafts of weed in the distance they began to be afraid that they were rocks or submerged ground, which made them even more impatient and outspoken in their complaints against me. Having seen the ships sailing through the weed, however, they

have lost their fear somewhat, though not entirely./² Everyone thought we were near some island, but I do not think it is the mainland, which by my reckoning is much further on.

Monday, 17 September

We continued on course w. Ran over fifty-three leagues in the twenty-four hours; I logged only fifty. We had a favourable current. We saw great quantities of weed. It was weed that grows on the rocks, and was coming from the west. Everyone thought we were near land, /which lifted the men's spirits and reduced their complaints. We have sailed 392 leagues from the island of Hierro, the westernmost point of the Canaries./¹

The *pilotos* took a sight on the north and marked it, and found that the needles were declining a full point NW. The men were disturbed and fearful, and would not say why. I recognized what was happening and ordered them to take another sight in the morning, and they found the needles pointing true. The reason appears to be that it is the star that moves, not the needles.

At dawn we saw much more weed. It looked like river weed, and we found a live crab in it, which I have kept. These are sure signs of land, for one does not find such things eighty leagues from land. The sea seems less salty since we left the Canaries, and the breezes sweeter all the time. We are all in good spirits, and the ships in competition with each other to be the first to sight land.

We saw large numbers of dolphins,² and they killed one from the Niña. These signs are coming from the west, where I trust that the great God in whose hands all victory lies will give us a landfall. This morning I saw a tropic bird, a white bird which does not normally spend the night at sea.

Tuesday, 18 September

Our day's run was more than fifty-eight and a half leagues; I logged only fifty-one. The sea lately has been calm, like the river at Seville. Today Martín Alonso in the Pinta, which is a fast ship, did not wait for the others; he told me that he had seen great numbers of birds flying westward, and that he was pressing on because he expected to sight land tonight. A great bank of cloud appeared to the north, which is a sign of land close by.

Wednesday, 19 September

We remained on course but ran only about twenty-six and a half leagues in the twenty-four hours, the winds being light. I logged twenty-three and a half. At ten o'clock a booby came to the ship, and in the evening we saw another. Normally they do not fly more than twenty leagues from land. /It was calm, and we took a sounding with a 200-fathom line. We found no bottom, but discovered that there was a sw current./[1] A few showers, with no wind, another sure sign of land. I do not wish to waste time beating about to make sure that there is land, but I am certain that there are islands to the north and south[2] and that I am sailing between them. However, I wish to maintain my course towards the Indies in this fair weather we are having, and with God's help we shall see everything on our passage homeward.

The *pilotos* gave me their calculated positions: the Niña's has us 466 leagues from the Canaries; the Pinta's makes it 445; my own man makes it 424. /I have been going around encouraging the men, always giving them the lower figure so as not to depress their spirits. The further we sail from Spain the greater grows their distress and unrest; they complain more every hour. They have been paying more and more attention to the signs we see, and although they took some heart from the birds, now that no land has appeared they believe nothing they see, and think that the absence of signs means that we are sailing to a new world from which we will never return./[3]

Thursday, 20 September

We sailed w by n and wnw in light, variable winds, about seven or eight leagues. Two boobies came to the ship, then another, a sign of being close to land. We saw a lot of weed, though there was none yesterday. We took a bird by hand, like a tern, /except that it was black with a white patch on its head; it had feet like a duck's, as water birds do. The crew killed a little fish./[1] Two or three little land birds settled on the ship, singing, and then flew away before dawn. Then a booby came, flying from wnw and on towards se, which is a sign that it had left the land to the wnw, for these birds sleep ashore and fly out to sea for food in the morning, but not more than twenty leagues. /These signs have raised the crews' spirits a little./[2]

Friday, 21 September

Flat calm, followed by high winds. Day and night together we ran about thirty-two leagues, partly on course and partly not. At dawn we saw so much weed that the sea seemed solid with it; it was coming from the west. We saw a booby. The sea is as calm as a river, with the pleasantest breezes in the world. We sighted a whale, a sign of land, since they always remain close to it [. . .][1]

Saturday, 22 September

Sailed about thirty-two leagues, generally wnw, with some variation either way. Very little weed. We saw some petrels and another bird. I needed this contrary wind; the crew were very restless, thinking that these waters never produce the wind to blow them back to Spain. No weed at all for part of the day, but later it became very thick.

Sunday, 23 September
Sailed NW, sometimes NW by N, sometimes on course due W, and made about twenty-three and a half leagues. We saw a turtledove, a booby, some small river birds and some other white birds. Large quantities of weed, with crabs in it. The sea was a flat calm, and the crew were complaining, saying that as the sea was never rough here there would never be a wind to take us home to Spain, but then they were astonished when a heavy sea rose with no wind. So this heavy sea came very opportunely for me; it was just like the Jews, on their way out of Egypt, arguing with Moses as he led them out of captivity.

Monday, 24 September
Remained on course W, day and night. We made about fifteen and a half leagues, and I logged thirteen. A booby came to the ship, and we saw many petrels /flying from the west. We saw fish around the ships, and killed a few with harpoons/.[1]

Tuesday, 25 September
Becalmed much of the day; a wind later, and we sailed W until nightfall. I talked to Martín Alonso Pinzón, captain of the caravel Pinta, and discussed a chart[1] which I had sent over to his ship three days ago and which has islands marked in these waters. Martín Alonso said that we are in the area, and I agreed with him. As we have not found the islands, it must be due to the currents which have set us back towards the northeast and caused us to run less than the *pilotos* say. I asked him to return the chart; he sent it across by a rope and I started to make calculations on it with my *piloto* and seamen.

At sunset Martín Alonso went up on the poop of his ship and called to me full of happiness[2] with the good news that he could see land. When he repeated it and said that it was definite, I knelt down to give thanks to God. Martín Alonso was saying the *Gloria in excelsis Deo* with his people, and mine did the same. The crew of the Niña all climbed up the mast and into the rigging, and all agreed that it was land. I thought the same, and that it was about twenty-five leagues away. Everyone kept on saying it was land until nightfall. I ordered a change of course from W to SW, the direction of the land. We had sailed W about five leagues, and in the night we made about eighteen leagues SW, a total of twenty-three. I told the crew fourteen.[3] The sea was very calm, and some of the crew swam. We saw many *dorados*[4] and other fish.

Wednesday, 26 September
Sailed on course w until after noon, then sw until we found that what
we had thought was land was only clouds. Our twenty-four hour run
was about thirty-three leagues; I told the men twenty-five and a half.
The sea was just like a river, with sweet, gentle breezes.

Thursday, 27 September
On course w, about twenty-five and a half leagues in the twenty-four
hours. I told the men twenty-one. We saw many *dorados*, and one was
killed. We also saw a tropic bird.

Friday, 28 September
On course w. Calms; sailed fifteen leagues in the twenty-four hours,
and logged fourteen. Not much weed. We caught two *dorados*, and the
other ships caught more.

Saturday, 29 September
Remained on course w and ran twenty-five and a half leagues; I told
the crew twenty-two. Little headway day and night because of calms.
We saw a frigate bird, which makes the boobies vomit up what they
have eaten and eats it itself. This is its only source of food. It is a sea
bird, but never settles on the sea, or goes more than twenty leagues
from land; it is common in the Cape Verde Islands. Later we saw two
boobies. Sweet, gentle breezes; the only thing missing is the song of
the nightingale, and the sea is as calm as a river. Later we saw three
more boobies and a frigate bird, three times. Large quantities of weed.

Sunday, 30 September
Remained on course w. Calms; we made only fifteen leagues in the
twenty-four hours. I logged twelve. Four frigate birds came to the
ship, a sure sign of land, because with so many birds of a kind together
it shows that they are not wandering about lost. Large amounts of
weed.
    NB: At nightfall the stars called the Guards are close to a line bearing
w, and at dawn they are on a line bearing NE, so it appears that in the
whole night they move only three lines, or nine hours. This is so every
night.[1] Also, at nightfall the needles deviate a point to the NW, and at
dawn they are right on the star, so it seems that the star moves like any
other, whereas the needles always point true.[2]

Monday, 1 October
Remained on course w. We made about twenty-six and a half leagues;
I told the men twenty-one. We had a great rainstorm. My *piloto*
reckoned that at dawn today we had sailed 602 leagues west from the

island of Hierro. My lower figure, which I show to the men, is 619; the true figure, which I keep to myself, is 750.

Tuesday, 2 October
Remained on course w. Forty-one and a half leagues in the twenty-four hours; I told the men about thirty-two. Still a good, calm sea, thanks be to God. There was weed drifting from east to west, the opposite to its usual direction. We saw many fish, and one was killed. We also saw a white bird like a gull.

Wednesday, 3 October
Course as usual. Fifty leagues; I told the men forty-two and a half. We saw petrels and a lot of weed, some very old and some fresh, bearing a sort of fruit. No birds. I think the islands on my chart are now behind us. I decided not to spend time beating about last week and this, when there were so many signs of land, even though I had information that certain islands lie in these waters, because I did not want anything to delay me in my aim of reaching the Indies; to delay would have been foolish.

Thursday, 4 October
Remained on course w. Our twenty-four hour run was sixty-seven leagues; I told the men forty-nine. More than forty petrels came to the ship together, and two boobies; a ship's boy threw a stone at one of them and hit it. A frigate bird came to the ship, and a white bird like a gull.

Friday, 5 October
Remained on course at about six and a half knots. Our twenty-four hour run was about sixty and a half leagues, because the wind grew less in the night; I told the men forty-eight. The sea calm and still, thanks be to God, and the air sweet and temperate. No weed; plenty of petrels. Large numbers of flying fish flew into the ship.

Saturday, 6 October
Remained on course w. Forty-two and a half leagues in the twenty-four hours; I told the men thirty-five. Martín Alonso said tonight that we would be best to steer sw by w. I think he had the island of Cipango in mind when he said this.[1] My own opinion is that if we miss Cipango we shall be a long time in making a landfall, and it is better to strike the mainland first and go to the islands afterwards.

Sunday, 7 October
Continued w. We ran at nine and a half knots for two hours and then at

six and a half knots. An hour before sunset we had sailed about twenty-four and a half leagues.[1] At sunrise today the caravel Niña, which was ahead of us, being a faster vessel, and was sailing as fast as she could to win the prize offered by the King, ran a flag up to the maintruck and fired a lombard as a signal that they had sighted land, as I had ordered. I had also given orders for all three ships to close up together at sunrise and sunset; these are the times when the visibility is best, the distance being less obscured by the mist. In the evening we could not see the land which the crew of the Niña thought they had sighted.

There was a great passage of birds from N to SW, which made us think that they were going back to the land to roost, or perhaps fleeing from the winter, which must have been arriving in the lands they had left. I know that most of the islands held by the Portuguese were discovered with the help of birds, so I decided to change course from due W to WSW,[2] and to follow this course for two days. Sailed about five and a half leagues in the night, which with the day's twenty-four and a half makes thirty.

Monday, 8 October
Sailed WSW, about twelve or twelve and a half leagues in the twenty-four hours. At times in the night we were running at almost twelve knots.[1] The sea has been like the river at Seville, thanks be to God, and the breezes as sweet as in Seville in April, so fragrant that it is a joy to smell them. The weed seems fresher. Many land birds; we caught one flying SW; terns,[2] ducks and a booby.

Tuesday, 9 October
Sailed SW for five and a half leagues. The wind then changed and I altered course to W by N for four and a half leagues. All told, we made eleven and a half leagues by day and twenty-two by night. I told the men eighteen leagues. We could hear birds passing all night long.

Wednesday, 10 October
Sailed WSW at about eight knots, sometimes up to nine and a half, occasionally only five and a half. Sixty-two and a half leagues in the twenty-four hours; I told the men only forty-six and a half. They could contain themselves no longer, and began to complain of the length of the voyage. I encouraged them as best I could, trying to raise their hopes of the benefits they might gain from it. I also told them that it was useless to complain; having set out for the Indies I shall continue this voyage until, with God's grace, I reach them.

Thursday, 11 October[1]
Course wsw. A heavy sea, the roughest in the whole voyage so far. We saw petrels, and a green reed close to the ship, /and then a big green fish of a kind which does not stray far from the shoals. /[2] On the Pinta they saw a cane and a stick, and they picked up another little piece of wood which seemed to have been worked with an iron tool; also a piece of cane and another plant which grows on land, and a little board. On the Niña too they saw signs of land, and /a thorn-branch laden with red fruits, apparently newly cut. /[3] We were all filled with joy and relief at these signs. Sailed twenty-eight and a half leagues before sunset. After sunset I resumed our original course westward, sailing at about nine knots. By two o'clock in the morning we had sailed about sixty-eight miles, or twenty-two and a half leagues.

When everyone aboard was together for the *Salve Regina*, which all seamen say or sing in their fashion, /I talked to the men about the grace which God had shown us by bringing us in safety, with fair winds and no obstacles, and by comforting us with signs which were more plentiful every day. I urged them to keep a good watch and reminded them that in the first article of the sailing instructions issued to each ship in the Canaries I gave orders not to sail at night after we had reached a point seven hundred leagues from there; I was sailing on because of everyone's great desire to sight land. /[4] I warned them to keep a good lookout in the bows and told them that I would give a silk doublet to the man who first sighted land, as well as the prize of 10,000 *maravedis* promised by Your Majesties.

I was on the poop deck at ten o'clock in the evening when I saw a light.[5] It was so indistinct that I could not be sure it was land, but I called Pedro Gutiérrez, the Butler of the King's Table, and told him to look at what I thought was a light. He looked, and saw it. I also told Rodrigo Sánchez de Segovia, Your Majesties' observer on board, but he saw nothing because he was standing in the wrong place. After I had told them, the light appeared once or twice more, like a wax candle rising and falling. Only a few people thought it was a sign of land, but I was sure we were close to a landfall.

Then the Pinta, being faster and in the lead, sighted land and made the signal as I had ordered. The first man to sight land was called Rodrigo de Triana. The land appeared two hours after midnight, about two leagues away. We furled all sail except the *treo*, the mainsail with no bonnets, and jogged off and on[6] until Friday morning, when we came to an island.[7] We saw naked people, and I went ashore in a boat with armed men, taking Martín Alonso Pinzón and his brother Vicente Yáñez, captain of the Niña. I took the royal standard, and the captains each took a banner with the Green Cross which each of my ships carries as a device, with the letters F and Y, surmounted by a crown, at each end of the cross.

When we stepped ashore we saw fine green trees, streams everywhere and different kinds of fruit. I called to the two captains to jump ashore with the rest, who included Rodrigo de Escobedo, secretary of the fleet, and Rodrigo Sánchez de Segovia, asking them to bear solemn witness that in the presence of them all I was taking possession of this island for their Lord and Lady the King and Queen, and I made the necessary declarations which are set down at greater length in the written testimonies.

Soon many of the islanders gathered round us. I could see that they were people who would be more easily converted to our Holy Faith by love than by coercion, and wishing them to look on us with friendship I gave some of them red bonnets and glass beads which they hung round their necks, and many other things of small value, at which they were so delighted and so eager to please us that we could not believe it. Later they swam out to the boats to bring us parrots and balls of cotton thread and darts, and many other things, exchanging them for such objects as glass beads and hawk bells. They took anything, and gave willingly whatever they had.

However, they appeared to me to be a very poor people in all respects. They go about as naked as the day they were born, even the women, though I saw only one, who was quite young.[8] All the men I saw were quite young, none older than thirty, all well built, finely bodied and handsome in the face. Their hair is coarse, almost like a horse's tail, and short; they wear it short, cut over the brow,[9] except a few strands of hair hanging down uncut at the back.

Some paint themselves with black, some with the colour of the Canary islanders,[10] neither black nor white, others with white, others with red, others with whatever they can find. Some have only their face painted, others their whole body, others just their eyes or nose. They carry no weapons, and are ignorant of them; when I showed them some swords they took them by the blade and cut themselves. They have no iron; their darts are just sticks without an iron head, though some of them have a fish tooth or something else at the tip.

They are all the same size, of good stature, dignified and well formed. I saw some with scars on their bodies, and made signs to ask about them, and they indicated to me that people from other islands nearby came to capture them and they defended themselves. I thought, and still think, that people from the mainland come here to take them prisoner. They must be good servants, and intelligent, for I can see that they quickly repeat everything said to them. I believe they would readily become Christians; it appeared to me that they have no religion. With God's will, I will take six of them with me for Your Majesties when I leave this place, so that they may learn Spanish.

I saw no animals on the island, only parrots.

Saturday, 13 October
In the early morning many of the islanders came to the beach, all
young, as I have said, tall and handsome, their hair not curly, but
flowing and thick, like horsehair. They are all broader in the forehead
and head than any people I have ever seen, with fine, large eyes. None
of them is black; they are rather the same colour as the folk on the
Canary Islands, which is what one might expect, this island being on
the same latitude as Hierro in the Canaries, which lies due E.

13 October   Canoe with several rowers

Their legs are very straight, and they are all the same height, not stout
in the belly but well shaped. They came out to the ship in *almadías*[1]
made from a tree-trunk, like a long boat, all of a piece, wonderfully
shaped in the way of this land, some big enough to carry forty or fifty
men, others smaller, with only one man. They row them with paddles
like a baker's shovel, very swiftly, and if the boat overturns they all
jump into the sea to turn it over again and bale it out with gourds.
They brought us balls of cotton thread and parrots and darts and other
little things which it would be tedious to list, and exchanged
everything for whatever we offered them.

I kept my eyes open and tried to find out if there was any gold, and I
saw that some of them had a little piece hanging from a hole in their
nose. I gathered from their signs that if one goes south, or around the
south side of the island, there is a king with great jars full of it,
enormous amounts. I tried to persuade them to go there, but I saw that
the idea was not to their liking.

I decided to wait until tomorrow and then to set off to the

southwest, for many of them seemed to be saying that there is land to the s and sw and nw, and that the people from the nw often come to attack them, and continue to the sw in search of gold and precious stones. This island is large and very flat, with green trees and plenty of water; there is a large lake in the middle, no mountains, and everything is green and a delight to the eye. The people are very gentle; they are so eager for our things that if we refuse to give them something without getting something in exchange they seize what they can and jump into the water with it. But they will give whatever they have for anything one gives them; they even bargained for pieces of broken plate and broken glasses. I saw them take three Portuguese *ceotís*, the equivalent of one Castilian *blanca*, for sixteen balls of cotton which must have contained more than an *arroba*[2] of thread. I had[3] forbidden anyone to take this, except that I had given orders to take it all for Your Majesties if it was in sufficient quantity. It grows on this island, though in the little time available I could not swear to this, and the gold they wear hanging from their noses is also from the island, but so as not to waste time I wish to set off to see if I can reach the island of Cipango.

It is now after nightfall and they have all gone ashore in their *almadías*.

Sunday, 14 October

I gave orders at daybreak for the small boat of the Santa María and the boats of the two caravels to be got ready, and went along the coast to the northeast to examine the eastward part of the island, and the villages, of which I saw two or three. The people kept coming down to the beach, calling to us and giving thanks to God. Some brought us water, some food; others, seeing that I did not wish to go ashore, swam out to us, and we understood them to be asking if we had come from Heaven.[1] One old man climbed into the boat, and the others, men and women, kept shouting, 'Come and see the men who have come from Heaven; bring them food and drink.'

Many men and women came, each bringing something and giving thanks to God, throwing themselves on the ground and raising their hands in the air. They called to us to go ashore, but I was afraid of a great reef which encircles the whole island, though between it and the shore there is a deep harbour big enough to hold every ship in Christendom, with a very narrow entrance channel. There are certainly shoals within this reef, but the sea inside it is as calm as a millpond.

I bestirred myself to explore all this this morning so as to be able to give Your Majesties a description of it all, and also of a possible site for a fort. I saw a piece of land which is virtually an island; there are six houses on it, and it could be converted into an island with a couple of days' work, although I do not see the necessity. These people have little knowledge of fighting, as Your Majesties will see from the seven I have had captured to take away with us so as to teach them our language and return them, unless Your Majesties' orders are that they all be taken to Spain or held captive on the island itself, for with fifty men one could keep the whole population in subjection and make them do whatever one wanted.

Near the islet I have described there are groves of the most beautiful trees I ever saw; so green, with their leaves like those in Castile in April and May. There is also plenty of water. I explored the whole harbour, and then returned to the ship and set sail. I saw so many islands that I could not decide which to go to first. The men I had captured told me by signs that there are so many that they cannot be counted; they gave me the names of over a hundred. I therefore looked for the largest, and decided to sail for it, which is what I am doing now. It must be about five leagues from this island of San Salvador. Some of the others are nearer, some further away. They are all very flat and fertile, with no mountains, and they are all populated and make war on one another, though these people are very simple, and very finely made.

Monday, 15 October
Last night I lay to for fear of approaching land to anchor before morning, not knowing if the coast was free from shoals, and intending to increase sail at dawn. The distance was more than five leagues, nearer seven, and the tide set us back, so that it would be around noon when I reached the island. I found that the arm of the island nearest San Salvador runs N–S, and is five leagues long, and the other, along which I sailed, runs E–W for over ten leagues.

From this island I sighted another larger one to the west, so I increased sail to press on all day until nightfall, for otherwise I could not have reached the western cape. I named this island Santa María de la Concepción.[1] I anchored off the western cape just before sunset to find out if there was any gold there. The prisoners I took on San Salvador kept telling me that the people of this island wore great gold bracelets and legbands, but I thought it was all invention to enable them to escape. However, my intention being not to pass by any island without taking possession of it, although taking possession of one might be taken to serve for them all, I anchored and remained there until today, Tuesday.

At daybreak I armed the boats and went ashore. There were numerous people, naked and similar to those on San Salvador. They let us go about on the island and gave us whatever I asked for. The wind was strengthening from the southeast, so I decided not to linger, but set off to return to the ship. A large *almadía* was alongside the

Niña, and one of the men from San Salvador who was aboard the caravel jumped into the sea /and went off in it (another had jumped overboard the previous night). Our boat set off after the *almadía*, which paddled away so fast that no boat ever built could have outpaced it, even with a considerable start./² Anyway, it reached the shore and they abandoned it. Some of my men landed in pursuit, and the islanders all fled like chickens. The *almadía* was taken back on board the Niña.

By now another small *almadía* was approaching the Niña from a different headland with one man in it who had come to barter a ball of cotton. He did not want to come aboard, so some of the sailors jumped into the sea and captured him. I saw all this from the deck of the sterncastle, so I sent for him; I gave him a red bonnet and put a few little green glass beads on his arm and hung two bells from his ears. I had him put back in his *almadía*, which had also been taken aboard the ship's boat, and sent him back ashore. I then made sail to go to the other large island which I could see to the westward, and I ordered the other *almadía* which the Niña was towing astern to be set adrift.

When the man to whom I had given gifts, refusing his ball of cotton, reached the shore I saw that all the others came up to him. He was amazed and thought that we were good people and that the other who had escaped was being taken with us because he had done us some harm. That was my purpose in giving him presents and letting him go: to make them think well of us, so that when Your Majesties send someone else here he may be well received. All the things I gave him would not be worth four *maravedis* if you put them together.

I set sail, then, at about ten o'clock with the wind SE, veering southerly, to cross to this other island. It is very large, and all the men from San Salvador tell me by signs that there is a lot of gold, which the people wear as bracelets and legbands, and in their ears and noses, and round their necks.

From the island of Santa María to this new one is nine and a half leagues, almost due W, and all this part of the island runs from NW to SE. There appears to be at least thirty leagues of coast on this side, very flat, without a hill anywhere, like San Salvador and Santa María. There are sandy beaches all the way, except that there are some underwater rocks near the shoreline, making it necessary to take care when anchoring and not to anchor close inshore, although the water is very clear and one can see the bottom. Two lombard shots from shore all around these islands one can find no bottom.

The islands are very green and lush, with sweet breezes, and there may be many things here which I do not know about, because rather than lingering I wish to explore and investigate many islands in search of gold. As these people tell me by signs that the folk wear it on their arms and legs – and it is gold they mean, for I showed them some pieces of my own – with God's help I cannot fail to find the source of it.

Halfway between these two islands, Santa María and this larger one which I am calling Fernandina,[3] we found a man alone in an *almadía* making the same crossing as ourselves. He had a piece of bread as big as his fist, a calabash of water, a piece of red earth, powdered and kneaded,[4] and a few dried leaves which must be something of importance to these people, because they brought me some in San Salvador. He also had a small basket with a little string of glass beads and two *blancas*, so I knew that he had come from San Salvador and called at Santa María on his way to Fernandina. He came alongside the ship and I let him come aboard at his request. I also made him bring his *almadía* on board with him. I let him keep all the things he had with him, and ordered him to be given bread and honey, and something to drink. I am going to take him to Fernandina and give him all his possessions so that he will give a good report of us, in order that when Your Majesties, with the grace of God, send men back to this place they will be received with honour, and we will be given whatever the island has to offer.

Tuesday, 16 October
I left the islands[1] of Santa María de la Concepción about noon for the island of Fernandina to the west.[2] It appears very large. Calms all day. We could not reach the island in time to see the bottom to find a clean anchorage, which is a thing one must take great care over if one is not to lose one's anchors, so I lay to until daybreak, when I came to a village and anchored. The man whom I found in the *almadía* in mid-crossing yesterday had come to the same village, and had given such a good report of us that there were *almadías* alongside the ship all night, bringing us water and whatever else they had. I gave orders for each of them to receive something: a few glass beads, ten or a dozen strung together, or little brass bells of the kind which sell for a *maravedi* in Castile, or a few lace ends, all of which made a great impression on them. When they came aboard ship I ordered them to be given sugar syrup to eat.

Later, at about the hour of terce,[3] I sent the ship's boat ashore for water, and the people willingly showed the men where to find it, and carried the full casks back to the boat for them, and took great delight in pleasing us.

This island is very large. I have determined to sail all round it, for as far as I understand there is a gold mine either in or near it. It is eight and a half leagues almost due w of the island of Santa María. The cape to which I sailed and all the coast on this side run NNW–SSE.[4] I have seen a good twenty leagues of the coast, but it went on further. Now, as I write this, I have set sail with a south wind to press on around the whole island and search until I find Samoet, which is the island or city where the gold is found, according to all the people who have boarded the ship here; the people on San Salvador and Santa María said the same.

The people here are like those on the other two islands, with the same language and ways, except that these seem rather more civilized and subtle in their dealings; when they have brought cotton and other little things to the ship I have noticed that they are better at bargaining over the price than the others. Also I have noticed woven cotton cloths here like kerchiefs, and the people are more lively, and the women wear a little cotton thing in front which just covers their private part.

The island is very green and flat, and extremely fertile; I can well believe that they sow and harvest millet[5] and their other crops the whole year round. I have seen many trees very unlike our own, many of them with a host of different branches emerging from the one trunk, one branch differing from another to such a degree that the variation is astonishing. For example, one branch had leaves like a cane and another leaves like a mastic tree, and on the same tree one finds five or six variations just as great. One cannot ascribe this to grafting; they have not been grafted, but are simply growing wild, untended by the people.[6] As far as I know the people have no religion. They would, I think, readily become Christians, for they are intelligent.

The fish here show amazing differences from our own. Some are like cocks, with the handsomest colouring in the world: blue, yellow, red, all colours; others are marked in a thousand different ways. No man could look at them without amazement and delight, the colours are so beautiful. There are also whales. Ashore I have seen no animals of any kind; only parrots and lizards. A ship's boy told me he had seen a large snake. I have seen no sheep, goats or other beasts. I have not been here long, for it is only midday, but if there were any I could not have failed to see some of them.

I will describe the circuit of this island when I have completed it.

Wednesday, 17 October
At midday I left the village where we had anchored and taken on water to sail around this island of Fernandina. Wind sw and s. It was my intention to follow the coast to the se, for the whole coast runs NNW–SSE and I wanted to take that course, s and se, because according to all these Indians I have on board, and another from whom I received directions, the island of Samoet, where the gold is, lies to the south. However, Martín Alonso Pinzón, captain of the caravel Pinta, in which I had put three of the Indians, came to tell me that one of them

had told him very clearly that he could sail round the island much more quickly by heading NNW. Seeing that the wind was unfavourable for the course I had planned, and favourable for the other, I set sail to the NNW. As we approached the headland of the island, two leagues from it, I found a fine harbour with a mouth, or rather two mouths, both very narrow, for there is a small island in the middle, and enough space inside to take a hundred ships, given sufficient depth of water and clean anchorage, and enough depth at the mouth.

I thought it wise to explore it properly and take soundings, so I anchored off the mouth and went in with all the ships' boats, and we found that there was no depth of water. I had thought when I first saw it that it was the mouth of a river, so I had had casks brought to take on water, and on land I found eight or ten men who came and showed us where the village was, close by. I sent the crew for water, some armed and others carrying the casks, and they came back with the water.

As it was some distance away I had two hours to wait, and I spent them walking in the trees, the most beautiful sight ever seen: so much greenery, as green as Maytime in Andalusia, and the trees all as different from our own as night is from day, as is everything else, the fruits, the plants and the stones. Certain trees, it is true, were of a similar type to some which grow in Castile, but this only increased the variety, and there were so many of the other kinds that no one could list them, nor compare them to any in Castile.

All the people are like the ones I have described earlier: the same appearance and height, and naked too. They exchanged their possessions for whatever one gave them; I saw some of the ship's boys giving

17 October   Hammock

them pieces of broken dishes and glass in exchange for darts. The men who went for the water told me that they had gone into the people's houses and found them very clean and well kept inside; the beds and containers are like nets made of cotton.[1]

The houses are shaped like a campaign tent, very high, with good chimneys,[2] but of the many villages I have seen none has exceeded twelve or fifteen houses. My men noticed that the married women here wear cotton breeches; not the girls, except a few aged about eighteen. There were mastiff dogs and hunting hounds, and one they saw had a piece of gold in its nose like half a *castellano*[3] with letters on it. I was angry with them for not having bargained for it and given whatever price was asked, so that we could have examined it and found out whose money it was; they told me they had not dared.

I returned aboard with the water, made sail and set off to the NW, continuing until I had explored all that part of the island as far as the coast which runs E–W, at which point all the Indians told me again that this island was smaller than the island of Samoet and that it would be better to turn back so as to reach it more quickly. The wind then fell away and veered WNW, which was contrary for retracing our course, so I went about and sailed ESE all last night, sometimes due E and sometimes SE, to get away from the coast, because there were heavy clouds and the atmosphere was very close.[4] The [wind] was light[5] and did not enable us to reach land to anchor.

After midnight it rained hard almost until dawn, and it is still cloudy and threatening rain. We are now off the southeastern cape, where I am hoping to anchor until it clears enough for me to see the other islands which I have to visit. There has been rain, light or heavy, every day since I arrived in the Indies. Rest assured, Your Majesties, that this land is the finest, most fertile, level, rich and temperate on the face of the earth.

Thursday, 18 October

When the weather cleared I followed the wind and sailed round the island as far as I could. When it was no longer suitable weather for sailing I anchored, but I did not go ashore, and at daybreak I made sail again.

Friday, 19 October

At daybreak I weighed anchor and sent the caravel Pinta off to the ESE, and the Niña SSE, and I in the Santa María[1] steered SE. I gave orders that they should stay on these courses until noon and then come about and sail back to rejoin me. After less than three hours' sailing we sighted an island to the E. We braced up and headed for it, and the three vessels reached it before noon at its northern point, where there is an islet and a reef running off it to the N, and another[2] between it and the island proper. The men from San Salvador whom I have on board told me that its name is Samoet; I have named it Isabela.[3] The wind was northerly, and the islet I mentioned is on course for the island of Fernandina, on a line E–W of my departure point from there. From the islet the coast ran westward[4] for twelve and a half leagues to a headland. I have called the cape here at the western end Cabo Hermoso,[5] and it is indeed beautiful, round and with plenty of depth of water, with no shoals. The shore is of low rocks, changing to sandy beaches further in, which extend along most of this coast. I anchored there last night, Friday, until this morning.

Nearly all the coast and the part of the island I have seen are sandy, and the island is the most beautiful sight I ever saw; the others are lovely, but this is lovelier. There are many tall, green trees, and the land is higher than on the other islands we have discovered, with a few hilltops – nothing one could call a mountain, but sufficient to make the rest more beautiful by contrast – and there appear to be numerous streams in the middle of the island.

On this side the coast turns NE, forming a large bay, with many dense, tall woods. I tried to anchor in the bay, to go ashore and explore all this beauty, but the bottom was shoaly. I could only anchor well offshore, and there was a fair wind for this cape where I have now anchored, which I have called Cabo Hermoso, for beautiful it is. That was my reason for not anchoring in the bay, and I could see this cape from there, so green and fair, like all the land and everything else on these islands; I do not know where to go first, and my eyes never weary of seeing such marvellous vegetation, so different from our own.

I have no doubt there must be many plants and trees which would be valuable in Spain for tinctures and medicinal spices, but I am very sorry to say that I am unfamiliar with them. As we neared this cape we were met by the soft, balmy smell of the trees and flowers ashore, the sweetest fragrance in the world.

Before I sail tomorrow I shall go ashore to see what there is on the cape. The village is not here, but further inland; the men I have with me say the king lives there, and wears a lot of gold. In the morning I plan to go far enough to find the village and to see or speak with this king. The men I have with me tell me by signs that he rules all these neighbouring islands and wears clothes and has a lot of gold about him. I have no great faith in what they tell me, partly because of my difficulty in understanding them, but also because I know they have so little gold themselves that whatever small amount the king has will seem a lot to them.

I believe that this cape I have called Cabo Hermoso is a separate island from Samoet, and that there is another, smaller one in between. I do not wish to explore too much in detail, for I could not do it in fifty years; I wish to see and discover as much as I can, so as to return to Your Majesties, with God's grace, in April. If I find any quantity of gold or spices, I shall, of course, linger until I have gathered as much as I can; at present I can only keep moving until I come across them.

Saturday, 20 October
At daybreak today I weighed anchor off the southwest cape of this island of Samoet. I have called the island Isabela and the cape Cabo de la Laguna.[1] My intention was to sail to the northeast and east via the southeastern and southern part, where I understand from these men I have with me that the village and the king are to be found. I found so little depth of water that I could not get in or sail to it, and seeing that the route by the southwest was a long way round I decided to return on the course I had taken towards the NNE on the western side and to sail back round the island . . .[2] The wind was so light that I was unable to keep along the coast except at night, and since anchoring in these islands is perilous except in daylight when one can see where one is dropping anchor, for the bottom is all patchy, some clean and some foul, I sailed off and on all night. The caravels anchored because they made land sooner, and they expected me to go in to anchor in response to their usual signals, but I decided against it.

Sunday, 21 October
I reached this headland of the islet at ten o'clock and dropped anchor. The caravels did the same. After eating I went ashore, where the only habitation nearby was an empty house. All the household equipment was still inside, so I think the people must have run away in fear. I ordered nothing to be touched; instead I set off with my captains and the men to explore the island. The ones we have seen previously were beautifully green and fertile, but this one is much more so, with great woods, very green. There are large lagoons, and the woods along the shore and all around are a wonder to behold. Here and all over the island the trees and plants are as green as in Andalusia in April, and the song of the birds makes a man want never to leave. There are flocks of parrots so big that they darken the sun, and birds of amazing variety, very different from our own. The trees, too, are of a thousand kinds, each with its own fruit and pleasant fragrance; it grieves my heart not to recognize them, for I am sure they must all be useful. I am taking samples of them all, and of the plants.

As we walked round one of the lagoons I saw a serpent[1] which we killed; I am bringing Your Majesties the skin. It jumped into the lagoon when it saw us and we chased it through the shallow water and

21 October   Iguana

killed it with spears. /It is seven feet long, and a good foot across the belly./[2] I think there must be many of them in this lagoon. I recognized aloe plants[3] here, and I have decided that tomorrow I will have ten quintals of it brought abroad, for I understand that it is valuable.

While looking for water we went to a village nearby, half a league from where I am anchored. When the people heard us coming they left their houses and ran away, hiding their clothes and possessions in the undergrowth. I forbade the men to take even the smallest thing. Then some of the Indians approached us, and one came up to us. I gave him a few bells and glass beads, which pleased him very much, and in order to foster friendship and ask for something in return I had a request put to him for water. When I had returned to the ship they came down to the shore with their calabashes full and gave us the water with signs of pleasure. I ordered them to be given another string of beads and they said they would return in the morning.

I should like to fill all our water containers while we are here, and then, if I have time, I shall set off to sail round this island until I find and talk to the king, and see if I may obtain from him some of the gold which I am told he wears. Then I shall set off for another, very large island which I think must be Cipango, judging by the indications given me by these Indians I have on board. They call it Colba,[4] and say that there are many big ships there, and seafarers,[5] and that it is very large. From there I shall go to another island called Bohío,[6] also very large, according to them. The ones in between I shall observe in passing, and depending on what store of gold or spices I find I shall decide what to do. But I am still determined to continue to the mainland, to the city of Quinsay, and to give Your Majesties' letters to the Great Khan and return with his reply.

Monday, 22 October

I have been waiting all last night and today to see if the king of this place or anyone else would bring me gold, or any other thing of importance. Many of the people have come, naked like those of the other island and painted in the same fashion, some white, some red, some black, in many different ways. They brought spears and some balls of cotton to barter with, and exchanged them with some of the crew for bits of glass, broken cups and pieces of earthenware dishes. Some of them were wearing little pieces of gold hanging from their noses; they were quite willing to exchange these for a sparrowhawk bell or a few glass beads, so insignificant as to be worthless, for really however little one gave them, they too were amazed by our arrival, and thought we were from Heaven.

We took on water for the ships from a lagoon near here, beside the headland of what I have called the islet. Martín Alonso Pinzón, captain of the Pinta, killed another serpent, like yesterday's.

Tuesday, 23 October

I should like to sail today for the island of Cuba, which I believe to be Cipango from the description these people give me of its size and riches, and I shall wait here no longer, nor shall I go round the island to the village as I intended, to speak with the king or leader. I do not wish to waste a lot of time, for I can see that there is no mine of gold here, and sailing around these islands needs many shifts of wind, which does not always blow to suit a man's wishes.

It is only sensible to go where there is good potential for trade. To my mind there is no point in lingering when one can set off and explore a large area until one finds a country which offers profit, although I do believe that the place where we are now may provide an abundance of spices. It is a source of great regret to me that I know so little about spices, for I see an enormous variety of fruit-bearing trees, all as green as the trees in Spain in May and June, and many kinds of plants and flowers, and the only one we have recognized so far is this aloe, of which I have had a large quantity brought on board today to bring to Your Majesties.

I have not yet set sail for Cuba for lack of wind; we have a flat calm and heavy rain. Yesterday too it rained hard, but it was not cold; in fact the days are warm and the nights balmy, like May in Spain, in Andalusia.

Wednesday, 24 October

At midnight last night I weighed anchor from where I was lying off the headland of the islet, on the north of the island of Isabela, and set sail for Cuba, which these people have told me is very large and busy, with gold and spices, and large ships and merchants. They told me I could reach it by sailing wsw, which I think is true; for if this is the case, as all the Indians on these islands and those I have on board tell me (by signs, for I cannot understand their language), I believe it to be the island of Cipango, of which such wonders are told, and which lies in this region on the globes and the maps of the world which I have seen.

So I sailed wsw until daybreak, when the wind dropped and it rained, as it had done much of the night.[1] There was very little wind until afternoon, when a breeze got up, fair and kindly, and I set all sail: maincourse with two bonnets, forecourse, spritsail, mizzen and topsail, and the boat's sail on the sterncastle. I continued on the same course until nightfall, when we were in sight of the Cabo Verde, the western headland of the southern part of Fernandina. It lay seven and a half leagues away to the northwest. It was blowing hard, and not knowing the distance to the island of Cuba I did not wish to seek it at night; all these islands are very steep-to all around, with no bottom until one is within a couple of lombard shots of the shore, and the bottom is foul, part rocky and part sandy, so that the only way one can anchor safely is by using one's eyes.

I decided to shorten sail to the forecourse. The wind was soon blowing up much stronger, with heavy cloud and rain, and we were sailing too fast for my peace of mind, so I had the forecourse furled and in the night we sailed less than two leagues /. . ./[2]

Thursday, 25 October
We sailed wsw from sunrise until nine o'clock, about five and a half leagues, then altered course to w. Sailed at six and a half knots until one in the afternoon and from then until three, making about thirty-five miles. We then sighted land, seven or eight islands, all in a line from north to south, about five leagues away /. . ./[1]

Friday, 26 October
We were off these islands, to the south. It was all shallow for five or six leagues, and I anchored. The Indians on the ship said that it takes a day and a half from there to Cuba in their *almadías*, which are small vessels made from a single piece of timber, with no sail.[1] I set sail again for Cuba, because judging by the signs made by the Indians about its size, and the gold and pearls there, I believe it to be Cipango.

Saturday, 27 October
At sunrise I weighed anchor from these islands, which I have called the Islas de Arena[1] because of the shallows extending six leagues to the south of them. Sailed ssw at six and a half knots until one o'clock, about thirty-two miles, and from then until nightfall about twenty-

two miles on the same course. We sighted land before dark, and spent the whole night jogging off and on because of heavy rain. Sailed eighteen leagues ssw by sunset.

Sunday, 28 October

I sailed ssw for the nearest point of the island of Cuba, and into a fine river free from shallows and other perils. The sea along the whole coast along which I sailed is deep right up to the shore, with a clean bottom. There is twelve fathoms' depth[1] in the mouth of the river, and it is good and wide for tacking. /There are two beautiful high mountains, like the Peña de los Enamorados, near Granada, and one of them has another little hill on the top shaped like a handsome mosque./[2] I anchored inside the river, a lombard shot in from the mouth.

I never saw a lovelier sight: trees everywhere, lining the river, green and beautiful. They are not like our own, and each has its own flowers and fruit. Numerous birds, large and small, singing away sweetly. There are large numbers of palm trees, different from our own and those in Guinea; they are of medium height, without the skirt round the base; the leaves are very large, and are used to thatch the houses. The land is very level.

I jumped into the boat and went ashore, and found two houses which I think belonged to fishermen, who fled in fear. In one of them was a dog which did not bark. In both houses I found nets of palm fibre, ropes, horn fish hooks, bone harpoons and other fishing equipment. I think many people must live together in each house. I gave orders for everything to be left alone, and nothing was touched. The grass is as long as in April and May in Andalusia, and I found quantities of purslane and spinach.[3]

I returned to the ship and sailed a good way upriver. It is a joy to see all the woods and greenery, and it is difficult to give up watching all the birds and come away. It is the most beautiful island ever seen, full of fine harbours and deep rivers. It appears that the sea must never be rough, for the grass on the beach comes down almost to the shoreline, which is not the case where there are rough seas. So far I have encountered no heavy seas anywhere in these islands.

There are splendid mountains everywhere on the island, not very long, but high, and the rest of the land is similar in height to Sicily. There are rivers and streams all over it, as far as I can gather from the Indians I brought with me from Guanahani. They tell me there are ten large rivers and they cannot sail round the island in their canoes[4] in twenty days. As our ships were approaching land two *almadías* or canoes came out towards us, but they fled when they saw the crew getting into the boat and rowing to look at the bottom of the river for an anchorage.

The Indians tell me that there are gold mines and pearls on this island, and I saw a likely spot for pearls, with clams, which are a sign of them. I understand that large vessels belonging to the Great Khan come here, and that the passage to the mainland takes ten days. I have called this river and harbour San Salvador.[5]

Monday, 29 October
I weighed anchor and sailed westward to look for the city where the Indians, I think, tell me that the king is to be found. The island has one headland six and a half leagues to my NW, and another eleven leagues E. After sailing a league I saw another river with a smaller mouth, which I called Río de la Luna,[1] and we sailed on until vespers. I saw another river, much bigger than the others, to judge by the signs made by the Indians, and nearby there were good-sized villages. I have called the river Río de Mares.[2]

I sent two boats to a village to make contact, one of them with one of the Indians from the ship. We can understand them a little now, and they seem happy enough to be with us. All the men, women and children ran away from the boats, leaving their houses and all their possessions unguarded. I gave orders that nothing should be touched.

The houses are better looking than the ones we have seen so far, and I expect the closer I come to the mainland the better they will be. They are built in the shape of a campaign tent, very large, and arranged not in streets but haphazardly, like tents in an army encampment. They are clean and well swept inside, with all their equipment neatly arranged. The houses are all made of beautiful palm branches.

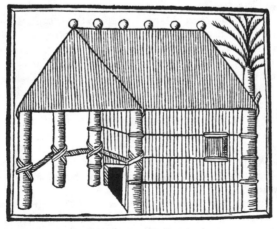

29 October   Indian house

We found many statues in the shape of a woman, and finely carved heads like masks. I do not know if they are for decoration or worship. There were dogs which never barked, and wild birds living tame in the houses, and wonderfully crafted fishing nets and hooks and other fishing gear. None of this was touched. I think all these people on the coast must be fishermen who take their catch inland, for the island is very large. It is so beautiful that I could go on and on in its praise. I found trees with wonderfully flavoured fruit, and there must be cows and other domestic animals, for I saw skulls like those of cattle. The birds, large and small, and the song of the crickets in the night are a great joy to us all; the night air is sweet and fragrant, neither too hot nor too cold. We had very hot weather coming from the other islands to this one, but here it is warm and pleasant, like May. The other islands were probably hot because they are very flat, and because as we were coming here we had easterly winds, which are warm.

The water in the rivers here is brackish near the mouth. I do not know where the Indians get their water; they have fresh water in their houses. Ships could tack about to enter and leave this river, and there are very clear leading marks. There is seven or eight fathoms' depth at the mouth and five inside. I think this whole sea must always be as calm as the river at Seville, and the water seems perfect for pearls. I found some large snails, different from those in Spain, with no taste.

On the SE side of this river and harbour where we are now lying there are two round mountains, and to the WNW is a fine level promontory.

Tuesday, 30 October

Sailed NW from the river Mares. After sixteen leagues I sighted a headland covered in palm trees and called it Cabo de Palmas.[1] The Indians on the caravel Pinta said that beyond the cape there is a river, and from the river to Cuba is a four-day journey. The captain of the Pinta said that he understood them to mean that this Cuba is a city, and that this is the mainland, running far to the north, and the king is at war with the Great Khan, whom they call Cami, and his country or city is called Fava, and they gave many other names.[2]

I have decided to sail to this river, and to send a gift to the king with Your Majesties' letter. I have a seaman for this purpose who has done the same task in Guinea, and some of the Indians from Guanahani are willing to go with him, provided that I take them back to their own land afterwards.

We are, I think, forty-two degrees north of the equinoctial line.[3] I am going to make every effort to find the Great Khan, who I believe is not far away, or reach the city of Cathay which belongs to him, and is very large, or so I was told before leaving Spain. All this land is low-lying and beautiful, and the sea is deep.

Wednesday, 31 October
Beating to windward the whole night. I saw a river which we could not enter, the mouth being too shallow; the Indians thought the ships would be able to sail in as easily as their canoes. I sailed on, and found a long headland surrounded by shallows, with a bay or cove which could take small ships. I could not sail into it because the wind had shifted due N, and the whole coast runs NNW and SE, and another cape ahead was even longer. For this reason, and seeing the sky threatening strong winds, I had to return to the river Mares.

Thursday, 1 November
I sent the boats ashore at sunrise, and the men found that all the people had fled. A good while later one man appeared, and I ordered him to be left unmolested, and the boats returned. When we had eaten I sent one of the Indians ashore. He shouted to the man from a distance, telling him that we were good people and were doing no harm to anybody, and were not from the Great Khan, but had been giving things away in all the islands which we had visited. Then he jumped into the water and swam ashore, and two of the islanders took him by the arms and led him to a house to question him. When they were sure that no harm was intended them, they were reassured and more than sixteen canoes came out to the ships with cotton thread and other small items. I gave orders for none of this to be taken, so that they would know that I am seeking only gold, which they call *nucay*. So they kept coming and going between the land and the ships all day, and my men went ashore quite safely.

I did not see any of them wearing gold, but I did see one with a piece of worked silver in his nose, so I deduce that there is silver here. They told me by signs that within three days many merchants will arrive from the interior of the island to buy the things we have brought, and they will give us information about the king of this land, who (as far as I can understand their signs) lives four days' journey from here, for they have sent many messengers throughout the land with news of my arrival.

These people are of the same type and customs as the others we have found. They appear to have no religion, for so far I have not seen the ones we have on board saying any prayers; in fact they say the *Salve* and the *Ave María* holding their hands up to Heaven as they are shown, and they make the sign of the cross. They all speak the same language and are all friends, as I believe are all these islands, and I think they are at war with the Great Khan. They call him Cavila, and the province Bafan. They go about naked, like the others.

This river is very deep, and at the mouth the ships can berth right up to the shore. It is brackish up to a league upriver, and above that the water is very sweet. I am sure that this is the mainland, and that Zayton and Quinsay lie ahead of us, each about a hundred leagues from here. This is evident from the sea, which is flowing differently from previously, and sailing NW yesterday I found that it was cold.

Friday, 2 November
I decided to send off two of my men, Rodrigo de Jerez, from Ayamonte, and Luis de Torres, who used to be with the Captain-General of Murcia and was once a Jew, and knows Hebrew and Chaldean and even Arabic. I sent two Indians with them, one from among those I brought from Guanahani and another from the houses by the river /who had come out to the ships in a little canoe./[1] I gave them strings of beads to buy food if they need it and told them to come back in six days. I also gave them samples of spices with instructions to look out for more of them.

I told them how to make enquiries after the king of this land, and what they are to say on behalf of the King and Queen of Spain, who have sent me to hand over their letters with a gift so as to learn of his status and make friends with him and assist him in whatever he may require of us. They are also to find out about certain areas and harbours and rivers of which I am informed, and their distance from here, etc.

I took a sighting of the altitude of the Pole Star tonight with a quadrant and found that we are forty-two degrees N of the equinoctial line.[2] By my reckoning we have sailed 1,317 leagues from the island of Hierro to this mainland.

Saturday, 3 November
In the morning I got into the boat and, because the mouth of the river forms a great lagoon, an exceptionally fine harbour, deep and free from rocks, with a good beach for careening ships and plenty of timber, I went upriver as far as the fresh water, about two leagues. I climbed a little hill to see something of the lie of the land, but I could see nothing for great woods. They were fresh and full of pleasant odours, and I am sure they must contain aromatic herbs. I could never tire of looking at all this beauty or of hearing the song of the birds.

Many canoes came to the ship today to exchange cotton thread and the nets in which the people sleep.[1]

¶ DEMONSTRACION
del Quadrante.

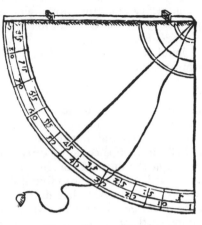

2 November   Quadrant

Sunday, 4 November
Immediately after daybreak I went ashore in the boat to catch some of the birds I saw yesterday. On my return Martín Alonso Pinzón brought me two pieces of cinnamon, and told me that a Portuguese sailor on his ship had seen an Indian with two big bundles of it, but had not dared to barter for it because I had said that I would punish anyone who engaged in barter. The Indian was also carrying red things like walnuts, and the bosun of the Pinta said he had found two cinnamon trees, but when I went to look I found that they were not. I showed some of the local Indians cinnamon and pepper,[1] which they recognized; they made signs to me that there is plenty of it to the SE of here.

I also showed them gold and pearls, and some of the old ones told me that in a place called Bohío there are endless quantities of gold, and the people wear it around their necks and arms and legs and in their ears, and pearls too. I also understood them to say that there are large ships and a trade in goods, all to the SE, and that a long way away there are men with one eye, and others with noses like dogs who eat human flesh; when they capture someone they cut his throat and drink his blood and cut off his private parts.

I decided to return to the ship to wait for the two men I sent off, and to go in search of these lands, unless they bring good news of what we are seeking. The people here are very timid and gentle, naked as I have described, with no weapons and no religion.[2] The land is very rich, and is planted up with *niames*,[3] which are like carrots and taste of chestnuts, and they also have various kinds of beans, quite different from our own, and plenty of cotton, not sown but growing wild. I think it must be there for the picking all the time, for I have seen the open heads and others just opening and the flowers all on the same bush. There are hundreds of other kinds of fruit, more than I can describe, and it must all be useful.

Monday, 5 November
At daybreak I had the ship careened and ordered the others to do the same, but not all at once, so that for safety's sake there would always be two where we were anchored; not that there is any danger from these people, and all three ships could be careened at the same time without any risk. While the ship was careened the bosun of the Niña came to ask for a reward[1] because he had found some mastic,[2] but he did not bring me a sample because he had dropped it. I promised him his reward and sent Rodrigo Sánchez and Master Diego to the trees and they brought me a little of the mastic and also a sample of the tree. We recognized it as mastic, although it has to be gathered in due season, and there is enough here to yield a thousand quintals a year. I have also noticed many of what I think are aloe plants.[3]

The harbour of Mares is one of the finest in the world, with the best climate and the gentlest people. It has a rocky headland, slightly elevated, on which one could build a fortress, so that if this place turns out to be productive and commercially important merchants from all over the world will be safe here. May Our Lord, in whose hands all victory lies, so dispose all things that they may be of service to Him.

An Indian told me by signs that the mastic is good for stomach ache.

Tuesday, 6 November
The two men I sent inland to explore came back last night and told me they had gone twelve leagues when they reached a village of fifty houses. There were about a thousand inhabitants, for they live many to a house. The houses are like big campaign tents. The men said they were received with great ceremony, according to the customs of the place. Everyone, men and women, came to see them, and they were lodged in the best houses. The people kept touching them and kissing their hands and feet in amazement, thinking they had come from Heaven, and so they gave them to understand. They were given food, and they told me that when they arrived the foremost men in the village led them by the arm to the most important house and sat them on /curious chairs, carved out of a single piece of wood in the shape of an animal with short arms and legs and its tail raised a little to form a

backrest, though this is as broad as the seat to give comfortable support; there is a head in front with eyes and ears of gold. They call these chairs *duhos.*/[1] All the men sat around them on the ground. The Indian who was with my men told them about our way of life, saying that we were good people. Then all the men went out and the women came in and sat around them in the same way, kissing their hands and feet and touching them to see if they were flesh and blood like themselves. /They gave them some cooked roots to eat which tasted like chestnuts./[2] They invited them to stay for at least five days.

My men showed them the cinnamon and pepper and other spices which I had given them, and were told by signs that there were plenty of spices nearby to the SE, but they did not know if there were any in the place itself.

Seeing that there were no great cities, my men came back. If they had allowed everyone to accompany them who wanted to, more than five hundred men and women would have come, thinking they were returning to Heaven. However, one important man of the village came with them, and his son and one of his men. I talked to them and received them with honour, and he told me about many lands and islands in these parts. I thought of bringing them back to Your Majesties, but for some reason, probably through fear and the darkness of the night, he took it into his head to leave the ship. Not wishing to distress him, and because I had the ship high and dry, I let him go. He said he would come back at daybreak, but he did not return.

My two men met many people crossing their path to reach their villages, men and women, carrying in their hand a burning brand and herbs which they use to produce fragrant smoke.[3] They came across no village of more than five houses, and they were treated with the same attention by all the people. They saw many kinds of trees, plants and scented flowers, and birds of many varieties, different from those of Spain, except that there were partridges, and nightingales singing, and geese; of these there are plenty. They saw no four-footed beasts except silent dogs. The land is very fertile and well worked, with *niames* and varieties of beans, very unlike our own; also millet and a great amount of cotton, picked, spun and woven. In one house they saw more than 500 *arrobas* of it, and they say that in a good year there could be 4,000 quintals. I do not think the people sow it; it produces all the year round, and is very fine with a large head.

They give whatever they have for the most miserable price; a big basket of cotton for a lace end, or whatever else one offers them. They are a most innocent and unwarlike people; men and women go about as naked as they were born. The women do wear a little cotton thing, just big enough to cover their private part and no more. They are good-looking, not very dark, in fact paler than the women on the Canaries.

I am quite sure, Your Most Serene Majesties, that if devout religious people knew their language well they would all readily be converted to Christianity, so I trust in Our Lord that Your Majesties will decide to make a resolute effort to convert these large populations and bring them into the Church, as you have destroyed those who refused to acknowledge the Father, the Son and the Holy Ghost; and that when your own days are done (for we are all mortal flesh) you will leave your realms in peace and cleansed of heresy and evil, and be received before the throne of the eternal Creator, who I pray will grant you a long life and a great increase in your kingdoms and territories, and the will and desire to increase the Holy Religion of Christianity, as you have done until now, *Amen.*

I refloated the ship today and am making haste to set off on Thursday in the name of God to sail to the southeast in search of gold and spices and to discover new land.[4]

Monday, 12 November
At the end of the dawn watch we left the harbour of the river Mares to sail to an island which the Indians on board have told me is called Babeque,[1] where according to their signs the people gather gold on the beach at night with torches and then beat it into bars with a hammer. To find it we must head E by s. /It is a little cold, and it would be unwise to sail north with winter coming on./[2]

Eight and a half leagues along the coast I found a river, and four leagues further on a second one, bigger than any of the others. I decided not to stop and sail into either of them for two reasons: the first and most important is that I have fair wind and weather for sailing in search of Babeque; the second is that if there were any large or notable city on the lower reaches we would see it, and to explore upriver would require smaller vessels than ours, and so much time would be lost. Such rivers as these deserve special exploration on their own. This whole area is populated, especially near the river, which I have called the Río del Sol.[3]

Yesterday, Sunday, 11 November, I thought it a good idea to take some of the people from the river to convey them to Your Majesties, so that they may learn our language and tell us what there is in their country, and learn our customs and matters of the Faith, and interpret for our people when they return, for I can see from my own observations that these people have no religion, nor are they idolators. They are gentle, and do not know the meaning of evil, nor killing, nor taking prisoners; they have no weapons and are so timid that one of our men can frighten away a hundred of them, just as a joke. They are ready to believe; they acknowledge that there is a God in Heaven, and are convinced that that is where we have come from, and they are quick to recite any prayer we tell them to say, and to make the sign of the cross.

Your Majesties should therefore determine to convert them to Christianity, for I believe that once this is begun a host of peoples will soon be converted to our Holy Faith, and great domains and their wealth and all their peoples will be won for Spain, for there is no doubt that these lands hold enormous quantities of gold. Not for nothing do the Indians I have on board tell us that there are places on these islands where they dig up the gold and wear it in their ears and round their necks and arms and legs, thick bands of it, and there are also precious stones and pearls and endless spices.

On the river Mares, which I left last night, there is certainly a great amount of mastic, and it could be increased if more were wanted, for these trees take easily if re-planted and there are plenty of them, very large, with leaves and fruit like the mastic tree, but both tree and fruit are bigger, as Pliny tells us.[4] I have seen many of these trees on the island of Chios, in the archipelago, and I had some of them tapped to see if they would give some sap to take away. It rained all the time I was in that river, so I was unable to gather any except a small amount which I am bringing to Your Majesties. It may also be that this is the wrong season for tapping them, which I think is best done when the trees are emerging from winter and preparing to flower; here the fruit is almost ripe.

One could also obtain great quantities of cotton, which I think could very well be sold here (rather than taking it to Spain) in the cities of the Great Khan which will no doubt be discovered, and in many of those of the other princes who will be pleased to serve Your Majesties, where they will be given goods from Spain and the lands of the east (for to us these lands are in the west). There is also an endless supply of aloes, though this is not something to make a fortune out of, whereas the mastic is really worthy of attention, being found only on the island of Chios which I have mentioned. They make a good 50,000 ducats from it there, if I remember rightly.

Moreover, the mouth of the river I have described is the finest harbour I ever saw, broad and deep and clean-bottomed, with a good location and site for building a town and a fortress where ships of all kinds could berth alongside the walls, and the land is high and temperate, with good fresh water.

A canoe came alongside us yesterday with six young men. Five of them came aboard, and I ordered them to be seized and have brought them away with me. I then sent men to a house on the west side of the river, and they brought back seven females,[5] some young and some adult, with three children. I did this because men behave better in Spain when they have women of their own land with them than when they are deprived of them. Men have often been taken from Guinea to Portugal to learn the language, and given good treatment and gifts, and when they were taken back with a view to employing them in their own country they went ashore and were never seen again. Others behaved differently. If they have their women they will be eager to take on whatever duties one asks of them, and the women themselves will be good for teaching our people[6] their language, which is the same throughout all these islands of India. They all understand each other, and go about from island to island in their canoes; quite differently from in Guinea, where there are a thousand different languages, incomprehensible to one another.

Last night the husband of one of these women, the father of the three children, a boy and two girls, came out to the ship in a canoe and asked me to take him with them, which I was very pleased to do. They are all happier now, so it appears that they are all related. The man is about forty-five.

By sunset today, Monday, I have sailed nineteen leagues E by S, and have reached a headland which I have named Cabo de Cuba.[7]

Tuesday, 13 November
I spent all last night tacking to and fro because I had sighted a division between one range of mountains and another. It was sighted just at sunset, when we could see two enormous mountains, and appeared to be the division between the land of Cuba and that of Bohío, which is what the Indians on board told me by signs. When it was clear day I filled away for the land, passing a point which appeared about two leagues off in the night, and entered a great gulf five leagues to the SSW, and it was another five leagues to the cape where there was a gap between two large hills. I could not tell if it was an arm of the sea.[1]

My aim was to sail to the island called Babeque, which lies to the east, and I could see no great settlement which would justify my fighting my way into a wind[2] which was now blowing up stronger than anything we had experienced so far, so I decided to gain sea-room and sail E with the northerly wind. We were running at six and a half knots, and from changing course at ten in the morning until sunset we made forty-four and a half miles E, or fifteen leagues, from the Cabo de Cuba.

Of the coast of the other island, Bohío, which we had to leeward, I explored sixty-four miles, or twenty-one leagues, from the cape of the gulf I have mentioned. The whole coast runs from ESE to WNW.

Wednesday, 14 November
I spent all last night jogging off and on; it is senseless to sail among these islands at night without exploring them first, and the Indians on board told me yesterday that it would be three days' sailing from the river Mares to the island of Babeque, that is to say three days in their canoes, which can make seven leagues a day. Also the wind was not what I needed[1] and I could only head E by S instead of due E as I wished. [. . .][2] At sunrise I decided to seek a harbour, the wind having veered from N to NE, and if I had not found one I should have had to go back to the ones I left in Cuba.

After sailing nineteen miles E by S in the night and [. . .] miles S, I reached land, where I saw many inlets and small islands and harbours, but with the strength of the wind and the heavy sea I did not dare attempt to sail into them. I therefore ran NW by W along the coast in search of a haven, and saw many, but none very accessible. After sailing fifty-one miles in this fashion I found a deep channel, a third of a mile wide, with a good river and harbour, into which I sailed. I put our bows to the SSW and then to the S and eventually to the SE, finding a good breadth and depth of water everywhere.

Here I found innumerable islands, of a good size and very lofty, covered with all kinds of trees and countless palms. I was amazed to see so many islands, all so mountainous. I assure Your Majesties that the mountains I have seen since the day before yesterday along these coasts and on these islands must be higher and lovelier and clearer than any in the world, with no mist or snow, and a great depth of water at their feet. These must, I think, be those islands without number which men depict in the farthest orient on their maps of the world. I believe they hold great riches, precious stones and spices, and that they stretch far to the south and spread out in all directions.

I am calling this the Mar de Nuestra Señora,[3] and the harbour near the channel leading to these islands Puerto del Príncipe.[4] Do not be surprised, Your Majesties, that I am so lavish in my praise; I assure you that I do not think I am telling you a hundredth part of it all. Some of the islands seem to reach the sky, and their tops are like the points of diamonds; others climb up to a sort of high, high plateau, and at their feet there is such an immense depth of water that a great carrack could berth hard alongside them; no rocky outcrops, and woods everywhere.

Thursday, 15 November
I decided to explore these islands in the ships' boats. [. . .][1] I found mastic trees and endless aloe plants. Some of the islands are tilled and planted with the roots from which the Indians make their bread, and I found traces of fires here and there. I found no fresh water. There were

a few people, who ran away. Everywhere I went I found fifteen or sixteen fathoms of water, and the bottom is clean sand everywhere.[2]

Friday, 16 November

I am leaving a cross planted everywhere I land in these islands and territories. I therefore went ashore in the boat at the channel leading into these harbours, and on a spit of land I found two large timbers, one longer than the other, lying across one another in the shape of a cross, as precisely as any carpenter could have placed them. We knelt before them in prayer, and I have ordered a great high cross to be made using the two timbers.

I found canes on the shore, but I could not see where they were growing. I think some river must bring them down and deposit them on the shore.[1] I went to a cove[2] inside the harbour entrance on the southeastern side, where there is a kind of high headland with rocky outcrops, and a great depth of water below it. The largest carrack in the world could berth hard up to it, and there is a little corner where six ships could lie without anchors as if they were inside a hall.[3] It would be a very easy place to build a fortress if this sea full of islands should ever turn out to be a great trading place. When I returned to the ship I found my Indians fishing for large sea snails. I ordered the men to go into the sea with them to see if there were any *nácaras*, which are the oysters which produce pearls,[4] and they found many of them, but no pearls. It must not be the season for them, which I think is May and June.

The men found an animal like a badger.[5] They also did some fishing with nets and caught large numbers of fish, including one just like a pig, different from a tunny. It has a stiff shell all over it; the only soft parts are its eyes and tail and a hole underneath through which it voids itself. I am having it salted to bring to show Your Majesties.

Saturday, 17 November

I set off in the boat in the morning to explore the island on the southwestern side which I had not yet seen. I saw many more, all green and pleasant, and found a great depth of water in between them. Some of them are separated by channels of fresh water; it must be flowing from springs high in the mountains. As I continued I found a most beautiful river of fresh water, flowing very cold because of its shallowness, and beside it a fair meadow with many lofty palm trees, the tallest I have seen so far.

I found large nuts, of the kind which grow in India,[1] and big rats[2] like the ones in India,[3] and some huge crabs. There were great numbers of birds, and a strong odour of musk; I am sure there must be some here.

Today the two eldest of the six young men I captured on the river Mares escaped. I had transferred them to the Niña.

Sunday, 18 November
I went ashore again in the boats with a large number of the ship's company to set up the great cross I have had made from the two pieces of timber at the mouth of the channel into the Puerto del Príncipe. We placed it in a space free from trees where it can be clearly seen. It is very tall and looks very fine.

The sea rises and falls much more here than in any other harbour I have seen in these waters, which is not surprising since there are so many islands. The tides are contrary to our own, for with the moon in the SW by S it is low tide here.[1]

I did not sail, today being Sunday.

Monday, 19 November
I set sail before sunrise, in a calm. Light winds from the E at midday, and I sailed NNE. At sunset Puerto del Príncipe was about seven leagues away to the SSW. Sighted the island of Babeque about fifty miles due E. Sailed all night just N of NE, about forty-eight miles, and another nine and a half by ten o'clock in the morning; total nineteen leagues NE by N.

Tuesday, 20 November
Babeque, or the islands of Babeque, lay ESE, right upwind of us, and seeing that there was no change in the wind and the sea was rising I decided to return to Puerto del Príncipe, from which I had come, twenty-six and a half leagues away. I did not go to the small island which I named Isabela, thirteen leagues away, where I could have gone to anchor today, for two reasons: first I had sighted two islands to the S which I wanted to see; and secondly I did not want the Indians I captured in Guanahani, which I called San Salvador, to escape, for it is only eight and a half leagues from Isabela. I have need of them, and mean to take them to Castile [. . .][1] They think that when I have found gold I am going to let them return home.

We came close to Puerto del Príncipe but could not get in, it being night and the strong currents taking us NW. We went about and steered NE with a strong wind, which lessened and changed in the third watch, when we headed E by N. The wind was SSE and at dawn veered S, with a little E in it. At sunrise I took a bearing on Puerto del Príncipe and found it SW, westerly, about thirty-eight miles away, or twelve and a half leagues.

Wednesday, 21 November
I sailed E at sunrise with the wind S. Made only a small distance because of the contrary sea, nineteen miles by the hour of vespers. The wind then backed to E and we sailed S by E, nine and a half miles by sunset. I took a sight and found us forty-two degrees to the north of the equinoctial line, the same as in the harbour of Mares, but I have now hung up my quadrant until we reach port where I can have it adjusted; we cannot be so far north.[1] I am disturbed by finding the Pole Star as high as in Castile; it is too warm for that.[2] The heat makes me think that these islands and the area through which I am sailing must contain a lot of gold.

Today Martín Alonso Pinzón has sailed away on his own in the Pinta without my permission, moved by greed. He believes that an Indian I ordered him to take aboard his ship will give him a lot of gold. He went without waiting, not through stress of weather but because he chose to. He has gone against me in word and deed many times before.

Thursday, 22 November
On Wednesday night I sailed S by E with the wind E, almost calm. In the third watch the wind backed NNE. I continued S to see the land which lies in that quarter, and at sunrise I found the land as far away as the day before, thirty-two miles, because of the adverse currents. Last night Martín Alonso Pinzón sailed on E for the island of Babeque, where the Indians say there are large amounts of gold. He was in sight about thirteen miles from us. I stayed on course for the land all night,[1] and I shortened sail and had a lantern hoisted because I thought he was sailing towards us; it was a bright, clear night with a favourable wind for rejoining us.

Friday, 23 November
Sailed S all day in light winds towards the land, set back all the time by the current, so that we were further from land at sunset than in the morning. The wind was ENE, a fair enough wind for sailing S, but light.

Close on this cape lies another land or cape, also running E. The Indians call it Bohío, and say it is very large and inhabited by another people with one eye in their forehead, and others whom they call cannibals, of whom they are very afraid. When they saw that we were sailing on this course they could not speak; the people eat them, and are very well armed. I believe there is some truth in this, but if they are armed they must be people of intelligence. I think they must have taken some captives, and when they did not return it was probably thought that they had been eaten. The Indians thought the same thing about me and the ship's company when some of them saw us for the first time.

Saturday, 24 November
Sailed on all night, and in the morning at the hour of terce reached the flat island,[1] in the same place as last week on our way to Babeque. At first I did not dare approach the land, for it appeared that the sea was very rough in that division between the mountains. At last we reached the Mar de Nuestra Señora, the one with the many islands, and entered the harbour[2] at the mouth of the channel to the islands. If I had known of this harbour at first and had not spent time exploring the islands in the Mar de Nuestra Señora, it would not have been necessary to turn back, although my time exploring the islands was not wasted.

On reaching land I sent the boat to take soundings in the harbour, and they found a good bar and a depth of between six and twenty fathoms, all clean sand. I sailed in with our bows to the sw and then turned w, with the flat island to the n. This island and another form a sea lagoon which would hold the whole Spanish fleet without hawsers, safe from every wind that blew.

This entrance on the southeastern side, which can be entered with one's bows heading ssw, has a way out, very wide and deep, at its western end, so that one can sail between the islands. To assist anyone coming from the north, which is the course for this coast,[3] to recognize the islands, they lie at the foot of a great long mountain which runs e–w, longer and higher than any of the others on this coast, which has many of them, and outside them is a reef running parallel to the mountain, like a bar as far as the entrance. All this is on the southeastern side, and there is another reef on the same side as the flat island, though this one is smaller, and between the two there is ample width and depth, as I have explained.

Later, at the entrance on the southeastern side, within the harbour itself, we saw a large and beautiful river, with more water in it than any we have seen hitherto, and it is fresh water down to the mouth. There is a bank at the mouth, but inside there is a depth of eight or nine fathoms. It is all surrounded by palm trees and woods like the others.

Sunday, 25 November
Before sunrise I went in the boat to look at a cape or point of land to the southeast of the flat island, about a league and a half away, where I thought there must be another good river. A couple of crossbow shots after doubling the cape, on its southeastern side, I found a large and beautiful stream of water rushing noisily down from a mountain. I went to the river and saw stones glittering in it, with patches of golden

colour in them, and I recalled that gold was found in the river Tagus at its junction with the sea. I felt sure this river must contain gold, and I ordered some of the stones to be gathered to bring home to Your Majesties.

While this was happening some of the ship's boys shouted that they could see pine woods. I looked up into the mountains and saw the trees, tall and splendid, bigger and straighter than I can well describe, like thick and thin spindles, and now I know that ships could be built here; there is an endless supply of planking and masts for the biggest ships in Spain. I saw oak and strawberry trees, and a good river and materials for water-powered sawmills.

The land and the breezes are cooler than hitherto, because of the height of these beautiful mountains. On the shore I saw many other stones the colour of iron, and others which some of the crew said had come from silver mines, all washed down by the river. I had a mizzenmast and yard cut for the Niña.

We came to the mouth of the river and into an inlet at the foot of the cape on the southeastern side, very wide and deep, the finest harbour a man ever saw; a hundred ships could lie there without mooring ropes or anchors. The mountains are very high, with many beautiful streams running down, and all the hills are covered in pine trees, and there are the most lovely and varied woods everywhere. We left another two or three rivers behind us.

It has given me incalculable pleasure and joy, Your Majesties, to see all this, especially the pine trees, for one could build as many ships here as one wished if one brought in the equipment; wood is here in plenty and pitch could be easily made. I am not giving it the hundredth part of the praise it deserves; it has pleased Our Lord always to show me something finer than before, and in all my discoveries things have grown better and better: the lands, the woods, the plants, the fruit and flowers, and the people; always different, wherever I have gone. I am full of wonder at the sight of it; how much more wonderful it will seem to those who hear of it, for no one will believe it unless they see it with their own eyes.

Monday, 26 November

Weighed anchor at sunrise from where we were lying in the harbour of Santa Catalina, on the inside of the flat island, and sailed along the coast with a light southwesterly wind towards the Cabo del Pico[1] to the southeast. We took a long time to reach the cape because the wind fell away. On reaching it we saw another headland lying SE by E about fifty miles beyond it, and another closer to us, about fifteen miles SE by S, which I have called the Cabo de Campana.[2] We failed to make it before nightfall because the wind fell away to a dead calm. The day's run was about twenty-four and a half miles, or eight leagues, in the course of which I sighted and marked nine notable harbours, which all the men agreed were very fine, and five large rivers. I was keeping close inshore so as to see everything.

The whole country consists of lofty and beautiful mountains, not dry and rocky, but all walkable, with fair valleys. Hills and valleys alike are covered in tall, fresh trees which are a glory to the eye; many of them look like pines. Behind the Cabo del Pico, on the southeastern side, are two small islands, each about two leagues in circumference, and to their landward side are three splendid harbours and two large rivers.

We have sighted no habitations from the sea anywhere on this coast. It may be populated, and there are indications that it is; wherever we went ashore we found signs of people and the remains of many fires.

The land which we sighted today to the southeast of the Cabo de Campana must be the island which the Indians call Bohío, because there is some distance between it and the cape. All the people I have found so far are terrified of the 'Caniba' or 'Canima', who they say live on the island of Bohío, which must be very large. I believe they come to seize these people's land and houses because they are so cowardly and unskilful in fighting. I think these Indians whom we have on board live away from the coast because they are so close to this island of Bohío; when they saw me altering course for there they could not speak for fear that they were going to be eaten, and I could not reassure them. They say the Bohío people have faces like dogs and only one eye. I think they are lying; the people who take them captive must be under the rule of the Great Khan.

Tuesday, 27 November

At sunset yesterday we were approaching a cape which I called Campana. The sky being clear and the wind light I decided not to sail inshore to anchor, although I had five or six excellent harbours to leeward, because I am lingering more than I intended, such are the appetite and delight aroused in me by the beauty and freshness of these islands everywhere I go, and I must not delay in my pursuit of my aims. I therefore spent the night hove-to or jogging off and on[1] until daybreak.

The tides and currents had carried us more than five or six leagues in the night from where we had been off the land of Campana at nightfall, and beyond the cape we sighted a great opening which appeared to divide one land from another, with what appeared to be an island in the middle. I decided to sail back, the wind being sw, and coming to where we had seen the opening I found that it was only a great bay, with a cape at the southeastern end of it and a high, square mountain[2] which looked like an island.

The wind veered suddenly N, and I changed course back to SE to run along the coast and see what it held. At the foot of the Cabo de Campana I saw an excellent harbour and a fine river, and a quarter-league from there another river, and a half-league on another, and a half-league on another, and after a further half-league another, and then a quarter-league on another, and a league further on yet another large river, about fifteen miles from Cabo de Campana. These are all to the SE of the cape, and most of them have fine entrance channels, wide and clear, and form splendid harbours for large ships, with no sandbanks or rocks or reefs.

On our way along the coast to the southeast of this last river I found a large village, the biggest so far, with huge numbers of people coming down to the shore shouting, all naked with assegais[3] in their hands. Wishing to talk to them, I furled all sail and anchored. I sent the boats ashore from both vessels with orders not to harm the Indians or to suffer any harm, and to give them a few trifles of barter goods.

The Indians made gestures of resistance, indicating that they would not let the men land, but when they saw that the boats were approaching the shore and our men were not afraid they ran away from the sea. Thinking that if only two or three men got out of the boats the Indians would not be afraid, two of my men went ashore and told them in their own language not to be afraid; they know a little of the language from the Indians we have with us. Finally all the Indians, men and boys, ran away.

The three [*sic*] men went to look at the houses, which are made of straw and similar to the others we have seen, and found them all empty of people and stripped of possessions. They came back on board and we made sail at noon to go to a handsome headland to the east, about eight leagues away. After sailing half a league across the bay I sighted a most excellent harbour[4] on the southern side, and to the southeast a most beautiful stretch of country, including a rolling plain surrounded by mountains, with large columns of smoke and villages in it, and the land well tilled. I therefore decided to go ashore in this harbour to see if I could have some converse or dealings with them.

Whatever I have said about the other harbours, this one is even finer, such is the lie of the land around it, the terrain so kindly and well populated. The beauty of the landscape and the woods is wonderful, with pines and palm trees, and so is the great plain running to the southwest. It is not completely flat, but is composed of low, rolling hills, the loveliest sight in all the world, with many streams running down from the mountains and out across it.

We anchored, and I got down into the boat to take soundings in the harbour, which is shaped like a flat dish. /Going[5] in the boats to the south of the harbour mouth, I found a river which a galley could row into comfortably. It was invisible except from close to, but was so beautiful that I was tempted to go a boat's length into it, where I found a depth of up to eight fathoms. I continued upriver in the boats for a good distance. The beauty and freshness of the river, so clear that we could see the sand on the bottom; all the various sorts of palm tree, taller and more beautiful than any I have encountered before; the endless variety of other trees, so tall and green; the birds; the greenness of the level ground – all this made me want to stay here forever.

The loveliness of this country, Your Majesties, is so marvellous; it surpasses all others in amenity and beauty as daylight exceeds night. I have said repeatedly to my men that, whatever efforts I make to tell Your Majesties about it, my tongue[6] could not tell the whole truth, or my hand set it down. Truly, I was dumbfounded by the sight of so much beauty, and find myself unable to describe it adequately. I have already written everything I could about the other places, their trees and fruits, their plants, their harbours and all their splendours, without doing them justice. Everyone has said that nowhere else could be more beautiful. I will write no more now; I hope that other men will see it and wish to describe it in writing, and do so rather better, if they can be as felicitous in describing it as the beauty of the place deserves./

I will not attempt to describe the extent of the benefits to be gained from this place. Certainly, Your Majesties, there must be countless useful things in lands such as these, but I am not lingering in any one harbour because I prefer to explore as many more lands as I can so as to describe them to Your Majesties. Moreover, I do not know the language; the people do not understand me, nor I them, nor any of my company. I often misunderstand what these Indians I have on board tell me, and I do not trust them, for they have tried repeatedly to escape. But now, God willing, I shall see whatever I can, understanding and learning gradually, and I shall have the language taught to one of my people, for I can see that so far the same language is spoken everywhere. Then it will be possible to find out which things are useful and to convert these people to Christianity. It will be easy, for they have no faith and do not worship idols; Your Majesties will have a city and a fort built here and these lands will be converted.

I assure Your Majesties that there can be no finer lands under the sun for their fertility, their freedom from extremes of heat and cold, and their abundance of healthy water; not like the rivers of Guinea, which are full of disease, for praise be to God not a single member of my company has had so much as a headache or taken to his bed ill, except one old man with the stone, which he has suffered from all his life, and he recovered in a couple of days. I am writing here of all three ships. So it will please God, Your Majesties, to see learned men come here or be sent by you, for they will then see the truth of it all.

I have written earlier of the site for a town and fortress on the river Mares, with its fine harbour and surroundings. All that I said was true enough, but there is no comparing the river Mares or the Mar de Nuestra Señora with this place. There must be large settlements inland here, with hosts of people, and things of great profit. For if Christendom is to enter into trade with all the places I have discovered so far, and hope to find before I return home, how much more, I say, must Spain, to whom it must all be subject. And Your Majesties, in my opinion, should not allow any foreigner to do business or gain a foothold here, but only Catholic Christians, for that is the beginning and end of the whole enterprise; it should be for the growth and glory of the Christian faith, and you should allow no one but good Christians to come here.

I went upriver and found several tributaries, and going around the harbour I found a beautiful wood at the mouth of the river, like a delightful orchard, and a canoe made from a single timber. It was as big as a twelve-seater *fusta*,[7] and had been drawn up under a boathouse or canopy of wood thatched with large palm leaves so that neither sun nor water could harm it.

This would be a fine place to build a town or city and a fortress, what with the good harbour, the sweet water and kindly land, the pleasant surroundings and the large supply of timber.

Wednesday, 28 November
Remained in harbour all day because of rain and heavy cloud, although the wind was sw. This would have been a favourable and following wind for running down the coast, but since it was difficult to make out the land and unfamiliarity with the coast only runs the ships into danger I remained at anchor. The men went ashore from both ships. Some of them went inland a little to wash their clothes, and found large villages with all the houses empty, the people having run away. They came back down a different river, larger than the one which flows into the harbour close to us.

Thursday, 29 November
Remained in harbour, the rain persisting and the sky still cloudy. Some of the men went to another village near the northwestern side of the harbour, but found the houses completely empty. On the way they came across an old man who had not been able to run away. They captured him but told him that they wished him no harm and gave him a few oddments of barter goods, then they let him go. I wish I had seen him, so as to have given him some clothes and asked him

questions, for I am very much taken with the attractions of this land and the possibilities it offers for colonization.[1] I am sure there must be large settlements here. In one house the men found a cake of wax, which I am bringing home to Your Majesties; where there is wax there must be a thousand other good things.[2]

In another house they found a man's head in a basket, covered by another basket, hanging on one of the posts, and another the same in a different village. They must be the heads of some important ancestor, for the houses are big enough for many people to live together in them, all probably descended from one man.

Friday, 30 November

We could not sail because of an E wind, directly contrary to my planned course. I sent eight armed men with two of the Indians from the ship to explore the villages inland and talk to the people. They found many houses, all empty, the inhabitants having fled. They saw four young men digging in the fields, who fled as soon as they saw them and could not be caught.

They walked a long way, seeing many villages. The land was very fertile and all in cultivation, with big rivers. Near one of them they came across a canoe ninety-five handspans long, beautifully made from a single timber, big enough to carry a hundred and fifty people.

Saturday, 1 December

The same contrary wind and heavy rain prevented us from sailing. I set up a large cross on an outcrop of rocks at the entrance to this harbour, which I have called Puerto Santo.[1] I put it on the point on the southeastern side of the entrance channel.

Anyone seeking to enter this harbour should approach closer to the point on the northwestern side than to the other one on the southeastern side. There is twelve fathoms' depth and a good clean bottom off both points on a line with the crag, but off the SE point at the entrance to the harbour there is a bank which dries out, although far enough from the point for a ship to pass inside it if necessary, for there is a depth of twelve or fifteen fathoms between the bank and the point, and when entering harbour the bows should be headed SW.

Sunday, 2 December

Still unable to sail because of adverse winds. There is a land breeze every single night. All the storms in the world need not trouble any ships anchored here; the force of the sea would be broken by the bank at the mouth [. . .][1] One of the apprentice seamen found some stones in the river which appear to have gold in them; I am bringing them back to show Your Majesties. There are other large rivers here, within a lombard shot.

Monday, 3 December
Still unable to leave harbour because of adverse weather. I decided to go to explore a beautiful headland a quarter of a league to the southeast of the harbour. I took a few armed men in the boats. Just beside the headland we found the mouth of a fine river, which one may enter with the bows to the southeast. It is a hundred yards wide,[1] with a fathom's depth at the mouth, but inside we found twelve fathoms, or five, or four, or two, and it would hold all the ships in Spain.

We went ashore from a tributary of this river, and making our way SE we found a cove where there were five very large *almadías*, which the Indians call canoes,[2] like *fustas*, beautifully worked. At the foot of the mountain the land was all tilled. The canoes were under some very thick trees, and we went up a track leading from them and found a boathouse, all neat and covered against the sun and rain, with another canoe made from a single timber like the others, like a seventeen-bench *fusta*. Its beauty and workmanship were a marvel to the eye.

We climbed up a hill as far as a flat area which we found sown with many kinds of vegetables and calabashes, very pleasing to the eye. In the middle of it was a large village. We came suddenly on the people of the village, who fled when they saw us, men and women alike. The Indian I had with me reassured them and told them not to be afraid, for we were good people. I told the men to give them some little bells and brass rings and green and yellow glass beads, with which they were very pleased, for I could see that they had no gold or other precious things about them, and I thought it enough to leave them feeling secure.

The whole area was populated, and the other people had run away in fear. I assure Your Majesties that ten men could put ten thousand of them to flight. They are so cowardly and timid that they do not even carry real weapons, just staffs with a little sharp stick burned to a point on the end. I decided to return. We took all the staffs away from them without difficulty, bartering for them all.

Returning to where we had left the boats, I sent a few men to where we had gone up the hill, for I thought I had seen a large beehive.[3] Before they came back a large number of Indians gathered and approached the boats, into which the men and I had withdrawn. One of them waded into the river as far as the stern of the boat and made a long speech which I did not understand, except that from time to time the rest of the Indians raised their hands high and gave a great shout. I thought they were reassuring us that they were pleased by our arrival, but then I saw that the Indian I had with me was turning as yellow as wax, and trembling, and he made signs to me that we should leave the river because they wanted to kill us. He went to one of my men who had a crossbow loaded and drawn, and showed it to the Indians, telling them, I think, that we would kill them all and that the crossbow could shoot a long way and was deadly. He also took a sword and drew it and showed it to them, saying something similar. When they heard this they all ran away, but our Indian went on trembling from faint-heartedness and cowardice, although he is a strong, well-built man.

I refused to leave the river; instead I made the men row the boat to the shore where the Indians were standing, a great crowd of them, all painted red and as naked as the day they were born, some of them with plumes on their heads, and other feathers, and all carrying bunches of assegais. I went up to them and gave them a few scraps of bread and asked them for the assegais, giving in exchange a little bell to some, a little brass ring to others, a few small beads to others. In this way I calmed them down and they all came down to the boats and gave us everything they had in exchange for whatever we chose to give them. The sailors had killed a turtle and the shell was in pieces in the boat, and the ship's boys were giving a piece the size of a fingernail and receiving a handful of spears from the Indians.

They are like the other people I have seen, with the same beliefs;[4] they thought we had come from Heaven. They will give you whatever they have, straight away, in exchange for anything at all, never saying that it is not enough, and I think they would do the same with spices and gold if they had them.

I saw one beautiful house, not very large, with two doors like all the rest, and when I went in I found a marvellous construction, divided as it were into chambers[5] in a way which I cannot describe, with shells and other things hanging from the roof. I thought it was a temple, and I called them and made signs to ask if they said prayers in it. They said no, and one of them climbed up and was giving me everything the place contained, some of which I accepted.

Tuesday, 4 December

Made sail in light winds and left the harbour of Puerto Santo. After two leagues I saw a fine river, the one I mentioned yesterday. I sailed along the coast, past the cape, and then all down the coast from ESE to WNW as far as Cabo Lindo,[1] which is E by S of Cabo del Monte. It is five leagues from one cape to the other. A league and a half from Cabo del Monte is a substantial, rather narrow river, which seems to have a good entrance channel and to be very deep. Three-quarters of a league from there I saw another very large river, which must be very long. At the mouth it is a hundred yards wide, with no bank across it, and a good entrance channel eight fathoms deep, for I sent the boat to examine it and take soundings. The water is fresh right down to the sea. It is one of the biggest rivers I have come across, and there must be large concentrations of people along its banks.

Beyond Cabo Lindo is a broad bay[2] which would be a good passage[3] ENE and SE and SSE.

Wednesday, 5 December
All last night I remained hove-to[1] off Cabo Lindo, which is where I was at nightfall, in order to explore the land to the east. At sunrise I saw another headland two and a half leagues E, and having rounded it I saw that the coast turned S and slightly SW. I then sighted another beautiful, high headland on that bearing, about seven and a half leagues on from the other.[2] I should have liked to sail to it, but I did not because of my desire to reach the island of Babeque, which the Indians tell me lies NE. I could not make for Babeque either, the wind being NE.

Sailing as I have described I looked SE and saw land, an island which the Indians tell me is called Bohío and is populated. The people of Cuba, or Juana, and all these other islands are very afraid of the people there, for it is said that they eat human flesh. The Indians have told me other remarkable things in sign language, but I do not believe them. The people of Bohío must simply be more intelligent and cunning in capturing them, for they are very faint-hearted.

So because the weather was NE and backing N, I decided to leave Cuba, or Juana,[3] and set off SE by E, although the land I had sighted lay due SE. I took this precaution because the wind here always veers from N to NE and from there to E and SE. The wind strengthened greatly and I was carrying all sail, and with the calm sea and the following current we were running at six and a half knots from morning until one o'clock, less than six hours because the nights here last almost fifteen hours. Later we were doing almost eight knots, and by sunset we had made about seventy miles, or twenty-three and a half leagues, all to the southeast.

As night was falling I ordered the caravel Niña, which is a fast vessel, to sail on ahead to examine the harbour in daylight. When she arrived off the mouth of the harbour, which is like Cadiz Bay, she sent in her boat to take soundings in the harbour, with a lantern. Before I came up to where the caravel was sailing off and on, waiting for the signal from the boat to enter harbour, the light in the boat went out. Seeing no light, the caravel gained some sea-room and signalled to me with a lantern, and when we reached her they told me what had happened. Then the men in the boat lit another light, and the caravel went in to join her. We could not, and spent the night sailing off and on.

Thursday, 6 December

At dawn we were four leagues from the harbour, which I have called Puerto de Santa María.[1] We sighted a beautiful headland about twenty-two miles s by E, which I called Cabo de la Estrella;[2] I think it is the southernmost point of the island. We also sighted land like a small island, about thirty-two miles to the east. About forty-three miles E by s was another handsome, shapely headland which I have called Cabo del Elefante,[3] and about twenty-two miles ESE another which I have called Cabo de Cinquín.[4] Just E of SE, about sixteen miles away, lay a great cleft or opening or inlet of the sea, which looked as if it must be a river.

Between Cabo del Elefante and Cabo de Cinquín there appeared to be a broad passage, and some of the men said it was a channel separating off an island which I have called Isla de la Tortuga.[5] The large island appears to consist of uplands, not mountainous and inaccessible but handsome, level, champaign country, all or most of it cultivated. The sown areas look like the wheat fields in the country around Córdoba in May.

We saw many fires in the night, and in the daytime many columns of smoke as if from watch towers. They appear to be on the alert, looking out for some people with whom they are at war.

The whole length of this coast runs E. At the hour of vespers we entered the harbour I have described, and I have called it Puerto de San Nicolás, in honour of St Nicholas whose feast day it is. As we sailed in I was overcome by its beauty and loveliness. I have said many fine things of the harbours of Cuba, but this one is certainly their equal or even better, and is unlike any of them. The mouth and entrance channel are a league and a half across. The ship should be headed SSE, though with so much width the exact heading is not important. The harbour continues SSE two leagues, and at the entrance there is a kind of corner on the southern side, and from there it continues in the same direction as far as the headland, where there is a most splendid beach and an area of open woodland with all manner of different trees. I think some of them are spice-bearing trees and nutmegs, but they are not ripe and it is difficult to tell. There is a river in the middle of the beach.

The depth of this harbour is remarkable. Right up to a [. . .] length[6] from the shore we could find no bottom with the lead at forty fathoms, and between there and the shore there is fifteen fathoms' depth, with a good, clean bottom. The whole harbour is the same; from both headlands inland there is a depth of fifteen fathoms just a step from the shore, with a clean bottom. It is the same along the whole coast, all good sailing depth[7] and clean, with not a bank anywhere, and hard in to the coast, just an oar's length from the shore, there is five fathoms.

At the landward end of the long part of this harbour running SSE, where a thousand carracks could beat to windward, there is an arm running inland a good half-league to the northeast, the same width all the way as if measured by a rope. It is about twenty-five yards wide, and its shape is such that the mouth of the main entry channel is invisible from it, so that it is like a closed harbour. From one end to the other there is eleven fathoms' depth, all good clean sand, and hard in to the shore, with the gunwales touching the grass, there is eight fathoms. The whole harbour is very breezy, open and clear of trees.

The entire island appears rockier than any other so far. The trees are smaller, and many of them are like Spanish trees – holm oaks, strawberry trees and others – and the same is true of the plants. The land is very high, and all champaign country or open, and the breezes are sweet. This is the coolest place we have found – not that it is especially cold, only so compared to the other islands. Facing the harbour is a fine level plain with the river I have mentioned running through it. There must be large settlements in the area, for we have seen many canoes, some of them as big as a fifteen-bench *fusta*.

All the Indians fled; they kept running away as soon as they saw the ships. The Indians I have brought with me from the small islands are so eager to return home that I think I shall have to take them back when we leave here. They now distrust me so much for not making for their homeland that I have no faith in what they tell me; I cannot understand them clearly, nor they me, but they are in great fear of the people of this island.

I should have liked to remain in this harbour several days in order to talk to these people, but I shall not linger because I have much to explore and I am afraid of running out of time. I trust in Our Lord God that the Indians I have here on board with me will learn my language and I theirs, and that I can return later to talk to these people, and that it may please His Divine Majesty to let me find some good source of gold for which to bargain before I go back home.

Friday, 7 December

At the end of the dawn watch I made sail and left Puerto de San Nicolás. Wind SW. Sailed NE two leagues to a headland[1] where there was a bay[2] to the southeast. The Cabo de la Estrella was nineteen miles away to the southwest. I then sailed E along the coast to Cabo de Cinquín, about thirty-eight miles, sixteen of which were E by N. The whole coast is high, with a great depth of water. There is twenty or thirty fathoms' depth right up to the shore, and a lombard shot out there is no bottom; I took soundings all along the coast, with the wind SW, and was very pleased with my findings.

The bay I have mentioned comes within about a lombard shot of

Puerto de San Nicolás, so that if the land in between were cut there would be an island of about [three to four]³ miles in circumference. All this land is very high, with no tall trees; only small ones like ilexes and strawberry trees, a true Castilian landscape.

Two leagues before reaching Cabo de Cinquín I discovered a small, rocky inlet like a cleft in the mountains, and through it a great valley all sown with something like barley. There must be large numbers of people, and beyond the valley there are great high mountains.

When we reached Cabo de Cinquín the end of Tortuga was to the northeast, about twenty-five miles away. Off Cabo de Cinquín, a lombard shot out, there is a rock above the water, in clear view.⁴ Cabo del Elefante was about fifty miles away E by S, all very high land.

Six and a half leagues on we came to a great bay, with broad valleys inland, champaign country and lofty mountains, all very much resembling Castile. After another six and a half miles we discovered a river, very deep and narrow, though it was wide enough to admit a carrack, and there were no banks or shallows at the mouth, and there were fifteen fathoms all along the sides, only three yards from shore. It goes inland a quarter of a league.

It was still early, about one o'clock in the afternoon, and we had a strong following wind, but because the sky was threatening rain and very cloudy, which is dangerous even when one knows the ground and much more so when one does not, I decided to enter the harbour, which I have called Puerto de la Concepción.⁵ I went ashore by a small river at the end of the harbour. It flows down through a broad valley and landscapes of amazing beauty.

I took fishing nets, and before we reached the shore a mullet just like those in Spain jumped into the boat, the first fish we have seen resembling any Spanish one. The crew did some fishing and caught more of them, as well as some sole and other fish like those of Spain. I walked some distance and found the land all tilled, and heard a nightingale and other small birds like the ones in Spain. We saw five men, but they ran away. I found some myrtle and other trees and plants like those of Castile, and the countryside and mountains are also similar.

Saturday, 8 December
Heavy rain and a strong northerly wind. The harbour is safe from all winds except from the north, but even this can do no harm because there is [no] great surge; neither the surge nor the flow of the river is enough to make the ship work at her moorings.¹ After midnight the wind veered NE and then E. The harbour is well sheltered from these winds by the island of Tortuga, which faces it twenty-eight miles away.

Saturday, 9 December

Rain and wintry weather, like Castile in October. The only habitation I have seen was a splendid house at the Puerto de San Nicolás, which was better built than the ones I have seen elsewhere. The island is very large; it would not surprise me if it were two hundred leagues around. It is all well cultivated. I think the villages must be well away from the coast, and the people see me coming and all run away and take everything with them, and make smoke signals like people at war.

The harbour is a thousand paces wide at the mouth, or a quarter of a league. There are no shallows or banks anywhere in it, in fact one can scarcely find bottom until one is almost hard in to the shore. The good, clean anchoring ground runs three thousand paces in from the mouth, so that any ship may sail in freely and anchor without fear of danger. At the end are the mouths of two small rivers, and inland from the harbour are the finest river valleys in the whole world, very like the lands of Castile, but even more lovely, which is why I have called the island Isla Española.[1]

Monday, 10 December

Strong winds from the northeast. We dragged our anchors half a cable, which astonished me. The reason, I think, was that the anchors were well out towards land and the wind was onshore.[1] Seeing that the wind was unfavourable for my purposes, I sent six men ashore, well armed, to go two or three leagues inland to try to talk with the people. They came back having found neither people nor houses, but they did find a few huts and broad tracks and many dead fires. The lands they saw were the finest in the world, and they found many mastic trees and brought back some mastic. They said it was there in plenty, but this is the wrong time to gather it because it does not set.

Tuesday, 11 December

I did not sail, the wind being still E or NE. Opposite this island, as I have said, is the island of Tortuga, which appears very large. Its coast runs more or less parallel to that of Española, with about ten leagues, at the most, separating them; that is to say from Cabo de Cinquín to the head of Tortuga, after which the coast turns away to the south.

I should like to explore the area between these two islands in order to look at Española, the fairest sight in all the world, but also because the Indians I have on board tell me that it is the way to the island of Babeque, which they describe as very large and mountainous, with great rivers and valleys. They also say that the island of Bohío is bigger than La Juana, which they call Cuba, and is not surrounded by water. I take this to mean that it is the mainland, lying here beyond this island of Española, which they call Caritaba,[1] and that it goes on and on. They must be right when they say that they are harassed by a cunning people, for all these islands are in great fear of the Caniba people, and as I have said before, Caniba means simply the people of the Great Khan, who must live very near here and will have ships; they must come to capture these people, and when they do not return it is supposed that they have been eaten. We understand these Indians better every day, and they us, although we have had many misunderstandings.

I sent some men ashore, and they found quantities of mastic, but it was not set. It must be because of the rains; in Chios they gather it in March, but it could probably be gathered in January in these temperate lands. We caught many fish like those of Castile: dace, salmon, whiting, John Dory, blue butterfish, mullet, meagre and prawns,[2] and we also saw sardines. We found many aloe plants.

Wednesday, 12 December

Remained in harbour with the same contrary winds. I have set up a great cross on the western side of the harbour entrance on a prominent hilltop, to indicate that Your Majesties are in possession of this land, and principally as a sign of Our Lord Jesus Christ and to the honour of Christendom. After we had set it up, three sailors went into the woods to look at the trees and plants, and heard a great gathering of people, all naked like the earlier ones. The men called to them and went after them, but the Indians ran away.

They finally succeeded in catching one woman. I had told them to capture a few of the people, in order to treat them honourably and calm their fears, and to see if they had anything useful, which can hardly be otherwise in view of the beauty of the land. So they brought a young, good-looking woman to the ship, where she talked to the Indians, their language being the same. I ordered her to be given clothes, and I gave her some glass beads and small bells and brass rings, and sent her back ashore, treating her honourably as is my custom. I sent some of the ship's company with her, and three of our Indians, to talk to the people. The sailors in the boat told me that when they were taking her ashore she did not want to leave the ship, but to stay aboard with the other Indian women whom I had ordered to be captured at Puerto de Mares on the island of Juana or Cuba.

All the Indians who came with the woman were in a single canoe,[1] /possibly fishing,/[2] and when they were just entering the mouth of the harbour and saw the ship they turned back and abandoned the canoe and went off to their village. The woman[3] indicated where the village is. She had a small piece of gold in her nose, which suggests that there is gold on this island.

Thursday, 13 December

The three men I sent off with the woman returned at three o'clock in the morning. They had not gone as far as the village with her, either because they thought it was too far or because they were afraid. They said large numbers of people would come to the ships another day, reassured by what the woman will have told them. As I wish to learn whether this land holds anything useful and to speak with the people of such a fertile and beautiful place, to induce them to become the subjects of Your Majesties, I decided to send more men to the village, for I am confident that the Indian woman will have taken the news that we are good people. I therefore chose nine men, well armed and capable of carrying out such an enterprise, and sent one of the Indians with them.

They went to a village four and a half leagues SE, in a great broad valley, and found it quite empty, the Indians having left everything and run away inland as soon as they detected the men's approach. The Indian accompanying my men ran after them shouting to them to have no fear, for my men were not from Caniba, but from Heaven, and were giving away many fine things to everyone they came across. What he said impressed them so much that over two thousand of them came back, and they all kept coming up to put their hands on my men's heads as a sign of great reverence and friendship.

The men said that when the Indians had lost their fear they all went off to their houses and each of them brought food: bread made from / roots which they sow for the purpose,/[1] fish and whatever else they had. It seems that because the Indians whom I brought in the ship had understood that I wanted a parrot or two, and the one who accompanied the men told the islanders as much, they brought parrots, and they gave the men whatever they asked for without seeking any payment. They begged them not to leave tonight, and promised them many other things which they had in the mountains.

While my men were with these people they saw a great throng or column of Indians approaching, including the husband of the woman whom I had sent home in honour. They were carrying the woman on their shoulders, and coming to thank us for the honour and gifts bestowed on her. My men told me that all the people were more handsome and fine than any they had seen hitherto; I do not know how this could be, for all the ones we have met on the other islands have been splendid people. My men say that there is no comparison with them in their beauty, both men and women. They are lighter skinned than the others, and they saw two young women among them light enough to be Spanish.

They also told me that the land they saw was so kindly and lovely that the finest areas of Castile are not to be compared with it. This I know for myself from the lands I have seen and the country here, but they told me that what I can see here does not approach the fairness of that valley, which exceeds the beauty of the countryside around Córdoba as the day exceeds the night. All the land there is worked, and a great wide river runs through the valley and irrigates all the fields. The trees are all green and laden with fruit; all the plants tall and in flower. The roads are broad and the air as sweet as April in Castile, and the nightingale and other little birds singing as they do in Spain in the same month, the sweetest joy in the world. At night there were small birds singing sweetly, and the noise of the frogs and crickets was everywhere. The fish were the same as in Spain. They saw many mastic trees and aloe and cotton plants, but found no gold. One could hardly expect it in so short a time.

I made a check on the length of night and day and the time from sunrise to sunset, which I found to be twenty half-hour glasses, though there may be some inaccuracy due to the glass not being turned immediately or to some of the sand not running through. I also found by the quadrant that we are thirty-four degrees from the equinoctial line.[2]

Friday, 14 December
Sailed from Puerto de la Concepción with the land breeze, which soon fell away to a calm, as it has done every day we have been here. We then had an easterly wind, and sailed NNE for the island of Tortuga, where we saw a point which I called Punta Pierna[1] about nine miles ENE of the head of the island, and from there we sighted another which I called Punta Lanzada,[2] about thirteen miles on the same course, NNE,[3] so from the head of Tortuga to Punta Aguda must be about thirty-five miles, or twelve leagues, bearing ENE. We sailed past long sandy beaches. This island of Tortuga is high, but not mountainous, a comely land and well populated, like Española, with the ground all under cultivation; it is like looking at the countryside around Córdoba.

The wind being unfavourable for the island of Babeque, I decided to return to Puerto de la Concepción. We were unable to make a river two leagues E of the harbour.

Saturday, 15 December
Left Puerto de la Concepción again. As soon as we were out of harbour the wind came E, contrary to my planned course, so I steered for Tortuga. Having come close to it I came about to explore the river which I wished to sail into and examine yesterday and could not.[1] Again I failed to make the river itself, but anchored half a league to leeward of it, off a beach, in a good clean anchorage.

We moored the ships and I set off in the boats to explore the river, entering first an opening less than half a league away, which was not the mouth of the river. We came out again and found the mouth, where there was less than a fathom's depth, and the river was running very swiftly.

We went in with the boats to try to reach the villages which the men I sent the day before yesterday saw. I had the mooring ropes taken ashore and the men pulled the boats two lombard shots upriver, but we could make no more progress because of the weight of the current. I saw a few houses and the big valley with the villages, and the river running through the middle; I never saw anything more beautiful. I also saw people near the mouth of the river, but they all ran away.

The people must suffer frequent attacks, for they live in terror; whenever we arrive somewhere they make smoke signals from their watch places all over the country, more so in this island of Española and in Tortuga than on the other islands we have been to. I have called the valley Valle del Paraíso, and the river the Guadalquivir, because it is the same size as the Guadalquivir at Córdoba. The banks are beautiful shingle, and all easy walking.

Sunday, 16 December
Set sail to leave the bay at midnight with a light breeze from the land. As we came along the coast of Española, sailing close-hauled because the wind came E at the hour of terce, we came across a canoe with a single Indian in it, halfway across the bay. I was amazed that he could stay afloat in such a wind. I had him and the canoe brought on board ship, and made much of him, giving him glass beads, hawk bells and brass rings. I took him as far as land, about thirteen miles, to a village[1] on the sea shore where we anchored in good ground, just off the beach near the village.

16 December   Canoe with single rower

The village appears newly built; all the houses look new. The Indian went ashore in his canoe and told the villagers that we were good people, though they already knew this from what happened in the other villages visited by my six[2] men. Over five hundred men came down onto the beach near the ships, which were moored close to shore, and shortly afterwards the king arrived, and singly and in groups they came out to the ship. They brought nothing with them, but some had their ears and noses pierced with small pieces of very fine gold, which they gave us quite happily.

I gave orders for them all to be received with honour. They are the finest and gentlest folk in the world, and I trust in Our Lord God that Your Majesties will make Christians of them all, and that they will all be your people, which indeed I now hold them to be.

When I saw that the king was on the beach, and that they were all paying him reverence, I sent him a gift which he accepted very ceremoniously. He is a young man of about twenty-one. He himself says little, having an old tutor and other counsellors who advise him and answer for him. One of my Indians spoke to him, telling him that we have come from Heaven and are seeking gold[3] and wish to go to the island of Babeque. He replied that it was well, and that there is abundant gold on the island. He told my marshal,[4] who took him the gift, how to find it, saying that it would take only two days to get there and that if we needed anything in his country he would gladly give it.

This king and his people go about as naked as the day they were born, including the women, quite without shame. They are the handsomest men and women we have yet found; quite pale, and if they wore clothes to protect them from the sun they would be as white as Spaniards, for this country is quite cold, and the finest one could describe.[5] It is quite high, but one could work the highest of its hills with a team of oxen, and it is all open country and valleys; nowhere in Castile can match it for beauty and kindliness. The whole island, and Tortuga too, are as fully cultivated as the area around Córdoba. They grow *ajes*,[6] little stems forming roots like carrots which serve them for bread; they grate them and knead them and make their bread, then they plant the same stem elsewhere and it forms four or five roots again. They are very tasty, just like a chestnut. They grow in Guinea too, but here they are bigger and better than I have seen anywhere else, as thick as a man's leg.

The people here are all stout and strong, not thin like those I have found elsewhere, and they are gentle in their speech. They have no religion. The trees are so lush that the leaves are losing their greenness and they are dark with foliage. It is wonderful to see these valleys and the rivers and the sweet waters, and the land so suitable for cereals[7] and for all kinds of flocks and herds, of which the Indians here have none at all, for vegetable-growing, and for everything else a man could want in this world.

In the afternoon the king came out to the ship. I received him with due ceremony and made my interpreters tell him that I was from the King and Queen of Castile, who are the greatest monarchs in the world. However, neither the Indians I have brought with me nor the king himself believed this; they think we are from Heaven, and that the realms of the King and Queen of Castile are not in this world but in Heaven.

We served the king some Castilian food and he ate a mouthful and gave the rest to his counsellors and tutor and the rest of the people he had with him. I assure Your Majesties that these lands, especially this island of Española, are so rich and fertile that no man could describe them; no one would believe it all without seeing it. Rest assured that this island and all the others are as firmly in your possession as Castile; we only have to establish ourselves and order the people to do whatever you wish. I, with my small company, could walk all over these islands unmolested, for I have already seen three of my seamen go ashore and a whole multitude of Indians flee from them without being threatened. They have no weapons or fighting skills, and all of them are naked. They are very timid; three men could put a thousand of them to flight, so they could easily be commanded and made to work, to sow and to do whatever might be needed, to build towns and be taught to wear clothes and adopt our ways.[8]

Monday, 17 December

Strong ENE winds in the night. The sea did not get up much because we are in the lee of the island of Tortuga, opposite, which provides shelter. Because of the wind I remained in harbour all day. I sent the crew fishing with nets. The Indians were much taken with the men, and brought them some arrows of the Caniba or cannibals made from the tops of cane stalks. The men also obtained from them some very long sticks, sharpened and burnt, and were shown two Indians who had pieces of flesh missing from their bodies, which they were given to understand had been bitten away by the cannibals, but this I did not believe.

I sent men to the village again, and they exchanged some glass beads for a few pieces of gold beaten into leaves. One of the Indians, who I think is probably the governor of this area,[1] was wearing a piece of this beaten gold as large as a man's hand, which he seemed to wish to exchange. He left the others in the square and went off to his house, where he had the gold beaten into pieces. He kept coming back with a piece and exchanging it, and when he had none left he made signs that he had sent off for more and that they would bring it another day. All this, together with their behaviour and customs, their gentleness and good sense, indicates that these people are more alert and aware than the others I have found so far.

In the evening a canoe arrived from Tortuga with a good forty men. As it approached the beach all the villagers who were gathered together sat down as a sign of peace, and most of those in the canoes went ashore. The leader stood up alone and made them go back to the canoe, shouting what appeared to be threats and splashing water at them, and throwing stones from the beach into the water. When they had all obeyed him and were back in the canoe, he took a stone and put it in the hand of my marshal so that he could throw it (I had sent the marshal ashore with the secretary and others to see if they could bring back anything useful). The marshal /laughed and/[2] refused to throw it. The leader showed signs of being very well disposed towards us.

When the canoe had gone away, I was told that there is more gold on Tortuga than on Española, because it is nearer to Babeque. It is my belief that there are no gold mines on Española or Tortuga, but that it is brought here from Babeque. They bring very little because the people here have very little to exchange for it, their land being so rich that they need not work hard to feed themselves, nor to clothe themselves either, since they go about naked. I believe I am now very close to the source of the gold, and that Our Lord God will reveal it to me.

I am told that from here to Babeque is four days' journey, probably about thirty or forty leagues; with fair weather one could sail it in a day.[3]

Tuesday, 18 December

I remained at anchor off the same beach, there being no wind, and also because the king[1] had told me that he would bring more gold; not that I am setting any great store by the gold he may bring, but I wish to learn more of its source. At daybreak I ordered both ships to be decked out with crests and banners, today being the Feast of Santa María de la O,[2] the commemoration of the Annunciation, and we fired lombards repeatedly. The king of this island of Española had risen early from his house some five leagues away, as I judge, and at the hour of terce he arrived in the village, which some of our company whom I had sent to see if any gold was arriving had already reached. They told me that more than two hundred men came with the king, and that four of them were carrying him on a litter. He is just a young man, as I have said.

Today, as I was eating under the sterncastle, the king came to the ship with all his people. /Your[3] Majesties would, I am sure, have been impressed by his dignity and the reverence in which he is held by them all, naked as they are. When he came aboard he found me eating at table under the sterncastle, and he came promptly to sit beside me without giving me time to go out to receive him, nor rise from table. When he came in under the sterncastle he made signs with his hands to tell all his people to stay outside, and they were very quick to obey him, sitting down on the deck; all except two elderly men whom I took to be his tutor and counsellor, who came and sat down at his feet.

They kept saying that this was the cacique.[4] I thought I should offer him food, and ordered some of what I was eating myself to be brought for him. Whatever I put before him he took just enough of it to taste, sending the rest out to his people, who all took some. He did the same with the drink, scarcely touching it with his lips before giving it to the others. All this was done with marvellous gravity and very few words, and what words he did utter, as far as I could judge, were full of sound good sense. The other two men watched his lips and spoke for him and with him.

After the meal one of his retinue, with great reverence, brought him a belt similar in shape to those in Castile, but of a different workmanship, and he gave it to me. He also gave me two pieces of worked gold, very thin; I think they acquire very little of it here, although I believe they live very near to a plentiful source of it. I thought he would like a coverlet which was on my bed, so I gave it to him along with some fine amber beads I had around my neck, some red shoes and a sprinkler of orange blossom water; his delight was wonderful to see. He and his tutor and counsellor are very distressed that they do not understand me, nor I them, but nevertheless I understood him to tell me that if I needed anything the whole island was mine to command.

I sent for a portfolio of mine on which I have as an emblem a gold *excelente*[5] bearing the portraits of Your Majesties, and showed it to him, repeating what I told him yesterday, that Your Majesties command and rule over the best part of the world and that no other ruler is your equal. I also showed him the royal standards and the banners of the cross, which greatly impressed him. He kept saying to his counsellors that Your Majesties must be great rulers, since you had not been afraid to send me from so far away, from Heaven. There was much more said which I did not understand, but I could see that he was greatly impressed by everything.

When it grew late and he wanted to leave I sent him ashore in the boat with great ceremony, firing lombards repeatedly. When he reached the shore he got into his litter and went off with all his men – over 200. His son was carried behind him on the shoulders of a distinguished Indian. Whenever he met sailors or others from the ships he ordered them to be given food and treated with honour. A sailor who saw him go past on the road told me that all the gifts I had given him were being carried ahead of the king by one of his important men. The son was some way behind the king, accompanied by just as many people, and one of the king's brothers was some way back again, but he was on foot, supported by the arm by a distinguished Indian on either side. This brother came to the ship after the king, and I gave him some of the barter goods./[6]

We obtained very little gold today, but I learned from an old man that there are many islands closely grouped a hundred leagues or more away, as I understood it, which are a plentiful source of gold. He even told me that one island is all made of gold, and in the others there is so much that they take it and sieve it out to make it into bars and work it in many ways. He made signs to show me how they do it, and indicated the location and the course to be followed. I have determined to go there, and if this old man were not such an important person of the king's I would seize him and take him with me, or if I knew the language I would ask him to come, for I do believe he would come willingly, judging by his friendliness to me and the men. However, since I now look on these people as subjects of Your Majesties, and do not wish to affront them, I have decided to leave him.

I have set up a fine, imposing cross in the middle of the square in the village. The Indians gave us great help, and prayed and worshipped before it. If one may judge by them, I trust in Our Lord that all these islands will be brought into Christendom.

Wednesday, 19 December
Last night I made sail to leave the channel between Española and the island of Tortuga. At daybreak the wind came E, which kept me between the two islands all day, and in the evening I failed to make a harbour which we had sighted. We saw four headlands and a great bay with a river, and from there a large inlet and a village with a valley behind it surrounded by lofty mountains covered in trees which I think were pines. Above the Dos Hermanos[1] is a high, broad mountain running NE–SW, and to the ESE of Cabo de Torres[2] is a small island which I have called Santo Tomás,[3] because tomorrow is the Eve of St Thomas.[4]

The whole coast of this island appears to consist of headlands and splendid harbours, if one may judge by its appearance from the sea. Before the island, on the western side, is a cape, partly low and partly high, running well out to sea. I have called it Cabo Alto y Bajo.[5] Some forty-five miles E by S of Cabo de Torres is a mountain, higher than another one,[6] which projects into the sea. From far away it looks like a separate island because there is a great cleft on the landward side. I have called it Monte Caribata[7] because the area is called Caribata. It is very lovely, covered in fresh green trees, with no snow or mist, and the breezes and temperature are like Castile in March, while the trees and plants are more like Maytime. The nights last fourteen hours.

Thursday, 20 December

At sunset today we entered a harbour[1] lying between the island of Santo Tomás and Cape Caribata, and anchored. This is a most splendid harbour; all the ships of Christendom could lie here together. From the seaward side, unless one has entered it before, it appears impossible to get into because there are rocky reefs running from the mountain almost as far as the island, not in a regular line but scattered here and there, some further out to sea and others nearer the shore, so that one needs one's wits about one to pass through certain wide channels which allow a vessel to come in without risk, with a depth of seven fathoms. Once through the reefs there is twelve fathoms, and the ship can lie moored with the worst rope aboard her, safe against any wind that blows.

At the entrance to the harbour is a channel[2] on the western side of a small, sandy island on which there are many trees. There is seven fathoms right up to the foot of the island, but there are many banks in the area and one must keep one's eyes open until one is inside the harbour. Once inside there is no need to fear the worst storm in the world.

From here one can see a great valley, all cultivated, running down to the harbour from the southeast. It is surrounded by the most beautiful mountains, so high that they seem to reach the sky, and covered with green trees. I am sure that some of them must be higher than the island of Tenerife in the Canaries, which is thought to be among the highest anywhere. A league away from this part of the island of Santo Tomás is another small island, and inside that is another, and they all have splendid harbours, though one must be wary of the shallows. I have also seen villages and columns of smoke.

Friday, 21 December

I explored the harbour with the boats. I have never seen a harbour to equal it. I have said such fine things about the earlier ones that it is difficult to find words to convey the excellence of this one properly, and I fear I may be condemned for exaggerating things beyond the truth. In my defence, I have old sailors in my company who say the same and will confirm it, and any seafarer will agree: my fine descriptions of the earlier harbours were true, and it is also true that this one is much better than all the rest. I have been a seafarer for twenty-three years, never staying ashore for any length of time worth mentioning; I have seen all the Levant and all the countries of the west;

I have made passages north to England and south to the Guinea coast, and nowhere in all those lands could a man find harbours as perfect as [on these islands, where we have]¹ found every one better than the last.

As I was writing the above I have been watching my words, and I say again that what I have written is true: this is the finest harbour of all, and all the ships in the world could lie here together; it is so sheltered that the oldest rope in the ship would hold her safe at her moorings. It must be five leagues from the harbour mouth to the landward end.

Some of the land we have seen is very well cultivated, though indeed all the land is well worked. I sent two men from the boats to climb a hill to see if there was a village. None was visible from the sea, but at ten o'clock last night some Indians came out to the ship in a canoe to marvel at us. I gave them some barter goods, with which they were well pleased.

The two men came back and told me where they had seen a large village some way inland. I ordered the men to row towards it, and when we had nearly reached land I saw some Indians coming down to the shore, looking frightened. I ordered the boats to stop, and told the Indians in the boat with us to tell them that I would not harm them. They came closer to the water, and we went closer to the shore, and when they had completely overcome their fear so many of them came down to the beach that they covered it, offering thanks for our arrival. Men, women and children came running from all directions to bring us bread made from yams, which they call *ajes*; it is good, very white. They also gave us water in gourds and clay pitchers like those in Castile, and brought us everything they had and thought we wanted, all with wonderful openness and gladness of heart. Let no one say that they gave freely because it was of little value, for those who gave us pieces of gold gave as gladly and willingly as those who gave us gourds of water, and it is easy to see when something is being given with true generosity.

These people have no staffs or assegais or any other weapons, nor do any of the others on this island, which I think is very large. They are as naked as the day they were born, men and women alike. Elsewhere, on Juana and some of the other islands, the women wear a little cotton thing in front to cover up their private part, the size of the flap on a man's breeches, especially when they are over twelve years old, but here neither girls nor women wear anything. Also, in the other places the men hide their women from us because of jealousy, but not here, and some of the women are very fine-bodied, and they were the first to come and give thanks to Heaven for our arrival and to bring us whatever they had, especially foodstuffs, *aje* bread, and peanuts,² and five or six kinds of fruit, which I have ordered to be preserved to bring to Your Majesties. The women in the other places did the same thing before they went away to hide, and I have given the men orders everywhere to take care not to do the least thing to displease them and not to take anything from them against their will, so they have paid them for everything. I cannot believe that any man has ever met a people so goodhearted and generous, so gentle that they did their utmost to give us everything they had, and ran to bring it to us as soon as we arrived.

Later I sent six men to explore the village. The Indians received them with all the ceremony they could and gave them whatever they had. They are in no doubt that we are from Heaven; the Indians I brought from the other islands think the same, despite having been told what they must believe, /namely that we are just like other men and live in a different kingdom called Castile./³

After the six men had set off some Indians arrived in several canoes to invite me on behalf of their leader to visit their village when I leave here. A canoe is the boat in which they travel; there are large ones and small ones.⁴ Seeing that the village of this leader was on my way, on a spit of land where many people were waiting for me, I went there. Before I set off an amazing crowd of people congregated on the beach; men, women and children, calling to me not to leave, but to stay with them. The messengers from the other chief who had come to invite me were waiting in their canoes to make sure that I would not leave without visiting him, so I went to see him.

When I arrived he was waiting for me with many items of food. He immediately told all his people to sit down, and had the food brought out to where I was waiting in the boats, just offshore. When he saw that I had accepted the gifts all or most of the Indians ran off to the village nearby to bring me more food, and parrots, and other things, showing generosity that astonished us. I gave them glass beads, brass rings and hawk bells, not because they demanded them but because I thought it only right, and above all because I look on them as already Christians, and subjects of Your Majesties even more than the people of Castile itself. All that is necessary is to learn their language and tell them what to do, for they will gladly do anything one tells them to.

As we set off for the ships the Indians, men, women and children, kept calling to us not to leave. After we had left, canoes full of them kept coming out to the ship; I received them honourably and gave them food and other things which they took away with them. Earlier another chief had arrived from a westerly direction, and many people swam out to the ship, a good half-league offshore. The chief I mentioned had returned, so I sent certain people to see him and seek information about these islands. He received them cordially and took them off to his village to give them some large pieces of gold. They came to a great river which the Indians swam across; my men could not, and had to come back.

This whole region is full of enormous mountains which seem to climb to the sky. Compared to them the one on Tenerife is nothing, in height or in beauty; they are all shapely and green and wooded, with delightful plains between them. Beside this harbour, to the south, is a plain running farther than the eye can see, uninterrupted by hills; it must be fifteen or twenty leagues long. There is a river running through it, and it is all populated and cultivated, as green now as Castile in May or June, in spite of the fourteen-hour nights and the land being so far north.

This harbour, then, is a good haven against all the winds that blow; deep and sheltered, with good, gentle people without any weapons, good or bad. A vessel could lie here at night without fear of being surprised by other ships; the mouth is a good two leagues across but it is greatly constricted by two reefs of rock, scarcely visible above the surface, which leave only a narrow channel, and one might almost think that the reefs were man-made, with just sufficient entrance left to allow the passage of ships. There is seven fathoms at the mouth as far as a small island with a beach and some trees at its foot; the entrance is on the western side and a ship can come hard alongside the rock in safety. On the northwestern side there are three islands, and a great river a league from the end of the harbour. I have called the harbour Puerto de la Mar de Santo Tomás, today being the feast of St Thomas. I called it a sea because it is so large.

Saturday, 22 December
Set sail at daybreak to pursue my course in search of the islands which the Indians tell me are rich in gold, some being more gold than earth. The weather being against us, I had to turn back and anchor. I sent the boat off with the net to do some fishing. The chief of this area, who has a village close to here, sent a large canoe to me full of his people, including one of his principal servants, to ask me to go in the ships to visit his land, where he would give me everything he had. With the servant he sent a sash; instead of a purse on it there was a mask with the nose, tongue and two large ears made of beaten gold. /The sash is made of very fine jewellery, like pearls, but actually white fish bones with a few red ones among them so that it looks like embroidery, sewn with cotton thread so skilfully that the reverse side is covered in delightful patterns, all white, as if it had been woven on a frame like the chasuble edgings produced in Castile by the embroiderers. It is so hard and strong that a shot from an arquebus would scarcely penetrate it. It is four fingers wide, like the sashes embroidered on a frame or

woven of cloth of gold for the kings and noblemen of Castile to wear in times past./[1]

These people are so open-hearted that, whatever one asks for, they give it with the best will in the world; they take it as a favour to be asked for something. They met the boat and gave the sash to a ship's boy, and then came alongside the ship to perform their embassy. Part of the day passed without my understanding them, and even the Indians we have with us do not understand them clearly, their words for some things being different, but eventually I understood by their signs that they were issuing an invitation. I have decided to set off there tomorrow. I do not normally set sail on a Sunday, not through superstition but through my religious devotion, but I wish to do whatever will please these people and am striving to do so in the hope that they will become Christians, for which their behaviour augurs well, and so that as the subjects of Your Majesties, which I already consider them to be, they will serve you with affection.

Before setting sail today I sent six men to a very large village three leagues away to the west, the chief of which came yesterday and told me he had certain pieces of gold. When the men arrived the chief took my secretary by the hand. I had sent my secretary to prevent the rest from doing anything untoward to the Indians, for they are so generous and my men so extremely greedy that they are not satisfied with getting whatever they want from the Indians for a lace end or even a piece of glass or pottery or other useless thing, but want to get everything with no payment at all, which I have always forbidden; though with the exception of the gold much of what they get is of trifling value. Considering the generosity of heart of the Indians, who would and do give a piece of gold for half a dozen glass beads, I have given orders that nothing shall be accepted without some payment.

This chief, then, took my secretary by the hand and took him to his house, accompanied by all the inhabitants of the village, which is very large. He ordered him to be given food, and all the Indians were bringing all manner of things made of cotton, and also balls of cotton thread. When it grew late the chief gave my men three fine fat geese and some small pieces of gold, and many of the people accompanied them on their way, carrying all the things they had acquired in the village and even trying to carry the men on their backs, which indeed they did through several rivers and some of the muddy places.

I ordered the chief to be given a few things, and he and all his people were delighted, truly believing that I had come from Heaven and thinking themselves fortunate to have seen us. Today more than 120 canoes have come to the ships, all laden with people, and all bringing us something, especially their bread, and fish, and clay pitchers of water, /beautifully made and painted on the outside like red ochre./[2] They also brought many kinds of seeds which are good spices.[3] They drop a seed in a dish of water and drink it, and the Indians I have on board tell me it is a most holy thing.

Sunday, 23 December

I was unable to set off in the ships for the land of the chief who sent his men to invite me, there being no wind, but I sent some men in the boats, led by the secretary, and accompanied by the three messengers who were waiting. While they were on their way I sent two of our Indians to the villages near the anchorage. They brought a chief back with them, and the information that there is a large amount of gold in this island of Española and that people come from elsewhere to buy it; they told me I would find as much as I wanted. Others came and said the same, that there is ample gold here, and they showed me the way in which it is obtained.

All this was hard to understand, but I have no doubt that there is a very large amount of gold in this area and that if we can only find the source we shall be able to obtain copious quantities, probably at no cost. There must be plenty of it, for we have had some good-sized pieces in the three days we have lain in this harbour, and I cannot think they bring it from elsewhere. May Our Lord God, in whose hands all things lie, see fit to guide me and to give me whatever may best serve Him.

I would say that over a thousand people have now been out to the ship, each bringing something. When they are half a crossbow shot from us they stand up in their canoes and hold up the things they are bringing and shout 'Here! Here!' I estimate that over five hundred have swum out to us because they had no canoe, and we are lying almost a league offshore. I think five chiefs or sons of chiefs have come to see us, with all their household, wives and children. I ordered something to be given to them all, for none of this is wasted. May Our Lord in His mercy guide my steps, that I may find this mine of gold, for there is no shortage of people here who tell me that they know it.

The boats returned after dark. The men told me that it was a long journey to the place they had visited. Beside Mount Caribata they met a lot of canoes from the village to which they were going, weighed down with people on their way to see us. I am sure that if we could remain in this harbour over Christmas the whole population of the island would come to see us, though I now believe it to be larger than England. The Indians all went back with my men to the village, which they tell me is bigger and better laid out in streets than any of the ones we have seen hitherto; it is in the area of Punta Santa,[1] almost three leagues to the southeast. As the canoes paddle very quickly they went on ahead to inform the cacique, as they call him. So far I have not been able to understand if cacique means 'king' or 'governor'. They have another word for their dignitaries: *nitayno*. I do not know if it means 'nobleman', 'governor' or 'judge'.[2]

Eventually the cacique came to them and they all gathered in the square, which was swept very clean; more than 2,000 men, the whole population. This king treated our men with great ceremony, and all the villagers brought them something to eat and drink. Then the king gave each of them some cotton cloths of the kind worn by the women, some parrots for me and some pieces of gold. The villagers also gave them these cloths and other things from their houses, exchanging them for the smallest things, which they seemed to look on as precious relics to judge by the way in which they received them.

When the men made to leave in the evening the king and all the people begged them to stay overnight, but seeing them determined they accompanied them much of the way, carrying all the gifts from the cacique and the others on their backs as far as the boats, which had been left at the mouth of the river.

Monday, 24 December

Weighed anchor before daybreak with an offshore wind. Among the many Indians who came to the ship yesterday and indicated that there is gold on the island, telling me the names of the places where it is found, I noticed one who seemed more willing and communicative than the rest, and more cheerful in his speech. I made much of him and asked if he would come with me to show me the mines of gold. He has brought a friend or relative with him, and the two of them, talking about where the gold is to be found, have mentioned Cipango, which they call Cibao; they say there is a great quantity of gold there, and the cacique's banners are of beaten gold, but it is far away to the east of us.[1]

Believe me, Your Majesties, there can be no better nor gentler people in the world than these. It should be a source of joy to Your Majesties, for you will soon convert them to Christianity and to a knowledge of the good customs of your kingdoms. There can be no better people and no finer land, and both are so plentiful that words fail me; I have praised the people and the land of Juana, which they call Cuba, in the highest degree, but Juana and its people are as inferior in every way to this island and its inhabitants as is night to day, and I am sure that anyone else seeing it would say the same. Things here, and the large villages of this island of Española, which they call Bohío, are truly wonderful, and all the people show a remarkable friendliness and are so gently spoken, not like the others whose speech sounds threatening; and they are all so well built, males and females, and not negroes.

They all paint themselves, it is true; some black, some other colours, but mostly red. I have been told that they do it to protect themselves from the sun. They have fine houses and villages, and they all have some kind of leader, like a judge or a chief, and obey him in everything. All these leaders are men of few words and great dignity of habit, exercising control by gestures and being immediately understood in a way which is remarkable to witness.

To enter the sea of Santo Tomás one must sail for a good league with the bows heading for a small island in the middle of the mouth. I have called the island La Amiga.[2] A stone's throw[3] from the island steer to the western side,[4] keeping the island to the east, but keep to the island side of the channel rather than the other side, because there is a large reef running out from the western side, and further out to sea on that side are three more banks. This reef ends only a lombard shot from La Amiga, but one may pass easily between the two with a depth of at least seven fathoms and a gravel bottom, and once inside there is a harbour where all the ships in the world could lie without moorings.

There is another reef and more shallows coming from the eastern side towards La Amiga; they are very large and run well out to sea, as far as the cape, almost two leagues. However, there appears to be an entrance channel two lombard shots from La Amiga, and at the foot of Mount Caribata on the western side is a fine, large harbour.[5]

Tuesday, 25 December: Christmas Day

Last night, while sailing in light breezes from the sea of Santo Tomás to Punta Santa, and with my ship a league off the point at the end of the first watch, around eleven o'clock, I decided to lie down to sleep, for I had not slept for two days and a night. Seeing it was calm, the helmsman gave the helm to an apprentice seaman and went off to sleep. /I[1] had strictly forbidden the helm to be handed over to the apprentice seamen throughout the voyage, wind or no wind. I had no reason to fear rocks or banks, for on Sunday, when I sent the boats to the king, they went a good three and a half leagues east of Punta Santa and the seamen saw all the coast and the shallows to a good three leagues ESE of the point, and saw where there was safe passage, which is something not done before in the whole voyage.

It was the Lord's will that at midnight, knowing that I had lain down to sleep, and seeing that the sea was like water in a bowl, a dead calm, everyone lay down to sleep and the helm was left to the boy, and the currents took the ship very gently onto one of the banks, which could be heard and seen a good league away even at night.[2] The boy, feeling the rudder grounding and hearing the noise of the sea, cried out, and I heard him and got up before anyone else had realized that we were aground. Then the master, who was officer of the watch, came on deck. I told him and the others to get into a boat we were towing, take an anchor and drop it astern. He jumped into the boat with a crowd of others, and I thought they were obeying my orders, but all they did was row off to the caravel half a league to windward.

When I saw my own men fleeing in the boat, the sea falling and the ship now in danger,[3] I had no alternative but to cut away the mainmast and lighten ship as much as we could to see if we could float her off. However, with the tide ebbing all the time there was no help for her; she took a list,[4] her seams began to open, and she filled up from below the waterline.[5]

Seeing no way of saving her, I transferred to the caravel, taking all the men with me for their safety. There was still a light offshore wind and much of the night was already gone,[6] so not knowing our way out of the banks I sailed off and on until daybreak, when I returned to the ship along the landward side of the reef. Before that I had sent Diego de Arana of Córdoba, the Marshal of the Fleet, and Pedro Gutiérrez, Butler of Your Majesties' Royal Household, to tell the king what was happening and to say that because of my wish to accept his invitation to go to his harbour to visit him, as he requested last Saturday, I had lost my ship on a reef on my way to his village, a league and a half away.

He burst into tears when he heard the news of our misfortune, and sent all his people from the village in numerous large canoes. With their help we began to unload everything from the ship. We received such help from the king that she was unloaded and everything cleared from the decks in no time. He supervised things himself with his brothers and relatives, both on the ship and in guarding what was taken ashore, making sure that all was safe. From time to time he sent one of his relatives to me in tears to console me and tell me not to be distressed or downcast, for he would give me everything he had.

I swear to Your Majesties that nowhere in Castile could everything have been better looked after; not a lace point went missing. The king had all our things put together beside his palace while they cleared several of the houses which he wanted to give us to store everything under guard, and he ordered two armed men to keep watch all night.

The king and all his people kept weeping as if deeply affected by our loss. They are of such a loving disposition, free from greed, friendly and willing to do anything; I swear to Your Majesties, I believe there can be no better people, nor a better land, anywhere on earth. They love their neighbours as themselves, and their speech is as gentle and kindly as can be, always with a smile. Men and women, it is true, go about as naked as they were born, but I assure Your Majesties that their behaviour among themselves is above reproach. The king is held in great majesty, and has a stateliness of bearing delightful to see. They remember things well, and are eager to learn about everything; their curiosity makes them ask about this and that, to find the cause and effect of it all./

Wednesday, 26 December
The king came to the Niña at daybreak to look, and almost in tears told me not to be downhearted, because he would give me everything he had. He told me he had given the men ashore two large houses and would give them more if necessary, and as many canoes as I might want to load and unload the ship and ferry people ashore, as indeed he did yesterday without a crumb of bread or anything else being lost, for these people are so loyal and uncovetous, especially this most virtuous king.

As I was talking to him a canoe arrived from another village with some pieces of gold which they wanted to barter for a hawk bell, for they love the bells above all else. Even before the canoe was alongside they were holding up pieces of gold and shouting *chuque chuque*,[1] which is what they call the bells; they go almost mad for them.[2] Afterwards, when the canoes from the other places were leaving for home, they called me and asked me to have a bell kept for them for another day, for they would bring me four pieces of gold as big as a man's hand. This news lifted my heart, and later a sailor who had been among those who took the clothing ashore[3] told me that the men ashore are receiving astonishing pieces of gold in exchange for next to nothing. For a lace end they are getting pieces weighing more than two *castellanos*, and this is nothing compared to what it will be a month from now.

/The[4] people look on things made of brass as more valuable than anything else, so for a lace end they will readily give whatever they have in their hands. They call it *turey*, meaning 'from Heaven', for *turey* is their word for the sky. They sniff it as soon as they take it, as if they know by the smell that it comes from Heaven, and by the smell they value it very highly. They do the same with a kind of low-quality gold of a purplish colour which they call *guanin*; the smell tells them that it is finer and more desirable./

The king was very pleased to see me in better spirits, and saw my interest in gold. He told me by signs that he knows a place near here where there is a large quantity, and that I should be of good cheer, for he will give me all the gold I want. He gave me details, telling me especially that there is so much gold in Cipango, which they call Cibao,[5] that the people set no value on it, and that he would bring it here, although here in Española, which they call Bohío, and in this province of Caribata, there is much more of it. He stayed aboard to eat with me, and then we went ashore together, where he treated me with great honour and gave me a feast of two or three kinds of *aje* with prawns and game and other food of theirs, and some of their bread which they call *cazabi*.

From there he took me to see some vegetables and trees near the houses; a good thousand people came with us, all naked. He was wearing a shirt and gloves which I had given him; he took more pleasure in the gloves than in anything else he was given. His manner of eating revealed his noble birth, being delicate and fastidious, and after the meal he was brought certain plants with which he rubbed his hands. I think he did it[6] to soften them; afterwards he was given water to wash his hands.

After our meal he took me to the beach. I sent for a Turkish bow and a handful of arrows and ordered a good archer from among the ship's company to do some shooting. Not knowing about weapons, since they neither use nor possess them, the king was most impressed. This arose out of our conversation about the Caniba people, whom they call 'Caribs', who come to capture them with bows and arrows. Their arrows are not tipped with iron. None of these lands seems to have any knowledge of iron or steel, or of any other metal except gold and copper; not that I have seen much copper. I used sign language to tell the king that the King and Queen of Castile would send men to destroy the Caribs and hand them all over to him with their hands tied.

I ordered a lombard and a spingard[7] to be fired. The king was astonished by their power and penetration, and when the people heard the noise they all fell down. They brought me a great mask with large pieces of gold in the ears and eyes and elsewhere; the king gave it to me, and he also put some other golden decorations on my head and round my neck. He gave many similar things to the men I had with me.

The sight of all these things was a great joy and comfort to me, and my misery at losing the ship has been somewhat tempered. I can see that Our Lord caused her to go aground with the purpose of establishing us here, for various things have come together so handily that it has been a piece of good fortune rather than a disaster. Certainly, if we had not run aground I should have gone on my way without anchoring, for the place is inside this great bay with two or three reefs, and I should not have left anyone here on this voyage. Even if I had wanted to leave them, I should not have been able to leave them so well found nor with so much equipment and stores and materials to build a fort. Truth to tell, many of the man I am leaving here had asked me, directly or through another, to give them permission to stay.

I have decided to build a fort with a tower, all good and sound, and a large moat; not that I think this is necessary on account of the people, for I am confident that with the few men I have with me I could subdue the whole island. I believe it to be larger than Portugal, with twice the population, but they are all naked and weaponless and irremediably timid. This tower should be built, and built properly, being so far away from Your Majesties, to show the people the skills and abilities of your subjects, so that the people will love, fear and obey you. So they are finishing planks to use in building the fortifications, and I shall leave supplies of bread and wine for over a year, and seeds to sow, and the ship's boat, and a caulker, a carpenter, a lombardier, a cooper, and many other men who are eager, in Your Majesties' service and with my approval, to discover the mine which is the source of the gold. So everything has coincided handsomely for us to make this beginning, especially the manner of the ship's grounding, so gently and with no wind or wave.

Her running aground was good fortune and the clear will of God, to cause me to leave people here. If further proof were needed, had it not been for the treachery of the master and crew members, most or all of them his countrymen, in refusing to take out the stern anchor to kedge the ship off, as I had ordered, she would have been saved and we would not have been able to get to know this area as we have done in these days we have spent here, and as those I intend to leave will continue to do. My constant aim has been discovery, and I was resting no more than a day in any one place except for lack of wind, in a heavy vessel ill-suited for exploration. The unsuitability of the ship was the fault of the people in Palos who did not fulfil their undertaking to Your Majesties to provide vessels suitable for this voyage.

Not a thing from the ship has been lost; not a lace point, not a single plank or nail, for she was left as sound as when we set off, except that we cut holes and broke in here and there to bring off the liquid stores[8] and all the trading goods, which we put ashore under guard, as I have said. And I trust in the Lord that when I return from Castile, as is my intention, I shall find a great barrel of gold for which the people I am leaving here will have bartered, and that they will have found the gold mine and the spices, and all in such quantities that Your Majesties will be able to make your preparations to go to recover the Holy Sepulchre, for Your Majesties may remember my request to you that all the proceeds of this voyage of mine should be used for the conquest of Jerusalem. Your Majesties laughed and agreed, and told me that such was your ambition in any case.

Thursday, 27 December
At sunrise the king came to tell me that he had sent for gold and that before I leave he will cover me in it. He begged me to stay; he and his brother and another close relative ate with me, and these last two told me that they wished to come to Castile with me. While we were eating

157

news came that the caravel Pinta was in a river at the end of the island. The king immediately sent off a /heavily crewed/[1] canoe with one of my seamen in it; his affection for me is remarkable. /I gave the seaman a letter for Martín Alonso, written in friendly terms and saying nothing about his going off on his own or the trouble he has caused me, but simply asking him to come to join me, since God has shown such great mercies to us all. The king went home after we had eaten, leaving me in good spirits and greatly cheered./[2]

I am now preparing with all possible speed for our departure for Castile.

Friday, 28 December

I went ashore to direct and speed up completion of the fort and to organize the people who are to remain behind. I think the king saw me coming in the boat, for he went secretively into his house and sent one of his brothers to greet me. The brother took me to one of the houses which the king has given to my men, the biggest and best in the village. They had prepared a dais of palm bark, and they sat me down / on one of their low chairs, very fine and brightly burnished, like jet, with a backrest; they call them *duhos*./[1] The brother sent off one of his squires to tell the king that I had arrived, as if he were unaware of the fact. I believe he was pretending, so as to do me greater honour. When he was told, he ran to me with a great plaque of gold in his hand and put it around my neck. I stayed with him until evening, considering my course of action.

Saturday, 29 December

At sunrise a young nephew of the king came to the caravel, an intelligent and spirited lad. I am making every effort to discover the source of the gold, asking anyone I can for information, in sign language, and this boy told me that four days' journey away to the east there is an island called Guarionex, and others called Macorix, Mayonic, Fuma, Cibao and Coroay, all with endless supplies of gold.[1] I wrote down the names. When one of the king's brothers found out what the king had told me he appeared to scold him for it. I have felt previously that the boy was trying to conceal the source of the gold from me so that I will not go off to buy it or barter for it elsewhere, but there is so much of it, in so many places, including this island of Española, as to be astonishing.

After nightfall the king sent me a great mask of gold, and asked me for a wash basin and a jug.[2] I think he has the idea of making another in the same shape out of gold, so I sent what he asked for.

Sunday, 30 December
I went ashore to eat, and arrived just after five kings who are the subjects of the king here. His name is Guacanagarí. All five were wearing crowns to indicate their great authority. Your Majesties would have enjoyed seeing them; /I believe King Guacanagarí must have ordered them to come to demonstrate his importance./[1]

As I reached the shore he came to greet me. He led me by the arm to the same house as yesterday, with the dais and chairs, and sat me down. Then he took off his crown and put it on my head, and I took off a necklace of fine red agates and beautiful multicoloured beads, all very handsome, and put it around his neck. I also took off a fine scarlet hooded cape which I was wearing, and put it on him, and I sent for a pair of red slippers which I put on his feet. I placed a silver ring on his finger, for I was told that they had been very eager to acquire a silver ring that one of the seamen was wearing.

He was very pleased, and two of the other kings each brought me a great plaque of gold.[2] While all this was happening, an Indian arrived who said that two days earlier he had seen the caravel Pinta in a harbour to the east of here.

I returned to the Niña, where Vicente Yáñez, the captain, told me he had found rhubarb on the island of Amiga, in the entrance to the sea of Santo Tomás six leagues away; they recognized it by the branches and the root. They say that rhubarb puts out a few little branches above the soil, with a few little fruits like dry brambles, and the stem near the root is as yellow and fine as the finest painter's colour, and below ground it forms a root like a great pear.[3]

Monday, 31 December
I have spent today supervising the loading of water and timber for our departure for Spain to bring the news to Your Majesties quickly, so that you may send ships to discover what is left to discover, as the enterprise now appears so splendid in extent and of such high promise. I should have liked to remain here until I had explored all the land to the east and sailed along the whole coast, to find the best crossing from Castile[1] for the shipping of cattle and other things. However, finding myself as I do with only one vessel, it seems foolish to subject myself to the possible dangers of exploration. All these problems and difficulties have arisen because the Pinta went off on her own.

Tuesday, 1 January 1493
I sent the boat off at midnight to bring the rhubarb from the island of Amiga. They came back at vespers with a basketful; they could not bring more for lack of a mattock to dig with. I am keeping it to show to Your Majesties.

The king tells me that he has sent off many canoes to bring gold. The canoe which went to look for the Pinta returned, with the seaman in it, but they had seen nothing of her. The man told me that twenty leagues from here they had seen a king with two great plaques of gold on his head, and that he took them off as soon as the Indians in the canoe spoke to him. He also saw many other people wearing gold. I believe King Guacanagarí has forbidden everyone to sell us gold, so that he can do all the dealing himself. However, as I have said already, I now know the places where there is so much of it that they set no value on it. The spices, too, are plentiful, and more valuable than the pepper and *manegueta* /from Guinea and Alexandria./[1] I am telling the men whom I am leaving here to gather as much as they can.

Wednesday, 2 January

I went ashore this morning to take my leave of King Guacanagarí and to depart in the name of God. I gave him a /very fine/[1] shirt of mine, and in order to show him the power and effect of the lombards I had one loaded and fired at the planking of the Santa María where she lay aground. This was after our conversation had come handily round to the Caribs, with whom these people are at war. The King saw the range of the lombard, the ball passing through the planking and carrying far out to sea. I also armed the ship's company and organized a mock skirmish,[2] telling the king not to be afraid of the Caribs even if they came. This was all done to make him look on the men I am leaving here as friends, and to put fear into him. /I also told him that I am going back to Castile in order to return with jewels and other gifts for him./[3]

I took the King and his companions to eat with me in the lodging he provided for me. I recommended Diego de Arana, Pedro Gutiérrez and Rodrigo de Escobedo to him warmly. These are the three whom I am leaving as my joint lieutenants in charge of the men who are staying on here, so that all may be well organized and supervised in the service of God and Your Majesties. He showed great affection towards me and sorrow at my departure, especially when he saw me making to embark. One of his close subordinates told me that the King had ordered a statue as tall as myself to be made from pure gold, and that it would arrive in ten days. I embarked intending to sail immediately, but the wind prevented it.[4]

I have left thirty-nine men in the fort on this island of Española, called by the Indians Bohío. Many of them are on friendly terms with King Guacanagarí. In charge of them, /I[5] have left Diego de Arana of Córdoba as captain, secretary and marshal, with the plenary powers which I myself hold from Your Majesties. In the event of his death I have named as his successor Pedro Gutiérrez, Butler of the Royal

Table and servant of the Lord Treasurer, and if he too should die, his office shall be assumed and executed by Rodrigo de Escobedo of Segovia, the nephew of Fray Rodrigo Pérez.

I have left them all the barter goods which Your Majesties ordered me to buy, a large quantity, so that they can exchange them and barter for gold, and the whole of the contents of the Santa María. They have biscuits for a whole year, wine, and plenty of artillery. I have also left them the ship's boat to enable them, being mostly good mariners, to go when they think fit to discover the mine of gold, so that on my return I may find quantities of it. They will also be able to look for a place to build a town, for this harbour is not quite what I would wish, especially since the gold is said to come from the east, and the further we go in that direction the closer we are to Spain.

I have also left them seed for sowing, and the necessary tradesmen: a secretary and marshal, a shipwright, a caulker, a good lombardier who knows about machinery, a cooper, a doctor, Master Juan, and a tailor; all good seafaring men./

When I was ready to leave I gathered them all together and addressed them. /I[6] told them first that they should consider the great mercies which God has granted them and me so far, for which they should always give thanks; that they should put their trust firmly in His goodness and mercy, taking care not to offend Him and placing all their hope in Him; and that they should pray to Him for my return, which I promised them would be as soon as possible, God willing, and which I trust to Him will bring joy to them all.

Secondly, I asked them and commanded them in Your Majesties' name, as I trusted in their goodness and loyalty, to obey their captain as they would obey me.

Thirdly, I told them to pay great attention and reverence to King Guacanagarí, his caciques and *nitainos* and lesser dignitaries, and to avoid like death committing any annoyance or grievance towards them, considering all we owe to him and to them, and how important it is to keep them happy, remaining as the men are in his country and under his rule; that they should, indeed, make every effort to earn his goodwill by pleasant and honest conversation and to preserve his love and friendship, so that on my return I may find him as friendly and well disposed as when I leave, or more so.

Fourthly, I ordered and begged them not to cause offence or injury to any of the Indians, male or female, and not to take anything against their will. I especially told them to avoid committing any insult or violence against the women which might cause outrage, or give a bad example, or bring us into disrepute among the Indians, who are sure that we have all come from Heaven and are ambassadors of the heavenly virtues.[7]

Fifthly, I told them not to spread out and separate, or at least not in ones and twos, nor to go inland, but to stay together until my return. Certainly they should not go outside the lands and territories of the King, who loves us so much and has been so good and kind to us.

Sixthly, I encouraged them to bear their isolation bravely. It will be almost like an exile, though it is their own choice. I told them to be virtuous, strong and vigorous in whatever tasks present themselves. I reminded them of the miseries which we came through on the voyage, and how God consoled us at last with the joy of a landfall, and then with all the wealth of gold we have found, each day bringing more. I told them that great enterprises are never achieved without great travail; when the work is done, the prize seems all the greater for it; the worse the problem and the harder the way, the deeper is the joy at the end of it.

Seventhly, I recommended that when the time seems right they should ask the King to send some Indians in canoes, and some of them should go up the coast with them in the boats, as if they want to observe the land, but keeping an eye open to see if they can discover the mines of gold. I think what the Indians bring us comes from the east, which is up the coast, and they indicate that that is the source of the gold. I also told them to look out for a good place to build a fort, for I am not satisfied with this harbour. Also, they should barter for all the gold they can get by honest means, so that when I return a great quantity will have been gathered.

Eighthly, and last, I undertook to ask Your Majesties to confer on them the great rewards which their service merits, if they behave as I have recommended. I promised that they will see how greatly they will be rewarded by Your Majesties and by the favour of Our Lord, once they are cheered by my return; that they may believe that I look on it as no small thing to leave them here as a pledge that I will come again, and that I will keep the memory of them in my soul night and day as a most urgent stimulus to me to make all possible haste to return./

Thursday, 3 January

I did not sail today because last night three of the Indians I brought from the islands, who had remained ashore, came to tell me that the others and the women would be coming at sunrise.[1] Also the sea was rather rough, and the boat could not rest on the beach. I have decided to sail tomorrow, God willing.

If I had only had the Pinta with me I should have had a great barrel of gold to take home, for I should have been able to explore the coasts of these islands, which I dare not do with a single vessel for fear that some accident could prevent my returning to Castile and giving Your

Majesties news of all that I have discovered. If I were sure that Martín Alonso Pinzón had got safe home to Spain in the Pinta, I should carry out my aims, but I have no news of him. When he arrives home he will be able to misinform Your Majesties so that you do not give him the punishment he deserves for going off alone without permission and disrupting the rewards which might have been conferred by Your Majesties in return for our efforts. I can only put my trust in God to grant me fair weather and put all to rights.

Friday, 4 January
At sunrise I weighed anchor in a light breeze with the boat going ahead of us to get beyond the reef by a wider channel than the one through which we entered. This one, and others, provide a safe departure from the town of Navidad; all the way the shallowest depth we found was three fathoms, with up to nine. The two channels run NW–SE, the length of the reefs which stretch from Cabo Santo to Cabo de Sierpe,[1] over six leagues, and three leagues out to sea and a good three off Cabo Santo, and a league off Cabo Santo there is only eight fathoms' depth. Inside this cape on the eastern side there are many shallows with channels enabling one to pass between them. This whole coast runs NW–SE, sandy all the way, and the land is very level for a good four leagues inland. Beyond that there are high mountains, and there are large villages with friendly people everywhere, to judge by their behaviour towards me.

I sailed E, heading for a high mountain which looks like an island but is not, being joined to low-lying land. It is handsomely shaped, like a campaign tent, and I have called it Monte Cristo.[2] It is about nineteen leagues due E of Cabo Santo. With the light winds we were still six and a half leagues short of it at nightfall.

I found four low, sandy islands, with a bank running a long way out to the northwest and on to the southeast. Inside it is a great bay stretching a good twenty leagues to the southeast of the mountain. It must be very shallow and shoaly. The coast of the bay has many unnavigable rivers, although the seaman whom I sent in the canoe in search of the Pinta says he saw a river which ships could enter.

I am spending the night here in nineteen fathoms, six and a half leagues from Monte Cristo, having stood well out to sea to avoid the many banks and reefs in the area. Anyone heading for the town of Navidad in the future should stand two leagues out to sea when he recognizes Monte Cristo, /which is round like a tent and resembles a reef, and sail W until he is off Cabo Santo. He will then be five leagues from the town of Navidad, and should enter by the channels which run through the banks lying off the town./[3]

Cipango is on this island, and there are large amounts of gold, spices, mastic and rhubarb.

Saturday, 5 January

I set sail with the land breeze just before sunrise. It then blew from the east, and I saw that to the SSE of Monte Cristo, between it and a small island, there appeared to be a good harbour in which to anchor tonight. I steered ESE and then SSE for a good six leagues until I was close to the mountain. After these six leagues I found a depth of seventeen fathoms, with a fine clean bottom, and this depth continued for another three leagues, reducing to twelve fathoms as far as the nose of the mountain, and a league off the nose I found nine, all clean, fine sand. I continued on course between the mountain and the island, where I found three and a half fathoms at low water, an excellent harbour where I anchored.

I went in the boat to the small island, where I found the remains of fires and indications that fishermen had been there. There were numerous stones painted in colours, or rather it was a quarry of such stones with beautiful natural colourings, suitable for religious buildings or other royal edifices; I found similar ones on San Salvador. There were also numerous mastic trees.[1]

This Monte Cristo is high and beautiful, easily walked, and handsomely shaped. The surrounding terrain is all delightful, low-lying countryside. The mountain is so high that from far away it looks like a separate island.

Beyond it, nineteen miles to the eastward, I saw a headland which I have called Cabo del Becerro.[2] Between it and the mountain, a good two leagues offshore, there are reefs. I think there are channels through which a vessel might pass, but only in daytime with a boat going ahead to take soundings. East of the mountain, towards the Cabo del Becerro, there is a beach, with handsome, level countryside for four leagues. The rest is all upland and high mountains, with a mountain range running NE–SE,[3] the fairest I have seen, like part of the mountains near Córdoba. Far away to the south and southeast one can see more very high mountains, with great green valleys and numerous rivers, all so pleasant and in such abundance that I cannot convey the thousandth part of it.

Later, to the east of Monte Cristo, I saw another mountain similar in size and beauty. E by N[4] from here there is lower ground stretching a good hundred miles, or almost.[5]

Sunday, 6 January

This harbour is well sheltered from all quarters except N and NW, from which the wind seldom blows here.[1] Even then one could shelter in the lee of the island, where there is from three to four fathoms.

At sunrise I set sail to pursue my course along the coast, which runs E all the way, though one must have an eye to all the reefs and banks. There are, however, fine anchorages inside them, with good entry channels.

/The land breeze lasted until noon, during which time we ran ten leagues./[2] After noon the wind came strongly from the east. I sent a lookout to the main-top to watch for the banks, and he sighted the caravel Pinta, running free before the wind towards us. She came to join us, but there was nowhere to anchor because of the shallows, so I sailed back the ten leagues we had run from Monte Cristo, and the Pinta came with us.

Martín Alonso Pinzón came aboard the Niña to make his excuses, saying that he had left me without meaning to and giving me his reasons, all false, for he left me that night through his own greed and pride. I do not know how he acquired the arrogance and dishonesty with which he has behaved towards me during this voyage. I have tried to ignore it, not wishing to assist Satan in his evil work and his desire to hinder this voyage as he has done hitherto. The fact is that among the Indians I gave Martín Alonso who are still on board his caravel one had told him that on an island called Babeque there was gold, and having a light and lively ship he decided to leave me and set out on his own, while I preferred to wait and to work my way eastward by exploring the coasts of the islands of Juana and Española.

It appears that when Martín Alonso reached the island of Babeque he found no gold, and that he came to the coast of Española, or Bohío, after the other Indians told him that there were larger quantities of gold here, and many gold mines. For this reason he came to within about fifteen leagues of the town of Navidad, more than twenty days ago, so it appears that the news the Indians brought, which led King Guacanagarí to send the canoe with my seaman, was correct, and the Pinta must have sailed before the canoe reached her.

I am told that the caravel has obtained large amounts of gold; they were given pieces of gold two fingers across, or even as big as a man's hand, Martín Alonso keeping half and sharing the other half among the crew.[3] So I now recognize, Your Majesties, that it was by the will of God that the Santa María went aground where she did, in the finest place on the island to build a settlement and the closest to the gold mines.

I have learned that beyond the island of Juana, to the south, there is another large island which has far more gold than there is here, and they gather lumps of gold bigger than beans, whereas on Española the mines produce pieces only as big as grains of wheat. Its name is

Yamaye.[4] To the eastward there is an island inhabited solely by women; I have heard this from many people. This island of Española and the other called Yamaye are only ten days' journey in a canoe from the mainland, probably about sixty or seventy leagues, and there the people wear clothes.

Monday, 7 January

The caravel has been making water, so I had the leak repaired and caulked. The crew went ashore for wood; they say they found numerous mastic trees and aloe plants.

Tuesday, 8 January

Strong E and SE winds prevented me from sailing. I therefore set the men to taking on water and wood and everything necessary for the remainder of the voyage. I should like to explore as much of the coast of Española as I can while maintaining my course. However, considering that the captains I appointed to both caravels are brothers, namely Martín Alonso Pinzón and Vicente Yáñez, who have the support of other greedy and insubordinate men who think that everything is now in their hands, ignoring the honour which I bestowed on them; and since they have disobeyed my orders and continue to do so, and indeed have said and done many unwarranted things against me, and Martín Alonso deserted me from 21 November to 6 January with no cause or reason beyond his own disobedience, all of which I have suffered in silence to bring this voyage to a successful conclusion; so, in order to escape from such evil company, with whom I must dissemble despite their rebelliousness, though I do have many decent men with me, I have decided to make no further stops, but to make all speed for home, this not being the time to speak of punishment.

I went ashore in the boat and went to the river near here where the crew were getting water, a good league to the SSE[1] of Monte Cristo. I found that at the mouth of the river, which is wide and deep, the sand is full of gold in amazing quantities, though the grains are very small. It must be ground small by being washed down by the river, although in a small area I found many pieces as big as lentils, and there are plenty of the finer grains.[2]

As it was high water and the river was brackish I told the men to take the boat a stone's throw upriver. They filled the casks from the boat, and when we returned to the caravel we found grains of gold in the hoops of the casks, and the same in the hoops of the big barrel. I have called the river Río del Oro.[3] The mouth is very wide and shallow, but once inside it is very deep. It is eighteen leagues from the town of Navidad. In between are many large rivers, three in particular

8 January   Indians panning for gold

which I believe will contain much more gold than this one, for they are bigger, though this one is almost as big as the Guadalquivir at Córdoba,[4] and they are less than twenty leagues from the gold mines.[5] I am not gathering any of the gold-bearing sand, since it is all on the threshold of Your Majesties' town of Navidad, and is as good as gathered; instead I am returning with all possible speed to bring you the news and to rid myself of the evil company in which I find myself, men who I have always said were insubordinate.

Wednesday, 9 January
I set sail at midnight with a southeasterly wind and sailed ENE[1] to a point which I have called Punta Roja,[2] forty-eight miles due E of Monte Cristo. I anchored in the lee of the point three hours before nightfall. There are reefs everywhere, and I dare not leave here at night without knowing where they are; they will, however, be useful later if there are channels through them, as I suppose, and if there is plenty of depth and a good anchorage sheltered from winds in every quarter.

The land from Monte Cristo to our anchorage here is high and level, a delightful champaign country, and beyond lie splendid mountains running from E to W, all green and cultivated and wonderfully beautiful, with many streams. Turtles are common everywhere; the crew caught some at Monte Cristo which had come ashore to lay their eggs, and they are as big as a great shield.

Yesterday, on the way to Río del Oro, I saw three mermaids rise well above the water, but they were not so beautiful as in the paintings, and their faces were not human at all. I have seen them before in Guinea, on the Manegueta coast.[3]

I shall set sail tonight, in God's name, and shall delay no further, for I have found what I was seeking. I wish to have no further annoyance from Martín Alonso Pinzón until Your Majesties hear the news of my

9 January   Manatee

voyage and of how he has conducted himself; and from then onwards I shall no longer put up with the actions of evil and wicked men who presume to do their own will in contempt of one who placed them in the position of honour which they hold.

Thursday, 10 January
I weighed anchor, and at sunset we came to a river three leagues to the southeast which I have called Río de Gracia.[1] I dropped anchor at the mouth, where there is good anchoring ground on the eastern side. To enter the river one must cross a bar with only two fathoms of water, and the entrance is very narrow. Inside there is a good, sheltered harbour, though there is a lot of shipworm.[2] The Pinta is in a poor state with it, having spent sixteen days here while Martín Alonso was bargaining for gold; that is what he was after, and he obtained a great deal. When he heard from the Indians that I was on the coast of the same island of Española and was bound to find him, he came to join me. He would like all his people to swear that he was here only six days, but his wicked behaviour is so clear to everyone as to admit no concealment. He has made his own laws, retaining half of all the gold he obtained. When he left here he took away four Indians and two girls by force. I have ordered them to be given clothes and taken ashore so that they may go home. Treating them thus can only be to Your Majesties' benefit, in all the islands but especially in this one, where you now have a settlement, for in an island with such a wealth of gold and spices and fine land the people must be treated honourably and generously.

Friday, 11 January
I left the Río de Gracia at midnight with the land breeze and sailed four

leagues to a headland which I called Belprado.[1] Eight and a half leagues SE of there is a mountain which I have called Monte de Plata,[2] and nineteen leagues E by S is a headland which I called Cabo del Angel.[3] Between this last cape and the Monte de Plata is a bay and some of the finest and fairest land in all the world, all beautiful upland country running well inland, and then there is a great range of mountains running E–W. At the foot of the mountain there is a fine harbour with fourteen fathoms at the mouth.[4] The mountain is high and lovely, and the whole area is well populated. I believe there will be good rivers and quantities of gold.

Four leagues E by S of the Cabo del Angel is a headland which I have called Punta del Hierro,[5] and four leagues further on the same course is another which I called Punta Seca,[6] and six leagues further on is a cape which I called Cabo Redondo.[7] To the E of this is another which I called Cabo Francés.[8] On the eastern side of it is a large bay, but it did not seem to offer a good anchorage. A league further on is another which I called Cabo del Buen Tiempo,[9] and a good league s by E of that is another which I have called Tajado.[10] From there I sighted another headland about fifteen leagues s.

A good day's sailing, helped by wind and currents. I did not dare to anchor for fear of the shoals, so I jogged off and on all night.

Saturday, 12 January
In the dawn watch I sailed E with a fresh wind and continued so until day. We made sixteen miles in that watch, and nineteen in the following two hours. I then sighted land about thirty-eight miles s, and we steered for it. In giving the ship sea-room[1] last night we must have gone twenty-two miles to the NNE.

When I sighted land I saw a headland which I called Cabo del Padre e Hijo,[2] because on the eastern side there are two vertical rocks, one bigger than the other. Two leagues to the east is a large and handsome gap between two mountains; it forms a very broad and splendid harbour, with a good entrance, but since it was still early morning, and I had a wind from the NNW, instead of the normal easterly, I did not wish to linger but continued E to a high and handsome cape, all sheer rock, twenty-five miles E of the harbour which I called Puerto Sacro.[3] I called it Cabo del Enamorado,[4] and as we were reaching it I discovered another cape nine miles to the east, much more splendid, higher and rounder, all of bare rock like Cape St Vincent in Portugal.

After drawing level with the Cabo del Enamorado I saw that between it and the other cape lay an enormous bay,[5] three leagues across, with a tiny island[6] in the middle of it. There is plenty of depth from the mouth to the shore. I anchored here in twelve fathoms and sent the boat ashore for water and to talk to the people, but they all ran away. Another purpose in anchoring was to find out if this land is all one island with Española, for I suspect that what I thought was a bay could be a channel between two islands. I am astounded by the size of Española.

Sunday, 13 January

There was no land breeze so I remained at anchor. I wanted to sail to find a better harbour, for this one is somewhat exposed. I also wish to see the outcome of the conjunction of the moon with the sun, which I am expecting on the 17th of this month, and its opposition to Jupiter and conjunction with Mercury, and the sun in opposition to Jupiter, which is the cause of great gales.[1]

I sent the boat ashore to a fine beach to gather *ajes* to eat, and they found some men with bows and arrows and stayed to talk with them. My men bought two bows and a large number of arrows and asked one of the Indians to come to talk to me in the caravel. He came, and he was stranger to look at than anyone else we had seen. His face was all blackened with charcoal,[2] although the people elsewhere also paint themselves with various colours. His hair was very long, gathered up and tied at the back of his head, and then put into a net made of parrot feathers. He was as naked as all the others. I believe he is one of the Caribs who eat other men's flesh,[3] and that the bay I saw yesterday is a channel separating off a different island.

I asked him about the Caribs and he pointed to the east, not far away, to the land[4] which I sighted yesterday before I entered the bay. He told me that there is gold there in plenty,[5] pointing to the caravel and saying that there were pieces of gold as big as the sterncastle. His word for gold was *tuob*; he did not understand *caona*, which is the word for gold in the first part of the island, nor *nozay*, the word in San Salvador and the other islands. In Española *tuob* means copper or base gold.[6]

The Indian told me that the island of Matinino is inhabited only by women, /and the men visit them at a certain season; if they give birth to a girl, they keep her, and if it is a boy he is sent to the men's island./[7] The women's island bears great amounts of *tuob*, which is gold or copper;[8] he said it lies to the east of Carib. He also told me about the island of Goanin, where there are quantities of *tuob*.[9] Many people told me about these same islands days ago.

In the islands we discovered earlier there was great fear of Carib, which was called Caniba in some of them, but is called Carib in Española. These Carib people must be fearless, for they go all over these islands and eat anyone they capture. I understand a few words, which enable me to acquire more information, and the Indians I have on board understand more, but the language has changed now because of the distance between the islands.

I ordered the Indian to be fed, and gave him some pieces of green and red cloth and some glass beads, of which they are very fond. I then sent him ashore, telling him to bring gold if he had any; I thought he had, because of certain trinkets he was wearing. When the boat reached the shore a good fifty-five men were hiding in the trees, all naked, with their hair very long, like women's hair in Spain. At the back of their heads they had plumes of parrot and other feathers, and they were all carrying bows.

The Indian got out of the boat and made the others put down their bows and arrows and the heavy pieces of wood they were carrying instead of swords, shaped like [. . .]¹⁰ They all came down to the boat, and the crew went ashore and began to buy the bows and arrows and other weapons, as I had told them to. After selling two bows the Indians refused to sell any more, but made as if to attack the crew and take them prisoner, running to pick up their bows and arrows from where they had left them and returning with ropes in their hands, apparently to tie up the men. The crew had their wits about them, for I always warn them to be on the alert for this, and when they saw the Indians running towards them they charged them, giving one of them a great sword-cut on the behind and shooting another in the chest with an arrow.¹¹ The Indians saw that they had little to gain, though there were only seven Christians and over fifty of them, and they all ran away leaving bows and arrows here, there and everywhere. The men would have slain a great number of them if the *piloto*, who was in charge, had not prevented them.

When they came back in the boat to the ship and told me the story, I was partly saddened, but also pleased, for it is as well for these Indians to be afraid of us. The people here are clearly evilly disposed; I believe that these are the Caribs, and that they eat human flesh. It is as well to leave them in fear so that they will think twice before harming the crew of the boat which I have left with the thirty-nine men in the town and fort of Navidad, if it happens to come here. If these are not the Caribs themselves, they must at least border with them, and their behaviour is the same; they are fearless and unlike the people of the other islands, who are ridiculously cowardly and defenceless. I should like to capture a few of them.

They have been making many smoke-signals, as is normal on this island of Española.

Monday, 14 January
I hoped to send men last night to look for the houses of the Indians, whom I believe to be Caribs, in order to capture some of them, but because of the strong E and NE winds and heavy sea I could not. After daybreak, however, we saw a large number of Indians on the beach, so

I ordered the boat ashore, with the men well armed. All the Indians came to the stern of the boat, including the one to whom I gave the trinkets when he came yesterday. He brought with him a king who had given him some beads to give to the men in the boat as a token of peace and safety. The king and three of his Indians got into the boat and came aboard the caravel. I ordered them to be given biscuits and honey, and gave the king a red bonnet and some beads and a strip of red cloth, and some pieces of cloth to the others too. The king told me he would bring a gold mask tomorrow, and indicated that there is plenty of gold here and in Carib and Matinino. I sent them back ashore in high good humour. /I was told today, as on other days, that there is a great deal of copper in these islands./[1]

Both caravels are making water fast by the keel. It is the fault of the caulkers in Palos who did not do their job properly. When I noticed the poor workmanship and tried to make them put it right they disappeared. However, notwithstanding the rate at which the ships are making water, I trust in the grace and mercy of the Lord, who has brought me to this place, to take me safe home again. He in His majesty knows the troubles I underwent before I was able to set off from Castile, when I had no other help but Him, for He saw into my heart, and after Him Your Majesties; everyone else was against me without justification. They have been the cause of a loss of a hundred *cuentos* of revenue to Your Majesties' Royal Crown since the date of my entry to your service on the 20th of this present month of January seven years ago, plus what it would have increased to from now onwards. But God in His power will set all to rights.

Thursday, 15 January

I intend to leave here, since there is no advantage in staying, and it appears that this unpleasantness is over. I have learned today that the bulk of the gold is in the area of Your Majesties' town of Navidad, and that the islands of Carib and Matinino are rich in copper,[1] though things will be difficult on Carib because it appears that the people are cannibals. The island is visible from here and I have determined to sail to it, for it lies on my course, and also to Matinino, which they say is populated entirely by women. I wish to explore them both and capture some of the people.

I sent the boat ashore. The king had not come, for his village is far away, but he sent his crown of gold as he promised, and many other Indians arrived with cotton, bread and *ajes*, all carrying bows and arrows. When the bargaining was over four young men came to the caravel. They appeared to give me such a good account of all the islands on my course eastward that I decided to take them back to Castile with me.

From what we have seen, they have no iron or other metal here, though in a few days one cannot learn very much about a country, partly through difficulties with the language, which I understand only by guesswork, and partly because in a few days the Indians do not fully grasp my intentions.

Their bows are as long as in France or England, and the arrows are just like the small spears of the people we have seen hitherto, made of young cane shoots, very straight and a yard and a half or two yards long. They are tipped with a sharp piece of wood about a palm and a half long, and some of them insert a fish tooth at the point. Most of them put poison on the tip, and they do not shoot as in other places, but in a way which is little danger to anyone.

There is plenty of fine cotton here, very long in the strand, and many mastic trees. I think the bows are yew. There is gold and copper, and plenty of *ají*, which is their pepper, and is more valuable; everyone aboard[2] eats it with everything, finding it very healthy, and this island of Española could fill fifty caravels a year with it.

I have found quantities of weed in the bay, the same as I found on my outward voyage of discovery, which makes me think that there must be more islands due E of where I first encountered them, for I am certain that this weed grows in shallow water close to land. If this is so, these Indies must lie very close to the Canaries, less than 400 leagues away from them.

Wednesday, 16 January

I sailed from the Golfo de las Flechas,[1] as I have called it, three hours before daybreak with the land breeze, which then veered w. I steered E by N for the island of Carib, the home of the people who put such fear into all these lands and islands. It appears that they travel all over these waters in innumerable canoes and consume whatever people they can capture. I was given the course by one or two of the four Indians I captured yesterday in Puerto de las Flechas. After about fifty miles they indicated that the island would be bearing SE. I decided to take that course, and had the sails trimmed accordingly, but after two leagues the wind freshened and stood well for our course to Spain. I noticed the crew were downcast at our change of course, for the caravels are leaking at such a rate that our only hope is the mercy of the Lord, so I had to abandon the course which I thought would take us to the island and set a course direct for Spain, NE by E, which I followed until sunset, making thirty-eight miles, or almost thirteen leagues.

The Indians have told me that this course will take me to the island of Matinino, inhabited only by women, which I should greatly like to see in order to bring five or six of them to Your Majesties, but I doubt if they know the course properly, and I cannot waste time because of the amount of water the ships are taking in. I am sure, however, that these women are there, and that at a certain time of year the men come to them from Carib, about ten or twelve leagues away, and if they bear a boy child they send it to the men's island, and if it is a girl they keep it.

These two islands must be less than fifteen or twenty leagues from where I set out; I think they lie SE, and that these Indians were mistaken about the course. After losing sight of the headland I named San Théramo, on Española,[2] seventeen leagues w of us, we sailed thirteen leagues E by N in fair weather.

Thursday, 17 January

At sunset last night the wind decreased somewhat. In the fourteen glasses to the end of the first watch, each of half an hour or slightly less, we were sailing at something over three knots, making about twenty-two miles. Then the wind freshened and we made something over six knots for the ten glasses of the new watch and the six following, until sunrise, our total run being almost sixty-seven miles NE by E. From then until sunset we ran E about thirty-five miles, or almost twelve leagues.

A booby came to the caravel, then another, and we saw quantities of floating weed.

Friday, 18 January

Last night we ran E thirty-two miles, almost eleven leagues, in light winds, then a further twenty-four miles SE by E, eight leagues, before sunrise. We had light winds all day, ENE and NE, occasionally veering slightly E, and our course was sometimes N, sometimes N by E or NNE. Taking all together I believe we ran about forty-eight miles, or sixteen leagues. There was only a little weed, but yesterday and today the sea has been teeming with tunny fish. I think they must go from here to the fisheries of the Duke of Conil and Cádiz.

A frigate bird[1] flew round the ship and then away to the SSE. I believe there are some islands in that direction. The islands of Carib and Matinino and many others lie ESE of Española.

Saturday, 19 January

Last night we ran forty-five miles N by E and fifty-one NE by N. After sunrise we had a fresh ESE wind, and ran NE and then NE by N about sixty-seven miles, just over twenty-two leagues. The sea was full of small tunny fish, and we saw boobies, tropic birds and frigate birds.

Sunday, 20 January

The wind fell calm last night. With an occasional puff of wind we sailed some sixteen miles NE. After sunrise we sailed about eight or nine miles SE, then twenty-eight miles, or nine and a half leagues, NNE. Small tunny fish were everywhere. A sweet, gentle breeze, like Seville in April or May, and the sea always smooth, thanks be to God. We saw frigate birds and petrels and many other birds.

Monday, 21 January
After sunset last night we sailed N by E, with the wind E or NE, at about six and a half knots until midnight, making about forty-five miles. We then sailed NNE at six and a half knots, so the full night's run was about eighty-three miles, or twenty-seven and a half leagues, N by E. After sunrise we sailed NNE with the wind still E, occasionally E by N. We ran about seventy miles, or twenty-three leagues, in eleven hours, having taken up an hour of the day to go alongside the Pinta to speak to them.

The winds are becoming colder now, and I expect to find them colder each day as we sail N and the nights grow longer with the narrowing of the sphere. We saw numerous tropic birds and other birds, but fewer fish because of the colder water. A great quantity of weed.

Tuesday, 22 January
After sunset last night we sailed NNE with the wind E and slightly southerly. We were making six knots for the first five glasses of the watch and the preceding three (making eight in all) and must therefore have run fifty-seven miles, or nineteen leagues.[1] We then sailed NE by N for six glasses, running about another fourteen miles, then for four glasses of the second watch we steered NE at four and a half knots, making over three leagues NE. In the eleven glasses from then until sunrise we sailed ENE at four and a half knots,[2] making eight leagues, and then ENE until eleven in the forenoon, running twenty-five and a half miles. The wind then fell away altogether and we were becalmed the rest of the day. The Indians swam in the sea. We saw tropic birds and a lot of weed.

Wednesday, 23 January
Very variable winds in the night. Sailing with care and taking all seamanlike precautions we made about sixty-seven miles NE by N, just over twenty-two leagues. I had to wait for the Pinta repeatedly. She is sailing very poorly when close-hauled, getting no help from her faulty mizzenmast. If her captain, Martín Alonso Pinzón, had been as eager to ship a good mast in the Indies, where he had so many good ones to choose from, as he was to leave me because he thought he was going to stuff his ship with gold, he might have put it right.

We saw many tropic birds and quantities of weed. The sky has been threatening rain for several days, but it has not come, and the sea has been as smooth as a river, thank God. After sunrise we sailed about twenty-four miles, or eight leagues, due NE, then the rest of the day the same distance ENE.

Thursday, 24 January
Repeated shifts of wind in the night; sailed about thirty-five miles, or eleven and a half leagues, NE. From sunrise to sunset, about fifteen leagues ENE.

Friday, 25 January
In the first part of the night, thirteen glasses, we sailed ten leagues ENE, then another four and a half miles NNE. After sunrise we made only a little over twenty-two miles ENE, or seven and a half leagues, the wind falling away. The crew killed a dolphin and a large shark. We were sorely needing them, for our supplies are now reduced to bread and wine and the *ajes* we loaded in the Indies.

Saturday, 26 January
Last night we made forty-four and a half miles, almost fifteen leagues, E by S. After sunrise we sailed sometimes ESE, sometimes SE. We made about thirty-two miles by eleven o'clock, when I went about and sailed close-hauled, making nineteen miles or six and a half leagues N.

Sunday, 27 January
From sunset last night I steered NE, due N, or N by E at about four knots, making about fifty-two miles, or seventeen and a half leagues, in the thirteen hours. From sunrise to noon I steered NE for nineteen miles, or six and one-third leagues, and from then to sunset about three leagues ENE.

Monday, 28 January
All last night I steered ENE, making about twenty-nine miles, or nine and two-thirds leagues. From sunrise to sunset, sixteen miles, or five and a half leagues, on the same course. Sweet, gentle breezes. We saw tropic birds and petrels, and great quantities of weed.

Tuesday, 29 January
Last night I sailed ENE, with winds from the south and southwest, about thirty-one miles, or ten and one-third leagues, and in the day about eight and a half leagues. Temperate breezes, like April in Castile, and a smooth sea. Fish which we call *dorados* came alongside.

The Journal

Wednesday, 30 January
Sailed about seven and a half leagues ENE in the night, and fourteen and a half leagues s by E during the day. We saw tropic birds and great quantities of weed; also many dolphins.

Thursday, 31 January
Last night we sailed N by E for twenty-four miles, and then NE for twenty-eight miles, making seventeen and a half leagues. From sunrise to sunset we made fourteen and a half leagues ENE. We saw a tropic bird and some petrels.

Friday, 1 February
Last night we sailed ten and a half leagues ENE. During the day we ran thirty-one leagues on the same course with smooth seas, thanks be to God.

Saturday, 2 February
Last night we sailed thirty-two miles, or ten and two-thirds leagues, ENE. Today, running free with the same following wind, we were making over five and a half knots; in eleven hours we ran sixty-one miles, or twenty and one-third leagues, with a smooth sea, thank God, and sweet breezes. The sea has been so thick with weed that if we had not seen it before we should have been frightened that it was shoals. We saw petrels.

Sunday, 3 February
Last night, running free with a smooth sea, thank God, we sailed about thirty-one leagues. The Pole Star appeared very high, as high as at Cape St Vincent. I could not take a sight of it with the astrolabe or the quadrant because of the swell. Remained on course ENE all day at about eight knots, making some twenty-nine leagues in eleven hours.

Monday, 4 February
Last night we sailed E by N, first at nine and a half knots and then at eight, making about a hundred and three miles, or thirty-four and one-third leagues. The sky was very stormy, with rain, and it was quite cold, which means that we are not yet in the Azores. After sunrise I changed course E, running about sixty-one miles, or twenty and one-third leagues, in the day.

Tuesday, 5 February
Last night I continued on course E, making about forty-three miles, or fourteen and one-third leagues. During the day we ran at about eight knots, making about eighty-eight miles in eleven hours, or just over

¶ S I G V E S E   L A   F I G V R A
del Aſtrolabio.

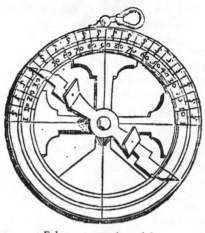

3 February   Astrolabe

twenty-nine leagues. We saw petrels and some little sticks, which is a
sign of land.

Wednesday, 6 February
Last night we sailed E at almost nine knots. In the thirteen hours we ran
about a hundred and thirteen miles, or almost thirty-eight leagues.
There were many petrels and other birds. Today we were running at
eleven knots, so we have made a hundred and twenty-two miles, or
forty and two-thirds leagues; a total twenty-four hour run of about
seventy-eight leagues.

Vicente Yáñez calculated this morning that we have the island of
Flores to the north and Madeira to the east. Roldán calculated that
Fayal or San Gregorio is to the NNE[1] and Porto Santo is E of us.
Quantities of weed.

Thursday, 7 February
Last night we sailed E at about eight knots, running about a hundred
and three miles, or thirty-four and one-third leagues. Today, sailing at
six and a half knots, we have made seventy miles in eleven hours, or
twenty-three and one-third leagues.

Our position this morning, by my calculation, was sixty-nine
leagues S of Flores. The *piloto*, Peralonso, thought that a line drawn
due N of us would pass between Terceira and Santa María, and one

due E would pass to the windward of Madeira, thirteen leagues off the northern tip of the island.

The crew saw a different kind of weed, of a type which grows abundantly in the Azores; later we saw more of the previous kind.

Friday, 8 February
Last night we sailed E at something over two knots for a while, then changed course to E by S, making thirteen leagues. From sunrise to noon we ran about twenty-one and a half miles, and from then to sunset the same again, making a day's run of fourteen and one-third leagues SSE.

Saturday, 9 February
Last night we sailed SSE for a while, making three leagues, then S by E, then NE until ten o'clock in the forenoon, another five leagues, and another nine and a half leagues E until nightfall.

Sunday, 10 February
After sunset last night we continued sailing E, making a hundred and three miles, or thirty-four and a half leagues. In the eleven hours from sunrise this morning until sunset, running at just over seven knots, we made seventy-nine miles, or twenty-six and two-thirds leagues.

In my caravel Vicente Yáñez, the two *pilotos* Peralonso Niño and Sancho Ruiz, and Roldán[1] have been pricking off our course on their charts. They all have us well to the E of the Azores, and taking a line N none of them has us level with the island of Santa María, which is the last of the Azores; they all make our position five leagues E, in the area of Madeira or Porto Santo.

My own reckoning is very different; I have us much further W, with Flores bearing due N and Nafe in Africa E of us, and the ship heading to pass [. . .][2] leagues to the windward of the northern tip of Madeira, so they have us 160 leagues closer to Spain. When we make our landfall, with God's grace, we shall see who is right. On our outward passage we had sailed 279 leagues from the island of Hierro before we saw the first weed.

Monday, 11 February
We stayed on course all night at nine and a half knots, making forty-one leagues, and today we have run seventeen and a half leagues. We saw many birds, and must be close to land.

Tuesday, 12 February
Last night we sailed E at six and a half knots, making about fifty-eight miles, or nineteen and one-third leagues. We ran into storms and

heavy seas, and if this were not a good, well-found ship I should be afraid of sinking. We made about eleven or twelve leagues today, in great difficulty and peril.

Wednesday, 13 February

From sunset to sunrise we were sorely beset by wind and storms, with very heavy seas. There were three flashes of lightning to the NNE, which means that a storm or tempest is coming from that or the opposite direction. We ran under bare poles all night, then set a little sail and made about forty-one miles, or almost fourteen leagues. Today the wind dropped a little, but then strengthened again, and the sea became terrible. The ships have been labouring badly in the crossing seas. We ran about forty-four miles, or fourteen and two-thirds leagues.

Thursday, 14 February

Last night the wind worsened and the seas were terrifying, crossing us from both sides and so distressing the ship that she kept losing steerage way and could not pull herself out of them, and they were breaking aboard her. I set the mainsail very low, simply to lift her out of the seas a little, and so ran about sixteen miles in three hours.

The wind and sea kept on worsening, and the danger was such that I was forced to let her drift astern wherever the wind took her; I could do nothing else. Martín Alonso, in the Pinta, did the same, and we lost each other, though I hoisted lanterns all night and he did the same until he appeared to give up through stress of weather and because he was well away from me. In the night we sailed forty-three miles, or fourteen and one-third leagues, NE by E.

After sunrise the wind increased, and the crossing sea grew even worse. The only canvas we were carrying was the lowered mainsail with no bonnet, to lift the ship out of the crossing seas in which she would otherwise have foundered. Our course was ENE, then NE by E, and eventually due NE. We sailed about six hours like this, around eight leagues.

I ordered lots to be drawn for a pilgrim to go to Santa María de Guadalupe[1] with a five-pound wax candle, and made everyone swear that whoever was chosen would carry out the pilgrimage. I told them to bring as many chickpeas as there were men aboard, and to cut the mark of a cross on one of them and put them all into a hat and shake them up. I put my hand in first, and drew the pea with the cross, so the lot fell to me and I consider myself obliged from now onwards to carry out the vow as a pilgrim.

We drew again to send a pilgrim to Santa María de Loreto, in the Ancona March in the lands of the Pope,[2] and the lot fell to a sailor from

Puerto de Santa María[3] called Pedro de Villa. I promised to pay his expenses. It was agreed to send another pilgrim to keep vigil for a night in Santa Clara de Moguer[4] and to have a Mass said; we put in the peas again, and again the lot fell to me. We then all swore together that when we first come to land we will go in procession in our shirts[5] to pray in a church dedicated to Our Lady.

As well as these communal vows, each man made his own personal ones, for none of us expected to survive; we had all given ourselves up for lost, so terrible was the storm. The danger was worse because we were short of ballast, the cargo having been lightened by our consumption of the stores, water and wine. I did not re-ballast the ship because I wanted to take advantage of the fair weather in the islands,[6] intending to have more ballast loaded for the island of women to which I meant to sail. To improve things we filled the empty wine and water casks with sea water when we could, which has made matters somewhat better.

/I[7] could have borne this storm more easily if I had been the only person in danger, for I owe my life to the great Creator, and I have been close to death, on its very threshold, on other occasions. The thing which caused me infinite pain and sorrow was the thought that Our Lord had seen fit to fill me with the light of faith and the conviction of this enterprise, and to give me victory, but that nevertheless, while our opponents remained convinced that they were right despite the glory and increase won for Your Majesties' high estate by my service, He in his Divine Majesty might wish to prevent it by my death. My own death would have been more bearable had it not also involved the death of these people whom I brought with me by the promise of a successful outcome. Seeing themselves so beset, they cursed not only the fact that they had come but also the fear, or the restraint, which in the face of my persuasion had prevented them from turning back, as they were often resolved to do.

Above all, my sorrow was doubled by the memory and the vision of my two little sons, whom I left at school in Córdoba, alone and helpless in a strange land, and the knowledge that I had not done, or at least had not revealed, the service for which one might expect Your Majesties to take thought for them.

I took comfort from my belief that Our Lord would not allow a matter of such importance for the exaltation of the Church to remain unfinished after I had brought it to the point of completion by such trouble and toil, and that He would not let me be destroyed. On the other hand, I thought that He had decided to torment me for my sins, or to prevent me from enjoying such glory in this world.

In this confused state of mind I did not forget the future interests of Your Majesties, who may still find a way to retain the victory if I die and the ship is lost. I thought that the success of my voyage might somehow be brought to your notice, and I therefore wrote down on a parchment, with the brevity imposed on me by the weather, how I had discovered the lands which I promised you, and the number of days it had taken, and the course; I also described the nature of the people and their kindness, and how Your Majesties' subjects were still in possession of everything I had discovered.

I sealed this account and addressed it to Your Majesties with an inscription promising a reward of five hundred *castellanos*[8] to anyone who presented it with the seal unbroken, so that if foreigners found it they would be prevented from gaining access to the information inside by the greed[9] aroused by the inscription. I then had a great cask brought, and having wrapped the account in a waxed cloth, which I then enclosed in a cake of wax, I put it in the cask, tightened the hoops and threw it into the sea. Everyone thought it was some kind of devotional offering. I thought it possible that it might not arrive safely, and the ships were still sailing towards Spain, so I made another package like the first and put it high up on the sterncastle so that if the ship foundered the cask would remain afloat at the mercy of the storm./

Later, with all the rainstorms and squalls, the wind changed to w and we sailed with the wind astern[10] for about five hours under just the foresail in a very confused sea, making about two and a half leagues NE. I had furled the *papahigo* of the mainsail[11] for fear that a wave might carry all away.

Friday, 15 February

After sunset last night the sky began to clear to the westward, as if it were about to blow from that quarter. I bent the bonnet on the mainsail. The sea was diminishing somewhat, though still very high. We sailed ENE at about three knots and made about thirteen leagues in the thirteen hours of the night. After sunrise we sighted land ahead to the ENE. /Ruy García, from the port of Santoña, saw it first from the crow's nest./[1] Some said it was Madeira, others the Rock of Sintra in Portugal, near Lisbon.

The wind then veered ENE, dead against us, with a heavy sea from the w. The caravel was about five leagues from land. By my reckoning we are around the Azores, and this land is one of the islands. The *pilotos* and seamen think we are already off the Spanish coast.

Saturday, 16 February[1]

We spent all Friday night tacking to and fro to reach the land which we now recognized as an island, sometimes NE, sometimes NNE, until sunrise, when we turned s to reach the island. We could no longer see it because of poor visibility; we then saw another island some nine leagues astern. From sunrise to sunset we beat to and fro, trying to reach land in strong winds and heavy seas.

As we were saying the *Salve* just on nightfall, some of the men saw a light to leeward, which looked as if it could be the land we saw first. We spent the night beating to windward, getting as close as we could and hoping to see one of the islands at sunrise. I slept a little, for I had not slept, nor had any chance of sleep, since Wednesday, and I was in great distress with my legs through being exposed to the wet and cold, and through lack of food.

At sunrise we steered ssw and at nightfall we reached the island. We could not identify it because of heavy cloud.

Monday, 18 February

After sunset last night I sailed along the coast of the island to find an anchorage and speak with someone on shore. I dropped a single anchor which was immediately lost. I made sail again and after beating to windward all night we reached the north of the island again after sunrise. I found a suitable anchorage, dropped a single anchor, and sent the boat ashore. The men talked to the people and found that it was the island of Santa María, one of the Azores, and were shown a harbour where we might take the caravel.

The islanders said that they had never seen such storms as in the last fortnight, and were astonished that we had survived. When they heard the news of my discovery of the Indies they gave great demonstrations of joy and offered thanks to God.

So my navigation was good and my reckoning sound, thank God; I had overestimated a little, but I was sure we were in the area of the Azores, and that this was one of them. I pretended to have sailed further in order to distort the reckoning of the *pilotos* and seamen who have been navigating, so as to remain sole master of this passage to the Indies, which indeed I am; not one of them knows the true course and none of them can be sure of the way to the Indies.

Tuesday, 19 February

After sunset last night three of the islanders came down to the shore and called to us. I sent the boat to bring them aboard. They brought us some chickens and fresh bread, today being Shrove Tuesday, and some other things from the Governor of the island, Juan de Castañeda.[1] He sent word that he knows me well and only night prevented him from coming to see me, but that he would come at dawn and bring more refreshments, along with three men who had remained ashore from the caravel. He had not sent them back earlier because he was so much enjoying hearing them talk about the voyage.

I ordered the messengers to be received with honour and given beds for the night, for it was late and the village was far away. Remembering the vows we made last Thursday in the anguish of the storm, and especially the vow that in the first land with a house dedicated to Our Lady we would go in our shirts, etc.,[2] I decided that half the company should go to fulfil the vow in a little building like a hermitage near the shore, and I would go later with the other half. Seeing no danger ashore, and trusting the Governor's promises and the peace between Portugal and Castile, I asked the three men to go to the village to bring a priest to say a Mass. When the men had gone in their shirts to carry out their pilgrimage, and were at prayer, the Governor and the whole population of the village on horse and foot surprised them and captured them all.

I waited unsuspecting for the boat to return in order to perform my own pilgrimage with the rest of them. At eleven o'clock, when they had not returned, I began to fear that they had been captured or that the boat had been wrecked; this island is surrounded by high rocks. My view was obscured because the hermitage lay behind a headland. I weighed anchor and set sail, and when we were directly off the hermitage I saw many men dismounting and getting into the boat with weapons. They came out to the caravel in order to take me prisoner, and the Governor stood up and asked me for safe conduct. I said he could have it, but asked him what was afoot since I could see none of my men in the boat. I told him to come aboard and offered to do whatever he wanted, planning to lure him onto the ship with friendly words and seize him in order to recover my people. I did not see this as a breach of the safe conduct, for he had already broken faith himself after offering us peace and security.

He was wary of coming aboard, as if he was up to no good himself. When I saw his unwillingness to approach the caravel I asked him to tell me why he had seized my men, saying that the King of Portugal would not be pleased, and that in the lands of the King and Queen of Castile the Portuguese were received with honour, entering freely and remaining as safe as in Lisbon. I also told him that Your Majesties had given me letters of introduction to all the princes, gentlemen and commoners in the world, which I would show him if he would only approach, that I was your Admiral of the Ocean Sea and Viceroy of the Indies, which now belong to Your Majesties, and that I would show him the documents bearing Your Majesties' signatures and seals. I showed them to him from a distance and told him that Your Majesties were on terms of great affection and friendship with the King of Portugal and had ordered me to pay all possible respect to whatever Portuguese vessels I might meet. I also said that, while I did not wish to leave my people in his hands, it would not prevent me from sailing to Spain, for I had ample crew to make Seville, and he and his men would be severely punished for the insult they had done us.

Their reply was that they recognized no King and Queen of Castile here, nor their letters, and had no fear of me, and they said in a threatening tone that they would show us what Portugal was made of. I was considerably angered by this, and I wondered if there had been some dispute between the two kingdoms since I set off on my voyage. I could not resist giving him a fitting reply. He stood up, still well away from the caravel, and told me to take her into harbour, saying that everything he had done and was doing was on orders from the King. I told everyone on the caravel to bear witness, and called to him and his men that I gave them my solemn personal promise not to disembark from this vessel until I had taken a hundred Portuguese to Castile and laid waste the entire island.

I dropped anchor in the same place as before, the wind and weather being unsuitable for any other purpose.

Wednesday, 20 February
I ordered the ship prepared for sailing and the casks filled with sea water for ballast, for it was an evil harbour to lie in and I was afraid my mooring ropes might be cut, which is just what happened. I therefore made sail for the island of San Miguel, although with the weather as it is there is not a safe haven in the whole of the Azores, and my only recourse was to find sea-room.

Thursday, 21 February
I left the island of Santa María yesterday for the island of San Miguel, to try to find a safe harbour against the foul weather. We sailed until nightfall without sighting any land because of the thick cloud and poor visibility caused by wind and sea, which were both very high. I was far from happy, having only three real seamen aboard, for the rest of them know nothing of the sea. We were hove-to[1] all night in severe storms and great peril and toil. By God's grace the sea was only coming from one direction; in the crossing seas we have had earlier we would have been in a much sorer plight.

After sunrise I could not see the island of San Miguel, so I decided to turn back for Santa María to see if I could recover my men and the boat and the anchors and cables which I left there.

I am amazed by the evil weather in the waters around these islands. I sailed all winter in the Indies without once anchoring[2] and the weather was always fair; I never saw the sea bad enough to prevent me setting sail /in a baker's trough/,[3] whereas here in these islands I have had these terrible storms. The same thing happened on my outward passage until I reached the Canaries, but once through them I had nothing but fine breezes and moderate seas.

The sacred theologians and wise philosophers were right to say that the earthly Paradise is in the farthest orient, for it is a most temperate place, and the lands which I have discovered are indeed the farthest orient.

Friday, 22 February

I anchored yesterday off the island of Santa María in the same harbour as before. A man appeared on the rocks overlooking it and waved his coat at us, telling us not to leave, then the boat arrived with five seamen, two priests and a clerk. They asked for safe conduct, which I granted them. It was late, so they remained on board to sleep, and I received them as cordially as possible.

This morning they asked to see my authorization from Your Majesties to make sure that I had made the voyage in your name. It appeared to me that they were attempting to justify their previous behaviour and show that they were in the right, after failing to take me prisoner. It had certainly been their intention to take me by main force, for they came in an armed boat, but then they saw that the game would be lost and took fright at my threats, which I would have put into action and, I believe, carried out successfully.

In order to recover my men I finally had to show them Your Majesties' general letter to all princes and gentlemen in authority and my other documents. I gave them presents[1] and they went ashore well content and released all my men and the boat. The men told me that if I had been taken I should never have been released, for they heard the Governor say that those were his orders from his lord the King.

Saturday, 23 February

Yesterday the weather began to show signs of improvement. I weighed anchor and set off to sail round the island to find a good anchorage to take on wood, and also stone for ballast. It was compline before I found an anchorage.

Sunday, 24 February

I anchored yesterday evening to take on wood and stones. There was a heavy sea which prevented the boat from going inshore, and at the end of the first watch it began to blow from the west and southwest. I gave orders to make sail because in these islands it is very dangerous to be riding at anchor with the wind in the south, and if it is sw it soon backs s. With the wind standing fair for Spain, I abandoned the idea of taking on wood and stones and gave orders to steer E. We were running at about five and a half knots for six and a half hours or so until sunrise, making some thirty-six miles. From sunrise to sunset – eleven hours – we sailed at a little under five knots, making fifty-two and a half miles, which with the thirty-six sailed in the night gives a total run of eighty-eight and a half miles, or twenty-nine and a half leagues.

Monday, 25 February
After sunset last night we remained on course E at four knots, making fifty-two miles, or seventeen and one-third leagues, in thirteen hours. From sunrise to sunset we made another seventeen and a half leagues, with a smooth sea, thanks be to God. A large bird like an eagle came to the caravel.

Tuesday, 26 February
After sunset last night we remained on course E, with a smooth sea, thanks be to God. For most of the night we were running at six and a half knots, and we made eighty miles, or twenty-six and a half leagues. From sunrise we had light winds and squally showers, and made about eight and a half leagues ENE.

Wednesday, 27 February
Last night and today I have been driven off course by adverse winds and a heavy sea. I make my position 132 leagues from Cape St Vincent, 85 from Madeira and 112 from Santa María. Such weather is distressing when we are nearly on the threshold of home.
/A swallow settled on the ship. It must have been driven out to sea by a storm./[1]

Thursday, 28 February
Last night, with repeatedly changing winds, we sailed s and SE, hither and thither, and NE and ENE, and the same all today.
/Many more swallows and other land birds came to the ship. We also saw a whale./[1]

Friday, 1 March
Last night we sailed E by N, twelve and three-quarter leagues, and today a further twenty-five on the same course.

Saturday, 2 March
Last night we ran on course E by N, twenty-nine and three-quarter leagues, and a further twenty-one today.

Sunday, 3 March
After sunset we sailed E. We were struck by a squall which tore all the sails, and we were in great danger from which the Lord saw fit to save

us. I drew lots for someone to make a pilgrimage in his shirt to Santa María de la Cinta in Huelva, and the lot fell to me. We all vowed to eat only bread and water on the first Saturday after we make port.

We had run about forty-eight miles when the sails carried away, and from then on we have run under bare poles because of the ferocity of the wind and the seas, which have been coming over the ship from two directions. We have seen some signs of approaching land, and we think we are off Lisbon.

Monday, 4 March
Last night we had a fearful storm, and thought that we were sure to founder, with heavy conflicting seas and winds which seemed to pick the caravel out of the water. There was heavy rain, with lightning on all sides. It pleased God to give me strength, and the weather continued the same until the first watch, when He gave me a landfall, and the crew saw land.

Not wishing to come inshore until I had identified it and found if there was some harbour, or place of refuge, I had no alternative to setting the *papahigo*, despite the risk, in order to gain sea-room, and God preserved us through the night, though with endless labour and terror.

At daybreak I recognized the land as the Rock of Sintra, near the Lisbon river. I decided to sail in, having no alternative. The storm was so terrible at Cascais at the mouth of the river that the people spent the whole morning saying prayers for us, and when we were inside they all came to see us and marvel at our escape.

And so, at the hour of terce, we reached Restelo on the Lisbon river, where the seafaring people have told me that this has been the worst winter for storms that ever was. Twenty-five ships have been lost in Flanders, and others have lain here unable to sail for four months.

I have written to the King of Portugal, who is staying nine leagues from here, telling him that the King and Queen of Spain have told me to be sure to enter His Majesty's harbours to request whatever I need, in exchange for payment, and asking him to give me permission to take the caravel to the city of Lisbon, in case desperate men should take it into their heads to do us some mischief in this deserted place, in the belief that we are laden with gold; also to let him know that I have come from the Indies, and not from Guinea.

Tuesday, 5 March
Anchored here in Restelo is a large ship of the King of Portugal, better equipped with cannon and weaponry than any vessel ever seen. The *patrón*,[1] Bartolomé Días of Lisbon,[2] came to the caravel in an armed boat and told me to get down into it to go to give an account of myself

to the King's officials and the captain of the ship. I replied that I was the Admiral of the King and Queen of Castile and that I do not render any such accounts to any such persons, nor do I leave any ship or vessel in which I find myself unless compelled by force of arms.

The *patrón* told me to send the master of the caravel, and I said I would send neither the master nor anyone else unless I was forced to it, for sending someone else was just the same to me as going myself, and the Admirals of the Kings of Castile are in the habit of dying rather than surrendering or handing over any of their people. The *patrón* moderated his tone and said that if that was my resolve, then so be it, but he asked to see any letters I might have from Your Majesties. I was happy to show him them, and he returned to his ship and reported to the captain, whose name is Alfonso Damán; he came to the caravel with a great show of celebration, including bugles,[3] trumpets and kettledrums, and we talked together. He offered to do whatever I ask of him.

Wednesday, 6 March
When it became known that I had been to the Indies an astonishing number of people came from the city of Lisbon to see me and to look at the Indians, all expressing amazement and praising God, telling us that He in His majesty has given us all this because of Your Majesties' faith in Him and desire to serve Him.

Thursday, 7 March
Today people have come to see the ship in enormous numbers, many of them of noble birth, including the King's officials. They all gave infinite thanks to Our Lord for granting Your Majesties so many good things and such an expansion of Christendom, which they said was appropriate since Your Majesties put so much endeavour and effort into spreading the Religion of Christ.

Friday, 8 March
I received today, by the hand of Don Martín de Noroña,[1] a letter from the King of Portugal asking me to go to see him, since the weather was not favourable for putting to sea in the caravel. I agreed, against my will, because I did not wish to give any grounds for mistrust, and have come to spend the night in Sacanben.[2] The King has ordered his officials to give me whatever I need for myself, the men or the caravel, without payment, and to see that whatever I want done is done.

Saturday, 9 March
I left Sacanben to go to meet the King, who is in Valle del Paraíso,[1] nine leagues from Lisbon. The rain prevented my arrival before

nightfall. The King had me received with great ceremony by the most important people in his household, and he himself greeted me very honourably and did me many courtesies, asking me to sit down and talking cordially with me.

He undertook unreservedly to have anything done which might be to the service of Your Majesties, paying more attention to it than if it were for himself. He expressed great joy that the voyage has been made and has had a happy outcome, but said that his understanding of the *capitulación* between Your Majesties and himself suggested that this conquest belonged to him. I replied that I had not seen the *capitulación*, but my only understanding was that Your Majesties ordered me not to go to La Mina, or to any part of Guinea, and that orders were given for proclamations to this effect in all the ports of Andalusia before I sailed. The King replied that he was sure that there will be no need for any arbitration in this matter.[2]

He has given me as my host the Prior of Crato, the most distinguished person here, who has shown me many honours and favours.

Sunday, 10 March
Today, after Mass, the King told me again that if I have need of anything he will give it me. We talked for a long time about my voyage, and all the time he refused to let me stand and had me treated most honourably.[1]

Monday, 11 March
I took my leave of the King today. He continued to behave most cordially to me, and gave me certain messages to convey to Your Majesties. When we had eaten I set off, and the King sent Don Martín de Noroña with me, and all the gentlemen there came to set me some distance on my road and do me honour.

I then came to the monastery of San Antonio, near a place called Villafranca,[1] where the Queen is staying. I went to pay my respects and to kiss her hands, for she had sent word that I should not depart without seeing her. The Duke and the Marquis were with her, and they received me with great honour. I set off after nightfall, and have come to Allandra[2] to sleep.

Tuesday, 12 March
I was on the point of leaving Allandra to go back to the caravel when a squire came from the King and offered, on the King's behalf, to accompany me overland to Castile if I wished, seeing to my lodging and providing animals and anything else I might need. When I left him he ordered me and my *piloto*, who was with me, to be given a mule

each. I learned that he also ordered the *piloto* to be given a further gift of twenty *espadines*. It was said that the King was doing all this so that Your Majesties would hear of it.

It was night when I returned to the caravel.

Wednesday, 13 March
At eight o'clock today I weighed anchor at high tide and with the wind NNW set sail on a course for Seville.

Thursday, 14 March
Last night, after sunset, we continued on course s. We were off Cape St Vincent in Portugal before sunrise, and then steered E for Saltés. Light winds all day; we are now off Faro.

Friday, 15 March
Yesterday, after sunset, we continued our course with light winds. We were off Saltés at sunrise, and at midday, on the flood tide, we crossed the bar into Saltés harbour, which we left on 3 August last year.

And so I bring this account to its end. I intend to continue by sea to Barcelona, where I am told Your Majesties are at present, in order to inform you fully about the voyage which God has allowed me to make and on which He has been my light. For surely, not only do I know firmly and unreservedly that His great majesty is the cause of all good things (of everything, that is, except sin), and that nothing can be guaranteed, or even thought of, unless it is His will; I know too that He has demonstrated this in a miraculous way, as may be seen in my account of the many notable miracles which He revealed during the voyage, and in my own person, after I had spent so long at Your Majesties' Court, opposed and denounced by so many prominent persons of your household. They were all against me and ridiculed my undertaking; I now trust in God that it will prove the greatest honour to Christendom that ever so easily presented itself.[1]

Appendix I

The Voyage Seen Through Other Eyes: the Pleitos de Colón

The *pleitos* were submissions in the dispute between the Crown and the Columbus family over the rights granted to the explorer in the agreement between him and Ferdinand and Isabella, their continued validity after his death, and the question of how far he had carried out his side of the bargain.[1] Much of the Crown case consisted of attempts to minimize the role of Columbus in conceiving the project of discovery, organizing the fleet and crews, and finding and exploring the islands. A central aim of the Crown Procurator was to stress the importance of the Pinzón family's part in things.

To this end a series of twenty-four questions was drawn up and put to a string of witnesses who included men who had sailed on the first voyage. The following are the questions concerning that voyage (questions 2–10 and 24, which have to do with later voyages and the discovery of the mainland, are omitted), together with samples of witnesses' statements in reply. Many of the answers include phrases such as *lo oyó dezir*, 'he heard it said', and in view of the gap of twenty-three years between the events and the testimonies the verbatim reports of conversations must be approached with caution. The strongest statements about Martín Alonso Pinzón's role are made by his own son. However, it is clear that the Pinzóns were important in the organization of the project, and were seafarers of experience and standing. Vicente Yáñez Pinzón emerged in the years following 1492 as a distinguished explorer in his own right.

Although some of the responses conflict with the detail of Columbus's account, there is very little in the questions themselves which is incompatible with the content of the Journal. If one severs the emotional bond with Columbus which one has grown to feel in reading the Journal, one begins to wonder as one reads the testimonies what picture would have emerged if Martín Alonso Pinzón had left us his own account.

It is interesting to compare the responses to questions 15–18 with the Journal entries describing the days immediately before the discovery (6–11 October), and those to questions 19–21 with Columbus's account of Martín Alonso's motives and activities while the Pinta was on her own (see the entries for 3–10 January). The reference to the Admiral of the Indies in the first paragraph is to Diego, the son of Columbus, who under the terms of the *capitulaciones* inherited the titles granted to his father.

Appendix I

1. First: Are they acquainted with the said Procurator and the said Admiral, and did they know his father, Admiral Christopher Columbus, and Juan de Fonseca, now Bishop of Burgos, and Martín Alonso Pinzón and Vicente Yáñez and their brothers, and Peralonso Niño, and Cristóbal Guerra, and Rodrigo de Bastida, and Diego de Lepe, and Juan de Solis, and Juan de la Cosa and Alonso de Hojeda? . . .

11. Item: Do they know that when the Admiral set off to explore those areas Martín Alonso Pinzón of Palos was on the point of setting off to discover them at his own expense with two of his own ships, and that he had reliable written information about the country, obtained in Rome that year in the library of Pope Innocent VIII, and that he had returned from Rome and begun the discussions for a voyage of discovery?

Juan de Ungría: This witness said that he heard it said that Martín Alonso Pinzón and one of his brothers went to Rome and that they had brought back some document with instructions for exploration, and that later he and the Admiral had joined forces and gone off exploring, and that they found the land mentioned in this question, and this was common knowledge.

Antón Fernández Colmenero: He said that he was in Palos, his home town, and that Martín Alonso Pinzón and Vicente Yáñez his brother told him that they were going exploring and asked him to go with them, because Columbus was going with them as captain in chief, and this witness said no . . . and he heard that they had found the island of Española, and then they came home, and this witness saw them, and they came straight to Palos, and he heard Martín Alonso and Vicente Yáñez say that they had found Española.

Arias Pérez: He said that he knows this because he is the son of Martín Alonso Pinzón, and when he was in Rome with some merchandise of his father's, the year before the voyage, Martín Alonso went to Rome, and one day in the Pope's library, having been there many times because of his great friendship with a servant of the Pope who was a great cosmographer and had many extensive documents . . . this witness and his father were told about these lands which were still undiscovered, and when they were together Martín Alonso, with his great energy and knowledge of the sea, told this witness repeatedly that he was organizing and equipping two ships to go to discover these lands; he knows this because of what he has said and what happened and because he saw it with his own eyes.

12. Item: Do they know that the said Martín Alonso Pinzón informed Christopher Columbus about the region and discussed with him the aforementioned document, which was said to be a judgement from the time of Solomon saying that if one sailed through the Mediterranean, past Spain and on to the westward . . . through ninety-five degrees one would find a land called Sypanso, fertile and rich, and larger than Africa and Europe together?

Antón Fernández Colmenero: He said that he heard of the documents from Martín Alonso himself, who had brought a copy from Rome, and he knows this because he returned from Rome with him.

Arias Pérez: He said that . . . when he was in the library of Pope Innocent VIII in Rome he gave him a document saying what is contained in the question, and his father took it and brought it back to Castile with the intention of going in search of the said land, and set about it . . . and then the Admiral came to Palos with this project to discover those lands . . . and saw fit to approach Martín Alonso, who agreed that the project was good and that he knew all about it, and that if Columbus had not arrived when he did he would have found him already gone with two caravels to discover those lands, and when the Admiral realized this he became very friendly with the witness's father and made a compact with him and asked him to accompany him, all of which this witness saw personally.

13. *Item: Do they know that when he had received this document the said Admiral increased his efforts and preparations for sailing to discover that land, and that Martín Alonso Pinzón made him come to the Court, paying his expenses so that he could negotiate for the voyage, since Martín Alonso had everything necessary in his house?*

García Ferrando: He said that . . . the Queen sent 20,000 *maravedis*, in florins, which Diego Prieto of this town brought with a letter asking this witness to give them to Christopher Columbus so that he could dress decently and buy a small beast to ride on and appear before her . . . and he came back with the authority to take over what ships he thought fit for the voyage, and that was when the friendship and pact with Martín Alonso and Vicente Yáñez came about, they being men of substance and experienced seafarers, and they advised Columbus and put many advantageous things his way for the voyage.

14. *Item: Do they know that after leaving the Court he went to Palos and could find no one to give him ships, nor to sail in them, and that the said Martín Alonso, in order to serve Their Majesties, gave him two vessels and decided to accompany him, with his relatives and friends, and the Admiral promised him half of all the benefits promised to him by Their Majesties for finding the country, and showed him the royal documentary undertakings?*

Juan de Ungría: He said that he repeats what he has said and that he heard many people say so and that it is common knowledge.

Garci Fernández: He said that what he knows is that Martín Alonso came to Palos, the witness does not know from where, and fitted out two vessels and gave them to the Admiral for the service of their Majesties. Asked how he knows that the ships were handed over fully fitted out, he said because he witnessed it and because he was purser on one of them, the Pinta.

Francisco García Vallejo: He said that to his knowledge, if it had not been for Martín Alonso helping with his relatives and friends, the Admiral would never have sailed on the voyage of discovery, and nobody would have gone with him, and Martín Alonso, in friendship and with the desire to serve Their Majesties, asked his brother and this witness and other men to go with him and the Admiral . . . asked how he knows this, he said that he was there and saw it, and went with the said Pinzón and his brother as part of the company.

Arias Pérez: He said that . . . when the Admiral came back from the Court he brought Their Majesties' order and authority to sail to discover those lands with three ships, and he found that there was not a single man in Palos who dared go with him or who would provide him with ships, for they said that he would never find land. After spending over two months making no progress he set to asking Martín Alonso, showing him the promises of rewards from Their Majesties if he should find land, and promising him a half share and the captaincy of one of the ships if he went with him, and suggesting that he should use his influence over his friends and relatives to serve Their Majesties, and Martín Alonso saw that the Admiral was helpless . . . and agreed to go with him, gave him the document he had brought from Rome, provided the ships and with his friends and relatives put the fleet together inside a month.

15. Item: Do they know that Martín Alonso Pinzón played a principal role on the voyage as captain of one of his two ships, and that his brothers were captains of the other two, and that they sailed 800 leagues west from the island of Hierro, and that 200 leagues earlier the Admiral thought he was near land but did not know which way to sail, and failing to find land he approached the vessel of Martín Alonso Pinzón to ask his opinion, saying that they had sailed 200 leagues more than he expected and should have had a landfall?

Manuel de Valdovinos: He said that . . . on the voyage he made with Vicente Yáñez he heard him and other men from Palos who sailed with him say that . . . they had gone 800 leagues west from Hierro, and that Vicente Yáñez and Martín Alonso brought their ships close to that of Columbus and said, 'Sir, where are we going? We have run 800 leagues without a landfall, and the crews are saying that they are doomed.' Columbus replied, 'Martín Alonso, bear with me this day and night, and if I do not find land for you before tomorrow morning, you may cut off my head and turn back, for you have ample time to return' . . . and then they changed course to southwest by west, and at sunset Columbus told everyone to keep a sharp lookout and they would see land, and the crew climbed into the maintops and stood on the poop and the fo'c'sle and looked into the setting sun, and no one saw land except Columbus himself, at sunset, and they all said to each other, 'Can you see it?', and none of the witness's shipmates saw it, and when they changed the watch at prime Columbus posted lookouts forward on the ships, and as they sailed on in the next watch a man from Seville called Juan Bermejo sighted land, and the first land was the island of Guanahani.

Pero Ramírez: He said that . . . he heard many of the men from Palos who sailed with Columbus say that they would have turned back, but Martín Alonso Pinzón made his relatives sail on another four days, and that was how they found land.

Juan de Moguer: He said that he heard as much from many people in Palos, and he heard it from Martín Alonso and Vicente Yáñez in Galicia when they returned from the voyage of discovery.

Garci Fernández: He said that he knows that Martín Alonso was captain of one of the ships called the Pinta, on which the witness was purser . . . and that after sailing . . . about 400 leagues Martín Alonso approached the Admiral and said, 'Sir, we should change course to southwest by west', and the Admiral agreed. The Admiral was always encouraging them and putting heart into Martín Alonso and the rest of them. They did not find land, and they changed course to southwest, and there they found the land called Guanahani, and the crew of the Pinta, on which the witness was sailing, sighted it first. As a sign of rejoicing Martín Alonso ordered lombards fired towards the Admiral's ship, which was following the Pinta, and they waited for him to catch them up, and the Admiral shouted, 'Martín Alonso, you have found land.' Martín Alonso replied, 'Sir, remember my reward!' and the Admiral said, 'I will give you 5,000 maravedis.' The witness knows all this because he was there.

Francisco García Vallejo: He said that . . . they sailed west from Hierro 800 leagues, and about 200 leagues before they sighted land the Admiral spoke to all the captains, including Martín Alonso, and said 'What are we to do?' This was on 6 October 1493. [*sic*] He said, 'Captain, what are we to do, for my crew is complaining? What shall we do, gentlemen?' Then Vicente Yáñez said, 'Sir, let us keep on until we have sailed 1,000 leagues, and if we do not find what we are seeking we can turn back.' Martín Alonso . . . said, 'What, sir, we have barely left Palos and you have had enough? Sail on; God will give us victory and a landfall, and for His sake let us not return in shame!' The Admiral replied, 'I hope you may not regret it,' and so they sailed on, because of what Martín Alonso had said.

16. Item: Do they know that the said Martín Alonso Pinzón shouted, 'Sail on! Sail on! This is a fleet and embassy of the great King and Queen of Spain; Spain has never lost her reputation, and please God she will never lose it through us. If you, sir, wish to go back I am resolved to carry on until I find land, or never to see Spain again!' and that they went on because of his opinion and his energy?

Juan González: He said that he heard so from a man of this town called Juan Quintero de Argurta, and from other men who were on the voyage, whose names he does not recall.

Juan Calvo: He said that he had heard that Martín Alonso said this to the Admiral; many of the sailors who went on the voyage told him so, but he does not remember their names.

17. Item: Do they know that the Admiral asked him if he thought they should stay on the same course, and that Martín Alonso said no, that he had told him many times that the course was wrong and that they should sail west southwest and would reach land sooner, and the Admiral said, 'So be it,' and that they changed course through the energy and opinion of Martín Alonso, who at that time was very skilled in everything to do with the sea?

Juan de Ungría: He said that he had heard this said publicly by men who said they had gone with the Admiral.

Juan González: He said that he was told that Martín Alonso Pinzón was very skilled in the ways of the sea, and that during the voyage he suggested the course mentioned in the question, and so they found land; he was told this by the sailors.

Francisco García Vallejo: He said that he knows, having witnessed it, that Martín Alonso said: 'Sir, it seems to me, and I feel it inside me, that if we steer more to the southwest we will find land sooner.' The Admiral answered, 'Well, Martín Alonso, so be it,' and they changed course to west southwest because of Martín Alonso's opinion. That navigational decision was reached through his effort and conviction. Asked how he knows this, the witness replied that he was there and saw it with his own eyes.

18. *Item: Do they know that three or four days after changing course . . . they reached the island of Guanahani?*

Herrando Esteban: He said that he heard this, and that it was public knowledge that that was the first land they discovered, and that they discovered it at night. When asked whom he heard say so, he said the people mentioned in the question and Bartolomé Roldán of Palos, the *piloto*.

Diego Fernández Colmenero: He said that he heard that when they were sailing west on the voyage, at the suggestion of Martín Alonso they changed course to west southwest, and Martín Alonso's reasons were that he saw birds over the sea which roost on land, and it was his effort and knowledge which made the Admiral take the course he suggested, Martín Alonso being such a skilled seafarer . . . and when asked how he knows this, he said that he talked with the men who came back from the voyage, and that his memory is clear.

Francisco García Vallejo: . . . Within three days of the change of course this witness was there when Martín Alonso saw some little birds flying by, called *gayeguillos* and *papagallos*, and Martín Alonso said, 'These birds mean something: there is land on either side of us,' and in three days they found the island of Guanahani in the Lucayos. On Thursday, 10 October, Pedro Niño the *piloto* said to the Admiral, 'Sir, let us not press on tonight, for according to your book I make us only sixteen leagues from land, twenty at most.' The Admiral was very pleased, and told him to say the same to Cristóbal García Sarmiento, *piloto* of the Pinta, which he did. Cristóbal García asked him for orders, and Pedro Niño said, 'We should shorten sail tonight and take things steadily; I make us close to land.' Cristóbal García replied, 'Well, if you ask me we should set a press of sail and make all the speed we can,' and Pedro Alonso Niño said, 'Do what you like, I will just follow you; when I hear you hail me I will stand off.' And that Thursday night the moon shone bright and as it came out a sailor on the Pinta called Juan Rodrigo Bermejo, from Molinos near Seville, saw a spit of white sand and looked up and saw the land, and then he fired a shot from a lombard; 'Land! Land!' and they held off until daybreak on the Friday, 11 October. It was Martín Alonso Pinzón who discovered Guanahani, the first island. The witness knows it because he saw it with his own eyes.

19. *Item: Do they know that after discovering that island they separated and the said Martín Alonso Pinzón went off and discovered the island of Española and seven other islands* . . . *and that he reached there seven weeks before the Admiral; that he anchored, and lay in the Martín Alonso river seven weeks before the Admiral reached the island and that the Admiral would never have found it had not Martín Alonso made efforts to summon him by sending letters by canoe when the Admiral was sailing northwest in the Lower Lucayos, and had by then lost his ship?*

Manuel de Valdovinos: He heard tell . . . that off the island of Guanahani some of the ships separated from the others, because it seems that they had been told by the Indians that there was an island called Haiti where there was a lot of gold, and they told them the course for that island. He heard that the island was discovered by Martín Alonso before anyone else, and that he sent word to the Admiral by sending letters by canoe, and when the Admiral arrived Martín Alonso was already there.

Antón Fernández Colmenero: He said that he heard Martín Alonso and his crew say so, and this witness was at the Martín Alonso river himself, and they asked him why he had stayed waiting for Columbus.

García Fernando: The witness said that what he knows is that Martín Alonso found a river on that voyage and called it Martín Alonso harbour . . . and he knows this because he was there himself and heard Martín Alonso and others say what is in the question. He went inland with some of the others and they came to a watering-place and stopped to drink, and there they learned about the gold. He took out a silver cup to drink with and an Indian took a fancy to it and went off with it, and he did not follow him or do him harm, but continued through the land, seeing the people and comporting himself well, and there were signs of gold.

Francisco García Vallejo: He said that one night Martín Alonso took his leave of the Admiral and sailed straight to an island called Baburcas, and from there he sailed more than two hundred leagues to the southwest and discovered Española, and sailed into the river called the Martín Alonso river and named it after himself. Forty-five days later he joined the Admiral at the island of Monte Cristo and told him that he had discovered Española and found the gold, and he gave the Admiral 900 *pesos* of gold which the Admiral did not accept. While the Admiral was at Monte Cristo, before Pinzón arrived, but after the loss of the *nao*, an Indian came and shouted that the *gutrunari*, an Indian king, wanted him to go back and that he would give him a *diaho*, which is a statue of a man made of gold. Vicente Yáñez . . . said, 'Sir, do you understand that?' and the Admiral replied that he understood some of it, and Vicente Yáñez said, 'I understand it; he is telling you to go back, and he will give you a golden man. Go back and get it, sir; it is worth 200 *cuentos* and it will be a fine sample of gold for you to take back to Their Majesties.' The Admiral thought for a while, and then he said, 'Let's leave here and set sail for Spain; I have enough under hatches to show to Their Majesties.' So they sailed, and the witness knows that Española, and the Martín Alonso river, and the gold, were all discovered by Martín Alonso Pinzón. Asked how he knows, he said that he was there and saw it all himself.

Arias Pérez: He said that he often heard his father and the other captains and masters and crewmen say that after they had reached Guanahani and sailed on to look for other islands and territory they had a great storm which separated them on the first night. At dawn they could not see each other, and Martín Alonso Pinzón, being a man of great energy and knowledge, set a different course from that being followed by the Admiral and discovered seven islands and the island of Española, where he entered a river and named it after himself. He saw such a quantity of gold in that land that they were all astonished, and he was so pleased that he went inland with twelve companions as far as the land of Caonabo, which later belonged to Behechio, and found amazing amounts of gold. He came back very pleased to the ship with his twelve men, and then went inland again towards what is now called the *vega* in Española, about thirty leagues, where again they found many signs of gold, and came back to the ship . . . and he despatched canoes to the area to which the Admiral had gone. The Admiral received the news in the island in the Lucayos where he was sailing, and he went immediately to Española, and when he arrived the witness's father, Martín Alonso, had already discovered it seven weeks earlier and found the gold. The witness knows all this because he heard it from his father, Martín Alonso, and all the other captains, and the men who went inland with him.

20. *Item: Do they know that in those seven weeks Martín Alonso explored Española and met the main chiefs of the country, reaching the home of Behechio and Caonabo in La Maguana, finding great amounts of gold and bartering for much of it before the Admiral arrived?*

> *Juan de Ungría*: He said that he heard this from Martín Alonso and the others who went with him.
> *Cristóbal García*: He said that he heard that Martín Alonso went inland from the river which he named after himself, and found and bargained for the gold which he brought back, before the arrival of Admiral Christopher Columbus, and that this is common knowledge and is not in doubt; he knows this because he has heard it from many people whose names he does not recall.

21. *Item: Do they know that, when the Admiral had received the letters sent by canoe by Martín Alonso, and when he had gone to Española and had seen the wealth which Pinzón had discovered and acquired, they set off immediately for Castile with the samples obtained by Martín Alonso?*

> *Juan de Ungría*: He said that this is what he heard from Martín Alonso and others who went with him. He saw some of the gold in Martín Alonso's possession.

Juan Calvo: He said that they came back to Spain after the discovery, and when the witness was on his way home from Flanders he found them in the port of Bayona, on the river Minho, and so he knows that this is the truth, and it is common knowledge.

22. Item: Are they aware that it is common knowledge that if it had not been for the said Martín Alonso Pinzón the Admiral would have turned back and would not have found land, and that the land was discovered through the wisdom and energy of Martín Alonso Pinzón, who explored the island of Española and its gold from the river called the Martín Alonso river, where he arrived and anchored before anyone else, and gave his name to that river and harbour?

Garci Fernández: What he knows is that Martín Alonso discovered the island in the ship Pinta, in which this witness was purser, and that the river was called the Martín Alonso river.

Juan Calvo: He said that he knows that it was discovered through the efforts of Martín Alonso, who told them to keep going, and that Española and its gold were discovered because Martín Alonso brought back the gold samples and anchored in the river which he named after himself. Asked how he knows this, he said that he knew Martín Alonso himself, and heard him tell it.

Francisco García Vallejo: He said that he knows the truth of this because he saw it with his own eyes. About 170 leagues from land the Admiral would have turned back, if Martín Alonso had agreed, but his energy and knowledge kept them going. Martín Alonso discovered the river named after him and the land before anyone else. Asked how he knows this, the witness said that he was a member of the crew on the voyage, and knows it because he saw it.

23. Item: Are they further aware that it is common knowledge that, if Martín Alonso Pinzón had not given his ships and made the voyage with the Admiral on the basis of the bargain between them that the Admiral would give him half of all the benefits granted him by Their Majesties for discovering land, the Admiral would have found neither ships nor the men to crew them, and that everything necessary was found after Martín Alonso Pinzón agreed to go, his reputation as a seafarer and a man of spirit and enterprise being so high?

Garci Fernández: He said that he knew Martín Alonso to be a man of great energy and spirit, and that if he had not given the Admiral the two ships the Admiral would not have sailed where he did, and would not have found a crew, the reason being that nobody knew the Admiral; it was through people's respect for Martín Alonso and because he provided the two ships that the Admiral made the voyage.

Antón Fernández Colmenero: He said that he heard everybody living in Palos say that Columbus would not have gone to the Indies, and nobody else would have dared to go, if it had not been for Martín Alonso and his brothers and relatives, all of whom helped him because they were men of spirit and energy, and experienced seafarers.

Diego Fernández Colmenero: He said that he knows that with royal authorization the Admiral obtained ships, and could find nobody to crew them except the criminals in the town gaol, and Martín Alonso made an agreement with him on a shared basis and through his wish to serve His Majesty, being a man of daring and experience and spirit who would always try to achieve what other men could not, so as to leave his mark in the world. He guided the Admiral and went with him and took many relatives and friends. The witness knows all this because he saw it with his own eyes.

Appendix II

The Payroll of the Voyage[1]

/Roll or List of Those who went with Christopher Columbus on
the First Voyage/

Jhesus cum Maria sit nobis in via

/Notarial Account of the Payments made by His Lordship to the
Men of Palos/

Jhesus 1498, on 16 November in Santo Domingo on the island of Española.

At the time when My Lord and Lady the King and Queen agreed that I should go to discover the Indies, which was in 1491, I established with Their Majesties that I would have one-eighth of the proceeds from the expedition, and that I would contribute one-eighth of the expenses, as is set out at greater length in the said agreement. In order that my costs should be made known I wished it to be done in the presence of a public notary in the town of Palos, where at Their Majesties' request I prepared three vessels, one *nao* and two caravels, and the money I spent was disbursed in the presence of the said notary, who wrote down all this document and the amounts with his own hand.

In this present year of 1498, when I was at their royal Court, Their Majesties exempted me from the expenses of the fleet which I gathered, as appears in their letter lodged with others in the Monastery of Las Cuevas in Seville, and the authorized transcription of it is here in a book with others. Although Their Majesties have exempted me, as stated, and although this document has expired, I wish it to be well guarded and signed by the said notary, after a transcript has been made here by a public notary who will swear to it, and I wish it to be taken to Palos and then lodged with the other important documents in Las Cuevas in Seville.

Even if this document should be lost, the people are there who received the money from me, and they will swear to it, and there too is the account of the *contadores mayores* who paid the same men what was due to them on their return from the Indies over and above the following which was advanced to them before the voyage, and they received the rest of their due in Barcelona in the May of [no date].

/In the town of Palos, Saturday 23 July in the year of Our Lord 1492. On this day aforesaid Christopher Columbus, Captain of Their Majesties, Our Lord and Lady the King and Queen, made payments of wages to the seamen and *grumetes* and other people who are sailing in the said fleet, and they are as follows:

Seamen
First to Sancho Ruiz de Gama, *piloto*, 20 ducats.
Juan de Moguer, seaman, 4,000 *maravedis*.
Gil Pérez, seaman, 4,000 *maravedis*.
Alvaro, the nephew of Gil Pérez, seaman, 4,000 *maravedis*. The said Gil Pérez stood surety for him, and *vice versa*.
Pero Sánchez of Montilla, seaman, 4,000 *maravedis*.
Pedro Arraez, seaman, 4,000 *maravedis*. Received for him by Vicente Yáñez.
Juan Ruiz de la Peña, from Biscay, 4,000 *maravedis*. Received by Vicente Yáñez.
Juan Arraez, son of Pedro Arraez, 4,000 *maravedis*. Received by Vicente Yáñez.
Juan Martínez de Azoque, from Denia, 4,000 *maravedis*. Received for him by Vicente Yáñez. Iñigo de la Orden, of Denia, stood surety for Juan Ruiz de la Peña and Juan Martínez de Azoque.
Juan de la Plaza, of this town, 4,000 *maravedis*.
García Fernández, of Illana, seaman, 4,000 *maravedis*.
Juan Verde de Triana, 4,000 *maravedis*. Received for him by Martín Alonso Pinzón.
Juan Romero, seaman of Pero González Ferrando, 4,000 *maravedis*.
Francisco García Vallejo, of Moguer, 4,000 *maravedis*.
Bartomolé Vives, of this town, 4,000 *maravedis*.
Juan de Medina, tailor, of Palos, 4,000 *maravedis*.
Cristóbal García Sarmiento, *piloto*, 8,030 *maravedis*.
Juan Quintero, son of Argueta Arraez [?], 18 ducats, 6,750 *maravedis*.
Juan Reynal, of Huelva, 12 ducats, 4,500 *maravedis*.
Bartolomé Roldán, of Moguer, seaman of Alonso López of Moguer, received 4,000 *maravedis*. He pledged as surety certain houses in the said town, bordered on the one side by Gonzalo Alonso Maldonado and on the other . . .
Martín Alonso received 4,000 *maravedis* for Juan Vezano.
The said Martín Alonso also received 4,000 *maravedis* for Antonio Calabrés, his servant.

Sancho de Rama, of this town of Palos, 4,000 *maravedis*. Martín Alonso Pinzón stood surety for him.

Grumetes

Juan Arias, Portuguese, son of Lope Arias of Tavira, 2,666 *maravedis*.
Alonso, servant of Juan Rodríguez de Guinea, son of Francisco Chocero, 2,666 *maravedis*. Received by the said Juan Rodríguez.
Juan, servant of Juan Buenaño, 2,666 *maravedis*. The said Juan Buenaño stood surety for him.
Pedro Tegero, 2,666 *maravedis*. Juan de Moguer stood surety.
Fernando de Triana, 2,666 *maravedis*. Vicente Yáñez stood surety for him.
Juan Cuadrado, 2,666 *maravedis*. Juan Guerrero, son of [?] stood surety for him.

[A leaf missing]

Miguel de Soria, servant of Diego de Lepe, 2,666 *maravedis*. His master, Diego de Lepe, stood surety for him. He was given 8 *doblas*.
Rodrigo Gallego, servant of Gonzalo Fuego, 2,666 *maravedis*.

[Material probably lost]
The said Martín, his master, stood surety for him. He was given 8 *doblas*.
Bernal, servant of Alonso, seaman of Juan de Mafra, 8 *doblas*, or 2,920 *maravedis*. Received by his said master.
Alonso de Palos, 8 *doblas*, 2,600 [altered to 2,900] *maravedis*. Martín Alonso Pinzón stood surety for him.
Andrés de Yrueñes, 7 ducats. Received by Juan Reynal. He is to have 2,666 *maravedis*.
Francisco Mendes, of Huelva, 2,666 *maravedis*.
Martín Alonso Pinzón received 2,666 *maravedis* for Fernando Mendes.

[On a separate sheet]
Diego de Arana, Marshal of Their Majesties' Fleet, has received 8,000 *maravedis*.
Francisco Martín Pinzón, Master of the Pinta, has received 8,000 *maravedis*.
Martín Alonso Pinzón, Captain of the Pinta, received 16,000 *maravedis*.

Notes

Introduction

Chapter 1

1 The Queen was probably reluctant to approve anything which might be seen as a contravention of the 1479 treaty of Alcaçovas, under which Spain agreed to leave Atlantic exploration to Portugal except in the area of the Canaries. See Florentino Pérez Embid, *Los descubrimientos en el Atlántico y la rivalidad castellano-portuguesa hasta el tratado de Tordesillas*, Seville, 1948, especially pp. 229–34.

2 His conviction that the voyage was divinely inspired is most apparent in his *Libro de profecías*, a conglomeration of Latin extracts from the Scriptures and the fathers of the Church, mostly alluding to islands and their discovery, or to evangelism. See the edition and Spanish translation by Francisco Alvarez Seisdedos, Madrid, 1984. The *Libro* was gathered later in life, and reveals an obsessive, self-justifying mania.

3 In his *Historia de las Indias*, at a point where Columbus instructs an Indian intermediary to tell a local ruler that the Spaniards have come down from Heaven and are looking for gold, Las Casas comments sarcastically on the unlikelihood of the combination. See Bartolomé de las Casas, *Historia de las Indias*, in Vol. 95 of the *Biblioteca de Autores Españoles*, Madrid, 1957, pp. 183–4. Future references to this work use the abbreviation 'LCH'. Las Casas (1474–1566) was one of the early colonists of the West Indies. After taking part in the exploitation of native labour in agriculture and mining, he became a Dominican friar, grew concerned at the abuse of the Indians, and became their outspoken champion. He had access to a copy of Columbus's Journal, his own recopying of which provides the closest available text to the original.

4 It is impossible to give exact equivalents for these, since they varied with the length of the day. Terce was three hours after sunrise, vespers an hour before sunset, and compline an hour after sunset.

5 The proliferation of such strongholds gave Castilla its name.

6 This is evident in sundry ways. In the siege of Cuzco the Inca army was defeated by the miraculous emergence from the clouds of St James of Compostela, *Santiago Matamoros* (the Moor-slayer), with the same white-clad angels who defeated the Islamic army at Hacinas in Castile in the tenth century. See the illustration in Felipe Guaman Poma de Ayala, *Nueva crónica y buen gobierno*, ed. John V. Murra and others, 3 vols, Madrid, 1987, fol. 404. The *Codex Mendoza*, a pictorial manuscript by an indigenous artist showing Aztec life and customs (and, more interestingly for the Spanish Viceroy who sent it back to Spain, the potential for taxation and commerce), has an explanatory commentary by a Spanish scribe. To denote aspects of Aztec religion, he uses Arabic

Notes

words: the pagan religious leader is not a bishop or a prelate, but an *alfaqui*, a Moorish high priest; the place of worship is not a church or temple, but a *mezquita*, a mosque. He sees the Aztec as a trans-Atlantic variety of Moor. See *Codex Mendoza*, ed. James C. Clarke, 3 vols, London, 1938. Columbus, similarly, uses words of Arabic origin to describe unfamiliar artefacts: *azagayas*, assegais, for the local weapons; *almadías* for the Indian canoes.

7 Columbus asked his heirs to continue to use them in the same form, describing them as an X with an S above, then an M with an A above it and an S above that, and then a Greek Y with an S above it. The manner of this description suggests that we may have three inverted abbreviations: XS, MAS, and YS, but expanding them is not easy. 'Christus' for the first, 'María' for the second, 'Iesus' or 'Yosue' for the third? None of this is at all convincing. The letters have also been interpreted as the initials of a Latin sentence, *Servus sum Altissimi Salvatoris* ('I am a servant of the Most High Saviour'), followed by the initials of Christ, Mary and possibly Joseph. See John B. Thacher, *Christopher Columbus: His Life, His Work, His Remains, as Revealed by Original Printed and Manuscript Records*, 3 vols, New York, 1903–4, Vol. III, p. 455 (future references use the abbreviation 'Thacher'), and Samuel Eliot Morison, *Admiral of the Ocean Sea: A Life of Christopher Columbus*, 2 vols, Boston, 1942, Chapter XXV (future references use the abbreviation 'Morison, *Admiral*').

8 The La Cosa chart is well reproduced in colour in Michel Mollat du Jourdin and others, *Les Portulans: Cartes marines du XIIIᵉ au XVIIᵉ siècle*, Fribourg, 1984 (English version, *Sea Charts of the Early Explorers*, New York, 1984), Plate 22.

9 In the early colonial period, when the Catholic Church took advantage of indigenous traditions of mural painting to convey Christian images to the Indians, the figure of St Christopher was painted as a colossus on the walls of various Mexican churches. See Emily Edwards, *Painted Walls of Mexico from Prehistoric Times until Today*, Austin and London, 1966, pp. 84–5.

10 Fernando Columbus, *Historie della vita e dei fatti di Cristoforo Colombo*, ed. R. Caddeo, 2 vols, Milan, 1930, Ch. 1.

Future references use the abbreviation 'FCH'. There is an English translation by Benjamin Keen, New Brunswick, 1959.

Chapter 2

1 On Behaim, see E. G. Ravenstein, *Martin Behaim: His Life and His Globe*, London, 1908.

2 Carlos Sanz, 'El mapa del mundo, según el proceso cartográfico de Occidente y su influencia en el de Oriente; y un mapa del mundo verdaderamente importante de la famosa universidad de Yale', *Boletín de la Real Sociedad Geográfica*, Vol. CII, 1966, pp. 38–42.

3 Sanz, 'El mapa . . .', suggests that the copy in the Yale University Library is printed, but it may be a manuscript with a printed border.

4 One could quote many similar examples. For a full translation see *The Travels of Marco Polo the Venetian*, ed. John Masefield, Everyman, London and New York, 1907. Future references use the abbreviation 'MP'.

5 For the full version of this episode, see MP, pp. 158–60.

6 He had previously, at Easter, kissed the Bible and made all his courtiers do the same.

7 The ensuing account of European involvement in the far east owes a considerable debt to L.-H. Parias, *Historia universal de las exploraciones*, Madrid, 1982, Vol. I, pp. 386 ff.; A. C. Moule, *Christians in China before the year 1550*, London, 1930; and the four volumes of the collection by Sir Henry Yule, *Cathay and the Way Thither*, 2nd edn, London (Hakluyt Society), 1913–15. Future references to the Yule collection use the abbreviation 'Cathay'.

8 *Cathay*, Vol. I, pp. 101–21.

9 *Cathay*, Vol. III, p. 5.

10 *Cathay*, Vol. III, p. 55.

11 For Montecorvino's letters, see *Cathay*, Vol. III, pp. 45–70.

12 Bibliothèque Nationale, Paris, MS Fr 2810, fols 136v ff.

13 *Cathay*, Vol. III, p. 102.

14 *Cathay*, Vol. III, pp. 137–73.

15 The Islamic geographer Ibn Batuta says that the journey from Sarai to Urgandi took 30–40 days. He walked the stage from Astrakhan to Sarai on the frozen river, taking 3 days. (*Cathay*, Vol. III, p. 146 n.)

Notes

16 *Cathay*, Vol. III, pp. 152–5.
17 'I was long tarrying among the Saracens, and I preached to them for several days openly and publicly the name of Jesus Christ and His gospel. I opened out and laid bare the cheats, falsehoods and blunders of their false prophet; with a loud voice, and in public, I did confound their barkings . . . and then these children of the Devil tried to tempt and pervert me with bribes, promising me wives and handmaidens, gold and silver and lands, horses and cattle, and other delights of this world. But when in every way I rejected all their promises with scorn, then for two days together they pelted me with stones, besides putting fire to my face and my feet, plucking out my beard, and heaping upon me for a length of time all kinds of insult and abuse' (*Cathay*, Vol. III, pp. 82–8).
18 'Cathay is a great country, fair, noble and rich, and full of merchants. Thither merchants go to seek spices and all manner of merchandise, more commonly than in any other part. And you shall understand that merchants who come from Genoa, or from Venice, or from Romania, or other parts of Lombardy, go by sea and by land eleven or twelve months, or more sometimes, before they reach the isle of Cathay.' *The Voyages and Travels of Sir John Maundevile Kt.*, ed. H. M., London, 1892, p. 133.
19 *Cathay*, Vol. III, p. 14.
20 *Cathay*, Vol. I, p. 121.
21 *Cathay*, Vol. I, pp. 173–4.
22 *Cathay*, Vol. IV, p. 198.
23 See F. Pérez Embid, *Los descubrimientos* . . .
24 Quoted by Armando Cortesão, *The Nautical Chart of 1424*, Coimbra, 1954, p. 39. This work is an invaluable and well illustrated source of information on the legendary Atlantic islands.
25 For an English version of the text, an excessively imaginative interpretation of the navigation involved in the voyage, and suggestions about the identity of the islands visited, see Paul H. Chapman, *The Man Who Led Columbus to America*, Atlanta, 1973.
26 Cortesão, *The Nautical Chart*, pp. 73–4.
27 Cortesão, *The Nautical Chart*, pp. 71–2.
28 FCH, Vol. I, Ch. 9.

Chapter 3
1 For a list of these, see Morison, *Admiral*, Vol. I, pp. 21–2.
2 FCH, Vol. I, Ch. I.
3 Ignacio B. Anzoátegui (ed.), *Los cuatro viajes del Almirante y su testamento*, 3rd edn, Buenos Aires, 1958, pp. 219–21.
4 See Morison, *Admiral*, Vol. I, pp. 20–1 n. 2.
5 *Cristoforo Colombo: Documenti e prove della sua appartenenza a Genova*, Bergamo, 1931. There is also an English–German edition, Bergamo, 1932. Later references to this collection use the abbreviation '*Documenti*'.
6 FCH, Vol. I, Ch. I.
7 *Documenti*, p. 105.
8 *Documenti*, p. 123.
9 *Documenti*, p. 125.
10 *Documenti*, p. 127.
11 Around 1445, according to Morison (*Admiral*, Vol. I, p. 13).
12 *Documenti*, pp. 109, 115.
13 *Documenti*, p. 115.
14 Morison, *Admiral*, Vol. I, p. 13.
15 See Cesare de Lollis (ed.), *Scritti di Cristoforo Colombo*, Part I, Vols i and ii, of the *Raccolta di documenti e studi publicati dalla R. Commissione Colombiana pel quarto centenario della scoperta dell'America*, 14 vols, Rome, 1892–4, I, ii, pp. 52–3, 199–200. Future references use the abbreviation '*Raccolta*'.
16 *Documenti*, p. 143.
17 *Documenti*, p. 147.
18 *Documenti*, p. 135.
19 *Documenti*, p. 149.
20 *Documenti*, pp. 109, 151.
21 *Documenti*, p. 133.
22 Morison, *Admiral*, Vol. I, pp. 17–18.
23 FCH, Vol. I, Ch. 3.
24 FCH, Vol. I, Ch. 3.
25 FCH, Vol. I, Ch. 4.
26 See Morison, *Admiral*, Vol. I, pp. 35–6 nn. 4–6.
27 For detailed references, see Morison, *Admiral*, Vol. I, pp. 36–7 n. 12. Fernando gives a rather garbled account (FCH, Ch. 5).
28 FCH, Vol. I, Ch. 4.
29 *Raccolta*, Part I, Vol. ii, p. 292.
30 The note in question says 26 fathoms. Even if one takes this to be the Genoese fathom of about 2 feet, or postulates a scribal transformation of feet to fathoms, the idea is outlandish.
31 *Documenti*, p. 137.
32 See Thacher, Vol. I, pp. 190, 193, for

the text of the Genoese chronicler Antonio Gallo; Cecil Jane, *Voyages of Columbus*, London, 1930, p. 309, for that of Andrés Bernáldez of Seville.

33 For the dating, see Morison, *Admiral*, Vol. I, p. 59 n. 19.

34 FCH, Ch. 5.

35 LCH, p. 348.

36 *Raccolta*, Part I, Vol. ii, pp. 294, 375.

37 *Raccolta*, Part I, Vol. ii, p. 407.

38 FCH, Ch. 4.

39 Alfragan was an Islamic geographer who computed the degree of longitude as 56⅔ miles. His mile unit was the Arabic one, equal to 2,164 metres. Columbus, in a typical piece of self-delusion, thought Alfragan was using the Roman mile of 1,480 metres, and thereby reached the conclusion that the degree, and therefore the world, were substantially smaller than they are. For a table of different geographers' calculations on the size of the degree, see Morison, *Admiral*, Vol. I, pp. 87, 103 n. 11.

Chapter 4

1 Juan Gil (in his *Colón y su tiempo*, Vol. I of *Mitos y utopías del descubrimiento*, Madrid, 1989) suggests that most of the works were gathered and annotated by Columbus after the second voyage, when his cosmography was questioned. See especially pp. 22–3, 121–45.

2 For a complete edition of his comments on Marco Polo see Juan Gil (ed.), *El Libro de Marco Polo anotado por Cristóbal Colón. Versión de Rodrigo de Santaella*, Madrid, 1987.

3 MP, pp. 388–9.

4 MP. pp. 347–8. This idea is also mentioned by other accounts of the orient, including those of Ibn Batuta and Jordanus (see *Cathay*, Vol. IV, p. 94).

5 Notably by Charles de la Roncière in *La Carte de Christophe Colomb*, Paris, 1924.

6 For a full translation of both letters, see Samuel Eliot Morison, *Journals and other Documents on the Life and Voyages of Christopher Columbus*, New York, 1963, pp. 12–15. Future references use the abbreviation 'Morison, 1963'.

7 FCH, Ch. 9.

8 Samuel Eliot Morison, *Portuguese Voyages to America in the Fifteenth Century*, Cambridge, Mass., 1940, pp. 44–7.

9 See Morison, *Admiral*, Vol. I, p. 105.

10 FCH, Ch. 11; LCH, pp. 106–8. Las Casas gives full details of Columbus's demands, which are largely reproduced in those later acceded to by Ferdinand and Isabella. It may well be that Las Casas simply assumed that they coincided.

11 FCH, Ch. 11; LCH, pp. 108–9.

12 On La Rábida, see Antonio Rumeu de Armas, *La Rábida y el descubrimiento de América*, Madrid, 1968; Angel Ortega, *La Rábida: historia documental crítica*, 4 vols, Seville, 1925–6.

13 See FCH, Ch. 12; LCH, pp. 110 ff.

14 On Columbus's movements in this period, see Henri Vignaud, *Histoire Critique de la grande entreprise de Christophe Colomb*, 2 vols, Paris, 1911, Vol. I, pp. 399–730; Vol. II, pp. 19–134; Juan Manzano Manzano, *Cristóbal Colón: Siete años decisivos de su vida, 1485–1492*, Madrid, 1964.

15 Las Casas appears to place this approach five years later, after Columbus's prolonged disappointment at the Court, though his wording is vague and it may be that he inserted his account of the discussions with the Duke as an afterthought. Fernando, too, says that application was made to the Duke after failure to convince the King and Queen. See FCH, Ch. 12; LCH, p. 114.

16 See Vignaud, *Histoire*, Vol. I, pp. 530–46.

17 LCH, p. 115.

18 *Raccolta*, Part I, Vol. ii, pp. 169 and 265.

19 LCH, p. 111.

20 Las Casas derides the idea, but even an advanced thinker like Martin Behaim could express a similar idea in 1492. He states on his globe that 'the inhabitants of India . . . sail to this island of Madagascar, normally in twenty days; it takes them three months' hard work to get back, because the slope of the sea takes them rapidly south.'

21 FCH, Ch. 12; q.v. for all this, with LCH, pp. 111–12.

22 LCH, pp. 113–14.

23 Published in the Real Academia de Historia's *Colección de documentos inéditos relativos al descubrimiento*, 2ª Serie, 25 vols, 1885–1932, Vols VII and VIII, 1892–4. Future references use the abbreviation 'Pleitos'. There is a new edition by Antonio Muro Orejón and others, *Pleitos*

colombinos, in at least 8 vols, Seville, 1964–.

24 For an English translation of these documents, see Morison, *Journals and other Documents* . . ., pp. 26–36.

25 He still had debts to Genoese merchants when he made his will in 1506. See Anzoátegui, *Los cuatro viajes* . . ., pp. 227–8.

26 Anzoátegui, *Los cuatro viajes* . . ., pp. 219–20.

27 LCH, p. 124.

28 On the financing of the voyage, see Vignaud, *Histoire*, Vol. II, pp. 110–28.

29 The royal document requisitioning the vessels from Palos is translated in Morison, *Journals and other Documents* . . ., pp. 31–3.

30 LCH, p. 124.

31 On the Pinzón family, see Alice Gould, 'Documentos inéditos sobre hidalguía y genealogía de la familia Pinzón', *Boletín de la Real Academia de Historia*, Vol. 91, 1927, pp. 319–75.

Chapter 5

1 A good summary of the history and nature of the two types may be found in José María Martínez Hidalgo, *Columbus's Ships*, ed. Howard I. Chapelle, Barre, Mass., 1966, pp. 20–34.

2 On the *nao* and carrack, see E. Manera Rodríguez, *El buque en la armada española*, Madrid, 1981, pp. 1–74.

3 See Martínez Hidalgo, *Columbus's Ships*, pp. 20–8; Manera Rodríguez, *El buque* . . ., pp. 76–84; Quirino da Fonseca, *A caravela portuguesa*, Coimbra, 1934.

4 See the entry for 23 January.

5 *Raccolta*, Part III, Vol. ii, p. 103.

6 Martínez Hidalgo, *Columbus's Ships*, p. 47.

7 Martínez Hidalgo, *Columbus's Ships*, p. 46.

8 Alice Gould, 'Nueva lista documentada de los tripulantes de Colón en 1492', *Boletín de la Real Academia de Historia*, Vols LXXXV, pp. 34–49, 145–59, 353–79; LXXXVI, pp. 491–532; LXXXVII, pp. 22–60; LXXXVIII, pp. 721–84; XC, pp. 532–55; XCI, pp. 318–75; XCII, pp. 776–95; CXVII, pp. 145–88.

9 Diego García de Palacio, *Instrucción náutica para el buen uso y regimiento de las naos*, Mexico, 1587, fol. 119v.

10 García de Palacio, *Instrucción náutica*, fol. 110.

11 Morison, *Admiral*, Vol. I, p. 197 n. 18.

12 Columbus mentions him in the entry for 7 February.

13 *Pleitos*, in *Boletín de la Real Academia de Historia*, Vol. XCII, p. 782 n. 3.

14 See Clifford W. Hawkins, *The Dhow: An Illustrated History of the Dhow and its World*, Lymington, Hampshire, 1977, p. 96. Hawkins mentions the dhow *Kanaktara*, of just over 150 tons, trading across the Indian ocean from Mombasa to Kenya in the early 1970s, with a total crew of 10, and a 50-ton dhow earlier in the century making voyages of over 2,000 miles with a crew of only 8.

15 A. B. C. Whipple, *The Clipper Ships*, Amsterdam, 1980, p. 81.

16 Alan Villiers, *The Way of a Ship*, London, 1954, pp. 17–19, 270.

17 See entry for 2 January.

18 *Raccolta*, Part II, Vol. ii, pp. 211–17.

19 From pp. 54–5 of the 'Carta escrita al licenciado Miranda de Ron, particular amigo del autor: En que se pinta un navío, y la vida y ejercicios de los oficiales y marineros de él, y como lo pasan los que hacen viajes por el mar', in *Cartas de Eugenio de Salazar escritas a muy particulares amigos suyos*, Madrid (Sociedad de Bibliófilos Españoles), 1866, pp. 35–57. Later references use the abbreviation 'Carta'.

Chapter 6

1 See above, my n. 19 to Ch. 5.

2 *Instrucción náutica*, fol. 109.

3 *Carta*, p. 54.

4 James E. Kelley, Jr, 'In the wake of Columbus on a portolan chart', in Louis de Voysey, Jr and John Parker, *In the Wake of Columbus: Islands and Controversy*, Detroit, 1985, pp. 77–111.

Chapter 7

1 Biblioteca Nacional, Madrid, MS Sig Vitrina 6, n. 7. The manuscript was published in facsimile in Carlos Sanz, *Diario de Colón*, Madrid, 1962. My working source has been the palaeographic transcription, with facing English translation, in the edition by Oliver Dunn and James E. Kelley, Jr, *The 'Diario' of Christopher Columbus's First Voyage to America, 1492–1493*, London and Norman, Oklahoma, 1989, referred to in footnotes as 'DK'.

2 See my n. 10 to Ch. 1.

3 See my nn. 5 to the entry for 18 December.

4 FCH, Vol. I, pp. 198–200.

5 DK, pp. 240–44.

6 The Journal text is obviously garbled at this point. See my n. 5 to the entry for 25 December.

7 FCH, Vol. I, pp. 202–5.

8 DK, pp. 276–80.

9 DK, pp. 196–8.

10 LCH, p. 175.

11 On the language of the Journal, see Ramón Menéndez Pidal, *La lengua de Cristóbal Colón*, Buenos Aires, 1947; Virgil I. Milani, *The Written Language of Christopher Columbus*, supplement to *Forum Italicum*, Buffalo, 1973; and the clear summary by Ralph J. Penny, 'The Language of Christopher Columbus', in the parallel texts edition of the *Journal of the First Voyage* by Barry W. Ife, Warminster, 1990, pp. xxvii–xl.

Journal

3 August

1 His word is *virazón*, translated by Dunn and Kelley as 'sea breeze'. The term is explained by Guillén Tato (p. 128) as 'a wind which follows the sun on certain coasts, blowing first from the east and then veering west until it becomes a land breeze'. In 1587 García de Palacio (*Instrucción náutica*, fol. 147v) explains it slightly differently: 'it is when at night or in the morning there has been a land breeze and at midday the wind veers to the sea.' Columbus's two changes of course are explained by the wind veering west late in the day; he sails as close to it as he can.

9 August

1 From now onwards Columbus spent a tiresome month in the Canaries, trying to ensure the seaworthiness of his fleet before setting out westward. Las Casas abandons the day-by-day account of the Journal and summarizes the content in a few lines. Fernando's account is much fuller (FCH, Ch. 17). According to him, having failed to make Gran Canaria, Columbus left Pinzón in the Pinta off the coast of the island, with instructions to try to exchange her for another ship while he himself, with the Santa María and the Niña, proceeded to Gomera for

the same purpose. He reached Gomera on Sunday, 12 August, and sent a boat ashore. It returned on the morning of the 13th with the news that no ship was to be had, but that the mistress of the island, Doña Beatriz de Bobadilla, was due to return from Gran Canaria with a suitable forty-ton ship. Columbus decided to wait for her, but sent a man off two days later on a vessel bound for Gran Canaria to tell Pinzón what was happening. After a frustrating wait, Columbus decided to set off back to Gran Canaria; he sailed on the 24th, overtook the vessel with his man aboard, and spent the night near Tenerife, which was in the throes of a volcanic eruption. He reached Gran Canaria on the 25th to find that Pinzón, after much difficulty, had arrived only the day before, and that Doña Beatriz had sailed on the previous Monday. Columbus decided to make the best of a bad job, refitted the Pinta's rudder, and took advantage of the delay to change the lateen sails of the Niña to the square rig more suitable for the following trade winds which he was expecting. Las Casas mistakenly says that the Pinta was the vessel whose rig was altered; see Morison, *Admiral*, Vol. I, p. 172.

15 September

1 LCH, p. 129.

16 September

1 The Las Casas text continues (DK, p. 32) 'and from then onwards', probably a comment by Las Casas, unless Columbus himself inserted it at some later date when reading over the Journal.

2 LCH, p. 130.

17 September

1 LCH, p. 130.

2 The word is *toninas*. See Morison, 1963, p. 97, 16 November, n. 5. Columbus's word for 'tunny fish' is *atún*.

19 September

1 FCH, I, pp. 142–3.

2 Las Casas adds (DK, p. 36): 'as indeed there were, and he was sailing in between them'.

3 LCH, p. 131.

20 September

1 FCH, I p. 143. Las Casas's text (DK, p.

36) reads: 'It was a river bird, not a sea bird; its feet were like a gull's.'
2 LCH, p. 131.

21 September

1 LCH (pp. 132–3) introduces here a long and sententious passage about the rebelliousness of the crew and Columbus's dignity and resolution in quelling it. The style and tone are so markedly different from Columbus's own that, while the passage may well be based on further comments by Columbus, it is clearly largely Las Casas's own creation, from which it would be risky to attempt any re-creation of the original. Fernando (FCH, I, p. 144) also says more about the discontent; he is almost certainly summarizing.

24 September

1 LCH, p. 133. In LCH Las Casas then expands again, very much in his own style and usual adulatory tone, on the fortitude of Columbus and the discontent of the crew, who plotted to throw the Admiral overboard and pretend that he had fallen while taking a sight with his quadrant or astrolabe. He also mentions the Pinzóns, their role in fomenting the discontent, and Columbus's repeated complaints about them.

25 September

1 LCH, p. 135: 'This chart is the one sent to him by Paolo the physician, of Florence, which is now in my own possession, along with more of the Admiral's things, and writings in his own hand.'
2 He shouted, 'Albricias!' The word means 'reward', and was shouted as a greeting in mediaeval Spain by a bringer of good news.
3 Las Casas interpolates (DK, p. 42): 'So he wrote down the distance run on the voyage in two ways, the shorter version being false and the longer one true.'
4 See Morison, 1963, p. 57 n. 4, for identification.

30 September

1 The Guards, a group of stars near the Pole Star, played an important part in early navigation. The reference to their position relative to the arms has to do with the idea of a human figure centred on the Pole with arms stretched east and west. For a fuller explanation, see DK, p. 47 n. 3, and Morison, 1963, p. 59 n. 2.
2 This difference in compass readings (see also the entries for 13 and 17 September) may be due simply to the revolution of the Pole Star around the celestial pole, though Dunn and Kelley (DK, p. 49, n. 1) suggest that the variation is so extreme in this case that it may have been due to proximity to some iron object on the ship.

6 October

1 The Las Casas text (DK p. 52) reads *al almirante parecio que dezia esto m. alonso por la Isla de cipango*; a word is erased after *que*. Alvar reads the sentence as *el almirante parecio que no. Dezia esto Martín Alonso por . . .*, i.e., 'the Admiral thought not. Martín Alonso was saying this with the island of Cipango in mind.'

7 October

1 Fernando's account of the events of this date says that land was sighted to the west at daybreak, but as it was indistinct nobody on the Santa María wished to claim the first sighting for fear of losing the reward of 10,000 *maravedis* promised by Ferdinand and Isabella, Columbus having said that anyone calling 'land!' who did not make good the claim in three days would lose the reward even if he did sight land later. This may well be an attempt by Fernando to take some of the glory of the first sighting away from the Pinta.
2 The Las Casas text (DK, p. 54) has *guesueste*, 'west southeast', a nonexistent bearing.

8 October

1 Las Casas interpolates (DK, p. 54): 'unless the handwriting is misleading'.
2 The Las Casas text (DK p. 54) has *grajaos* instead of the usual *garjaos* (probably through confusion with *grajo*, 'crow').

11 October

1 This entry includes 12 October.
2 FCH, Vol. I, p. 158.
3 FCH, Vol. I, p. 159. The Las Casas text (DK, p. 56) has *un palillo cargado descaramojos*. Dunn and Kelley (DK, p. 57) translate *escaramojos* as 'barnacles'; Morison as 'rose hips'.
4 FCH, Vol. I, p. 159.

5 The mysterious light now described is a controversial subject. The uncharitable have suggested that Columbus invented it because of his wish to be considered the first man to make visual contact with the New World. Others have accepted that it was a light on shore, sometimes with the aim of bolstering ideas on Columbus's landfall, or suggested that it was a firebrand in an Indian canoe. The navigational details in this entry suggest that the source of light must have been well out in the Atlantic, over thirty miles from the landfall. A strong possibility is that what Columbus saw was part of the reproductive process of a marine annelid of the genus *Odontosyllis*, whose evening or nocturnal courting procedure, on the surface, involves the extrusion by the female of streams of brilliantly luminous matter along with the ova. She does this several times over a period of a few minutes, the purpose of the luminosity being to guide the males to the ova for fertilization. The display occurs in the winter months, and is linked with the third quarter of the moon. For more details, see L. R. Crawshay, 'Possible Bearing of a Luminous Syllid on the Question of the Landfall of Columbus', *Nature*, Vol. 136, 1935, p. 559.

6 To jog off and on is to make short tacks towards and away from the coast. It was a procedure commonly carried out at night off an unfamiliar coast which it would have been dangerous to approach in the dark.

7 Las Casas (DK, p. 62) inserts: 'one of the Lucayos, which was called Guanahani in the Indians' language'. The first land sighted is generally thought to have been Watling Island, but the landfall has been the subject of controversy. Recently a computer-generated reconstruction of Columbus's course, taking into account magnetic variation, meteorological data, the effect of currents and historical ship drift information led American scholars to the conclusion that Guanahani was, after all, probably Watling island (Philip L. Richardson and Roger A. Goldsmith, 'The Columbus Landfall: Voyage Track Corrected for Winds and Currents', *Oceanus*, Vol. 30, 1987, pp. 3–10).

8 See Dunn and Kelley (DK, p. 67 n.) for a discussion of the ambiguity of this passage.

9 *cejas*. Compare FCH, Vol. I, p. 168: *i*

capelli . . . tagliati sopra le orecchie, 'their hair cut over their ears'. There has evidently been a scribal confusion between *cejas* and *orejas*.

10 This is probably a reference to the Guanches, a people of African origin occupying the Canaries before the conquest by the Spanish.

13 October

1 This is a Spanish word of Arabic origin, used in the fifteenth century to describe the dugout canoes of north Africa. The word 'canoe' is derived from *canoa*, a Caribbean Indian word which Columbus does not learn until 26 October. I have therefore preserved the use of *almadía* until this later date, and translated *canoa* as 'canoe' thereafter.

2 *Ceotís* and *blancas* are coins; an *arroba* was a trading weight, approximately a quarter of a hundredweight.

3 The transitional state of fifteenth-century tense use, coupled with Columbus's rather opaque syntax, makes this ambiguous in the Las Casas text (DK, p. 72); it could mean 'would have'.

14 October

1 *Del cielo* (DK, p. 74) means both 'from Heaven' and 'from the sky'.

15 October

1 Rum Cay.

2 This passage is obscure and probably garbled (DK, pp. 78–80). My version is in accord with the restoration proposed by Dunn and Kelley, which is supported by the amplified account given in LCH, p. 148: 'One of the Indians . . . jumped into the sea, climbed into the canoe and went off in it, with the boat in pursuit, which could not overtake it however hard the men rowed . . . He says that another Indian had escaped the previous night.'

3 Long Island.

4 FCH, Vol. I, p. 173: '. . . and a piece of earth similar to cinnabar, with which the people paint their bodies . . . and some dried leaves which they greatly value for their perfume and health-giving properties'.

16 October

1 The Las Casas text reads *las isla*. The *s* of *las* may be a scribal error, but it has been taken to mean that Columbus was thinking of more than one island (see

Oliver Dunn, 'Columbus's First Landing Place', p. 44). Vigneras suggests Rum Cay and Conception Island.

2 He forgets that he has told us this.

3 I.e., mid-morning.

4 The Las Casas text has *sursudueste*, 'ssw'; probably a scribal error for *sursueste*.

5 *panizo*. The word normally means 'millet', but the crop alluded to was probably maize, *maíz*. The word *panizo* is now applied to maize in parts of Latin America.

6 *ni estos son enxeridos porque se pueda dezir que el enxerto lo haze* (DK, p. 88). Both Dunn and Kelley (p. 89) and Morison (1963, p. 72) mistranslate this, ignoring the subjunctive and taking *porque* to mean 'because'. Morison's version is the worse: 'Nor are these grafted, for one can say that the grafting is spontaneous.'

17 October

1 Las Casas gives a long explanation of the construction and use of these *hamacas*, 'hammocks', in LCH, pp. 150–1.

2 *chimeneas*. This can mean 'fireplaces' or 'chimneys'. Either appears possible, but Las Casas, at least, takes it to mean the latter, explaining in a marginal note that Columbus is wrong: 'These chimneys are not for smoke; they are little crowning pieces (*coronillas*) on the roofs of the Indians' straw houses . . . though they do leave a slight opening for smoke to get out through the roof' (DK, p. 93).

3 A Spanish coin.

4 Dunn and Kelley (DK, p. 95) translate this as 'the weather very dirty'.

5 *el era poco*. A word is missing after *el* (DK, p. 94). It was probably *viento*, 'wind', though Dunn and Kelley suggest *tiempo*, 'time'.

19 October

1 He says simply *en la nao*, 'in the ship', his habitual way of alluding to the Santa María, as distinct from the two *caravelas*. The usage is similar to that of a nineteenth-century seafarer talking of 'a ship' as opposed to 'a barque', though the technical basis for the distinction is, of course, different.

2 *y otro*. Dunn and Kelley (p. 97 n.) suggest that *otro* (masculine) refers to *restinga*, 'reef' (normally feminine, but used earlier in the sentence with the

masculine article *un*), rather than to *isleo*, 'islet' (masculine); i.e., that there was another reef, rather than another islet. This seems logical. Morison's version is ambiguous (1963, p. 75), though he is probably thinking along the same lines.

3 The identity of Isabela is disputed. The name appears to refer to Crooked Island and Fortune Island jointly, and possibly also to the other island in the group, Acklins. See DK, p. 99 n.

4 *al gueste*. Dunn and Kelley (DK, p. 99 n.) suggest that this is an error for *al sueste*, 'southeast'.

5 It means 'Cape Beautiful'; probably the southern tip of Fortune Island.

20 October

1 The southwestern point of Crooked Island, opposite the northern point of Fortune Island.

2 An obscure passage. See DK, p. 103 n, and Morison, 1963, p. 77, for somewhat different versions.

21 October

1 Probably an iguana.

2 FCH, Vol. I, p. 177, says that they were amazed by the beast's ugliness and hostility, but that they later came to look on its soft, white flesh as a delicacy. He also says that the Indians call it Giovanna, the Italian form of Joanna.

3 Columbus was wrong about the aloe plant, to which he refers frequently later. He had read in Marco Polo that *lignum aloe*, a kind of wood, was common in the orient, and confused it with the medicinal aloes from which a purgative was produced. The plant he found in the Indies was almost certainly the agave, which has similar spiky leaves. See Morison, 1963, p. 78 n.

4 Cuba.

5 *marcantes*. Dunn and Kelley (p. 109) interpret this as *marchantes* and translate 'traders'. I prefer Morison's interpretation, *mareantes*.

6 Santo Domingo.

24 October

1 An obscure sentence: *Y asi navegue fasta el dia al guesudueste y amaneciendo . . .* [lacuna] *calmo el viento y llovio y asi casse toda la noche.* Dunn and Kelley, p. 113, translate: '. . . and at dawn the wind died down and it rained, and it continued in this way almost all night.' This seems to

make nonsense of the time sequence. The word *casse* is odd, the normal form being *casi*. A verb may have been omitted.
2 The entry ends with 'etc.', which suggests that Las Casas may have omitted some navigational details.

25 October
1 Again the entry ends with 'etc.'

26 October
1 I have omitted the words *estas son las canoas* (DK, p. 114), 'these are canoes', assuming that this is a comment by Las Casas.

27 October
1 The name means 'Sandy Islands'. They are now the Ragged Islands.

28 October
1 Dunn and Kelley (DK, p. 117 n.) state, with no convincing evidence, that Columbus's fathom was equal to the *aune* of Provins and measured 2.7 English feet. While it may have been less than the English 6-foot fathom, the mere etymology of the word would suggest that it was longer than they argue: it is based on the reach of a man's outstretched arms (*braza* is a plural, 'arms', turned into a singular).
2 The content of this sentence is positioned here in LCH, p. 155, as part of the same sentence as the preceding and following words in my translation. In DK Las Casas appears to add it as an afterthought in the last sentence of the 29 October entry. I think he probably omitted it in transcribing the 28 October entry, and included it in the next entry after realizing the omission.
3 *verdolagas y bledos*. Purslane is a medicinal and salad plant. I am less sure of the exact meaning of *bledos*. The word is derived from the Latin *blitum*, which is a genus of widespread, generally weedy plants with spinach-like leaves, including the Peruvian quinoa, Good King Henry and orache. As Columbus tends to mention only usable resources, he is probably referring to an edible plant.
4 This appears to be where Columbus himself begins to use the word *canoas*, 'canoes'. In the next sentence, possibly realizing that this may be obscure, he gives a paraphrase for clarity.
5 Now Bahía Bariay.

29 October
1 It means 'Moon River'. Now Río Jururu.
2 Puerto Gibara. *Mares* means 'seas'.

30 October
1 'Palm trees Cape'. Now Punta Uvero.
2 LCH, p. 157, comments extensively on the gullibility and self-deception of men.
3 Las Casas (DK, p. 124) hints that the text from which he transcribed this could be corrupt.

2 November
1 FCH, Vol. I, p. 181, says that this Indian had paddled out to the ships in a canoe.
2 Morison's explanation of this mistake (commented on by Las Casas in the margin) is that Columbus simply mistook another star for the Pole Star (Morison, 1963, p. 87 n.).

3 November
1 The text continues: *que son hamacas*, 'which are hammocks'. It is not clear whether this is Columbus or Las Casas; probably the latter.

4 November
1 Las Casas inserts (DK, p. 130): 'apparently from samples he had brought from Castile'.
2 *ley*, possibly 'law'.
3 The manuscript has *mames*, probably a copyist's error. The allusion is to cassava.

5 November
1 *albricias*. See my note to the entry for 25 September.
2 Columbus sets great store by the commercial potential of this so-called mastic tree (*almaciga*), which he thought was the same as the commercial variety he had seen in Chios. It was, in fact, the gumbo-limbo tree, *Bursera simaruba*.
3 See my note to the 21 October entry.

6 November
1 FCH, Vol. I, p. 183. His Italian word is *duchi*; LCH calls them *duhos*.
2 FCH, Vol. I, p. 183.
3 This is the earliest allusion by a European to tobacco, to which some Spaniards soon became addicted. Las

Casas, writing only a few decades later, sounds superior and mystified in his description of the practice: '. . . these are dried herbs wrapped in a certain leaf, also dried, like the *mosquetes* [this normally means 'musket', but here is probably some sort of firework] the boys make at the Feast of the Holy Spirit. They set fire to one end and suck and inhale the smoke into their body. This soothes their flesh and almost intoxicates them, and apparently prevents them from feeling weary. These *mosquetes*, or whatever we may call them, are called *tabacos*. I have known Spaniards in this island of Española who grew habituated to them, and when criticized for this vice answered that it was beyond their power to give them up. I do not know what pleasure or benefit they found in them' (LCH, p. 162).

This is restrained by comparison with Benzone's attack a few decades later: 'In this island, as in certain other areas of these new countries, there are certain small shrubs like canes which produce a leaf like a walnut leaf, but rather larger. It is greatly valued by the people of the country . . . and much prized by the slaves transported from Africa by the Spaniards. When the leaves are mature they are gathered and hung in bunches over a fire until they are thoroughly dry, and when the people want to use them they take a leaf of their corn and roll up one of these other leaves inside it like a tube, set fire to one end of it, and with the other end in their mouth they suck in their breath so that the smoke enters their mouth, their throat and their head. They suck in all they can, and take pleasure in it, filling themselves with this bitter smoke to the extent of losing their wits. Some of them inhale so much that they fall down as if dead, and remain stupefied for most of the day or night; others are content to take in only enough to make their head spin. Consider what a foul and pestiferous poison of the Devil this is! It has often happened to me that, while travelling in Guatemala or Nicaragua, I have gone into the house of an Indian who had been inhaling this herb, which in the language of Mexico is called *tobacco*, and suddenly smelling the foul stench of this truly diabolical and stinking smoke I have been forced to run out of the house and go elsewhere.' (Benzone,

Historia del Nuovo Mondo, 1572, fols 54v–55r).

4 The Journal says nothing of the next 5 days. Las Casas (DK, p. 140) adds the comment: 'He intended to sail on the Thursday, but the wind was wrong and he could not leave until 12 November.' LCH, p. 163, repeats this, and goes on to bemoan, at great length, Columbus's attitude to the Indians. FCH, too, is silent about these 5 days. Possibly Columbus spent them in careening the Pinta and the Niña.

12 November

1 Probably Great Inagua island.
2 I have moved this sentence forward from the end of the entry, where it is introduced by Las Casas with the phrase *dize tambien arriba que* . . ., 'he also says above that . . .' (DK, p. 148).
3 'Sun River'.
4 Columbus's obsession with mastic may have been due to Genoese domination of the mastic trade based on Chios. Jourdain Cathalá de Sévérac tells us in his *Mirabilia Descripta* (ed. Henri Cordier, Paris, 1925), 'I saw an island called Chio where the mastic tree grows in great quantity. If the trees are planted elsewhere they will not produce mastic, which is the gum of a most noble tree. A powerful Genoese called Martin Zacharie held that island; he killed or took prisoner over ten thousand Turks' (p. 97). He goes on to say that the annual crop was more than 150,000 pounds in weight, and that the Mediterranean mastic trade in the fourteenth century was controlled by the Genoese (pp. 98 n., 99 n.).
5 *siete cabezas de mugeres*, literally 'seven head of women' (DK, p. 146).
6 The Las Casas text reads *los nuestros*, which can mean either 'our men' or 'our people' (DK, p. 146). In LCH, p. 164, Las Casas changes this to *las nuestras*, 'our women'.
7 LCH, p. 166: 'According to what I have gathered about his whole voyage down the coast of Cuba and back again, and from the original maps drawn by the Admiral himself, which are in my possession, this is the cape which we now call Cape Maici, 3 leagues from Baracoa, which the Admiral himself called the river or harbour of Mares'.

13 November

1 Vigneras suggests that this was possibly the entrance to Nipé Bay.

2 *para ponerse al rigor del viento* (DK, p. 150). Dunn and Kelley, accepting an assertion by Julio Guillén Tato (*La parla marinera en el diario del primer viaje de Cristóbal Colón*, Madrid, 1951), translate 'where he could shelter himself from the force of the wind' (DK, p. 151 n.). This is the direct opposite of the normal meaning of the phrase, and Columbus could not shelter in a settlement; he needed a harbour.

14 November

1 This is a compromise translation of *el viento . . . le escaseava* (DK, p. 150). Dunn and Kelley, following Guillén Tato, translate 'the wind was against them'. Morison, Jane and Thacher interpret it as 'the wind was falling off', which is closer to the normal meaning of *escasear*. The wind is said to be initially in the north, which would be a fine beam wind for ships sailing E, but at some point in the night it veered NE and Columbus had to head s by E, and at sunrise he decided to head s. Certainly on the 13th and by the time he sighted land on the 14th the winds were heavy.

2 Columbus wrote more about his reasons; Las Casas (DK, p. 150) cuts him short and mentions 'other inconveniences which he includes here'.

3 'Sea of Our Lady'. Now Tanamo Bay.

4 Las Casas has probably excised a passage of description here (DK, p. 154), replacing it with: 'He says so many and such remarkable things about the beauty and fertility and loftiness of these islands which he found in this harbour that he tells the King and Queen . . .'

15 November

1 More abbreviation by Las Casas (DK, p. 154): 'and he says wonderful things about them'.

2 Columbus's phrase is *y todo basa* (DK, p. 154); it is followed by an explanation, possibly his own, possibly inserted for laymen by Las Casas: 'which means that the bottom is sand, with no rocks, something which sailors greatly desire because the rocks cut their anchor cables'.

16 November

1 Las Casas adds the comment: 'and he was right' (DK, p. 156).

2 *cala*, explained (possibly by Columbus, but more likely by Las Casas) as 'a narrow entrance through which the sea enters the land' (DK, p. 156).

3 *sala*. Morison, 1963, p. 96, translates it, unjustifiably, as 'dry dock'.

4 This explanation could be an addition by Las Casas.

5 DK has 'like a *taso* or *taxo*', p. 156. Probably an italianism; the Italian for 'badger' is *tasso*, the Spanish being *tejón*. See Las Casas's marginal note, referred to in my n. 3 to the next entry.

17 November

1 The Las Casas text (DK, p. 158) is ambiguous, and certainly contains some words added by Las Casas: *hallo nuezes grandes delas de yndia creo que dize*. This could mean 'he found large nuts, of the kind which grow in India; I think it says', or 'large nuts; I think he means the kind which grow in India'.

2 *ratones*. Normally this means 'mice', but it is here better interpreted as an augmentative form of *rata*, i.e., 'big rat'.

3 A marginal note by Las Casas (DK, p. 158): 'They must have been *hutías*.' He gives a different name in LCH, p. 168: 'These were *guaminiquinajes* . . . little animals like dogs, very good to eat'; earlier (LCH, p. 162) he has compared their flesh favourably with hare and rabbit.

18 November

1 Dunn and Kelley explain in a note (p. 161) that this is an allusion to a method of specifying time, and specifically the tide time for a particular port on the first day of the new moon, by viewing the compass rose as a kind of 24-hour clock face, sw by s representing 14:15; they confirm that this was the time of high tide in the Huelva–Palos area.

20 November

1 In DK the sentence ends with 'etc.', which may indicate that Las Casas is abbreviating.

21 November

1 Las Casas inserts (DK, p. 162): 'and he was right, for to believe the quadrant was working properly these islands would have to be on a latitude of [. . .] degrees. If this were true it would put him very close to Florida, and on the same latitude, but where then are these islands which lay around him?' Dunn and Kelley

Notes

punctuate differently (DK, p. 163).
2 Las Casas's comments continue (DK, p. 163): 'Obviously if he were off the coast of Florida it would be cold, not hot, and it is manifest that nowhere in the world is it hot on a latitude of 42 degrees unless by some accidental cause hitherto unknown to. me.' The allusions to Florida, certainly, are by Las Casas.

22 November
1 *anduvo* . . . *la buelta de la tierra.* Dunn and Kelley, using the explanation of the phrase given by Guillén Tato, translate this as 'went . . . on a course parallel to the land' (see DK, p. 165 n.). Morison, 1963, p. 100, translates 'toward the land'. The *Diccionario marítimo español* (p. 563) makes the point crystal clear: '*Ir de la vuelta de fuera, de la de la tierra, o tomar o llevar la una o la otra,* "navegar o ponerse a navegar en una de estas dos direcciones"'

24 November
1 Cayo Moa Grande.
2 Probably Puerto Cayo Moa.
3 *ques su travesia desta costa.* Dunn and Kelley (DK, p. 168) translate 'which is perpendicular to'. *Travesía* means 'voyage', 'passage', but also, in modern Spanish, 'cross-street'.

26 November
1 'Cape of the Peak'. Now Punta Guarico.
2 'Bell Cape'. Now Punta Plata or Punta Baez.

27 November
1 *a la corda y temporejar.* The *Diccionario marítimo español* suggests that while these may sometimes be synonymous, they are not always so: '*estar a la cuerda*: véase *estar a la capa*' (p. 196); '*capa*: . . . la disposición de la embarcación que hallándose en el mar . . . no anda o no navega, y está poco menos que parada' (p. 140); '*temporejar*: aguantarse a la capa en un temporal . . . mantenerse de vuelta en vuelta en cualesquiera otras circunstancias' (p. 515).
2 El Yunque.
3 *azagayas,* a berber word familiar to fifteenth-century Spaniards. It seems wisest to translate with the cognate word, rather than 'javelins' (DK, p. 179) or 'darts' (Morison, 1963, p. 104).

4 Baracoa Harbour.
5 The rest of this paragraph and the whole of the next are in the first person in FCH, Vol. I, pp. 191–2.
6 The Las Casas text (DK, p. 182) reads *no bastara mill lenguas,* 'a thousand tongues would (possibly will) not suffice'. Fernando's source must have read *no bastara mi lengua,* 'my tongue would (possibly will) not suffice'. Both readings are ambiguous with regard to tense because early written Spanish does not indicate stress.
7 The *fusta* was a small, multi-oared vessel like a galley. A medieval Spanish ballad preserved into the twentieth century by the Sephardic Jews of Tetuán, Morocco, includes a sailor singing a song in which he asks for deliverance from storms, rocks and *las fustas de los moros, que andaban a saltear,* 'the *fustas* of the Moors, which go about to seize ships' (R. Wright, *Spanish Ballads*, Warminster, 1987, pp. 32–3).

29 November
1 The verb *poblar* is common in documents relating to the Spanish reconquest of lands held by the Moors. It implies, essentially, an influx of people, but also the cultivation of the land which that was aimed to achieve.
2 Las Casas comments in the margin (DK, p. 188): 'This wax was brought there from Yucatán, which makes me think that this land was Cuba.'

1 December
1 Las Casas (DK, p. 190) continues: 'which I believe he called Puerto Santo'. This may be another allusion to illegible handwriting. Fernando states explicitly in his account of events of 27 November that his father did so name the harbour (FCH, Vol. I, p. 191).

2 December
1 Las Casas (DK, p. 190) ends the sentence with 'etc.', which again suggests that he may have omitted something.

3 December
1 Dunn and Kelley (p. 193 n.) suggest that a *paso* was 5 Roman feet, and point out that in the entry for 9 December 1,000 *pasos* are said to equal one-quarter of a league.

2 The explanation could be an addition by Las Casas.

3 Dunn and Kelley (p. 195) translate *colmenar* as 'beehive'; Morison, 1963 (p. 109) as 'apiary'. In standard Spanish nowadays *colmenar* is the place where the hives are kept; the hive itself is *colmena*. In various localities in Huelva, Granada and Almería the traditional hive is called *colmena* when it has a colony of bees in it, and *corcho* or *bazo* when empty, which makes me wonder whether Columbus could be referring here to a wild bees' nest. See *Atlas lingüístico y etnográfico de Andalucía*, Vol. II, Map 627.

4 *creencia*. It could perhaps means 'credulity'.

5 Interpretations of this have varied, some translators taking it to mean that the interior of the house was partitioned, others seeing it as a description of a segmented altar inside the house (see DK, p. 197 n.)

4 December

1 'Cape Pretty'. Now Punta del Fraile.

2 The Windward Passage.

3 'Passage' is for *paso*. The word has also been read as *pozo*, 'well' and *poso*, 'stopping place'. Dunn and Kelley read *pozo*, suggest that this is an error for *poso* and translate 'a good stopping place for [ships coming from] the east-northeast' (p. 199 n.).

5 December

1 DK, p. 199: *anduvo a la corda*. Dunn and Kelley translate it as 'stood off and on'. See my n. to the 27 November entry.

2 Las Casas adds in the margin (DK, p. 198): 'This must be Maysi Point, the easternmost point of Cuba.' This is repeated in LCH, p. 176. Fernando, however, says that Columbus called the point Alpha and Omega (but see my next n.)

3 Another note in the margin by Las Casas (DK, p. 200): 'It appears that the Admiral must have called Cuba Juana.' LCH, p. 176: 'When he left the easternmost point or cape of Cuba, he called it Alpha and Omega, meaning "beginning and end", because he thought it was the limit of *terra firma*, going east; he considered the beginning to be Cape St Vincent in Portugal . . . He wrote this in a letter to the King and Queen from Española.'

6 December

1 'St Mary's Harbour'. Columbus changed the name to Puerto de San Nicolás; it is now Port Saint Nicolas.

2 'Cape of the Star'. Now Cape Saint Nicolas.

3 'Elephant Cape'. Now either Grande Pointe or Pointe Palmiette.

4 The meaning of this is a mystery. Now Pointe Jean Rabel.

5 'Turtle Island'. Now the Ile de la Tortue.

6 A gap in the manuscript. Dunn and Kelley (DK, p. 193 n.) suggest *passada*, a unit of length equal to 5 Roman feet. This seems unlikely, given the great depth of the water. Morison, 1963 (p. 113 n.), comments from his own investigations that the 40-fathom line is between 300 and 700 yards from the shore at this point.

7 *hondable*, literally 'soundable'. *Diccionario maritimo español* (DME), Madrid, 1831, p. 317: 'It is applied to the coast . . . where one can find bottom, but with sufficient depth of water for sailing.'

7 December

1 The Las Casas text continues: 'which forms the careenage'. This is presumably inserted by Las Casas from his own knowledge.

2 *angla*. Dunn and Kelley (DK, p. 209 n.) interpret this as 'cape', as does Morison, 1963 (p. 114). In view of the succeeding paragraph 'bay' makes better sense.

3 The manuscript reads '34', which is too many. Navarrete suggests '3 or 4'; Dunn and Kelley say this is too few, but Morison says it is about right.

4 Morison, 1963 (p. 114 n.), says that there is now no such rock, but also mentions that certain eighteenth-century maps mark it.

5 'Conception Harbour'. Now Moustique Bay.

8 December

1 See Morison, 1963, p. 115 n. 1.

9 December

1 It means 'Spanish island'; not, as is sometimes thought, 'little Spain'.

10 December

1 *las anclas estavan mucho a tierra y venia sobre ella el viento*; a perplexing passage. To attempt to lie with the anchors

between the ship and the coast in an onshore wind would be nonsense. It may mean that the bow and stern anchors, instead of being out to sea close to the perpendicular line from the shore, were closer to a stem-to-stern line through the ship, so that the force of the wind exerted a twisting action on them and caused them to lose their hold and drag.

11 December

1 LCH, p. 180: '*Caritaba* or *Caribana*'.
2 The list in the original reads: *albures salmones pijotas gallos pampanos lisas corvinas camarones* (DK, p. 216). The debatable one is *lisas*. The dictionary definitions of *lisa* give the Latin name *Cobitis taenia*, which is a freshwater fish, the spined loach, but the *Atlas lingüístico y etnográfico de Andalucía* (Vol. IV, Maps 1106, 1107) reveals that *lisa* was given by informants in various Andalusian ports, including those of the Huelva coast, as the name of different kinds of mullet. See also Maps 1111, 1112 of the same work for *corvina* and *pampano*.

12 December

1 The Las Casas text (DK, pp. 218–20) continues: 'which is their caravel in which they sail' – possibly an insertion by Las Casas. It is unlikely that Columbus would so misuse a precise nautical term.
2 This detail is from LCH, p. 181.
3 This is ambiguous in DK, and could possibly mean 'the canoe', but is more explicit in LCH, p. 181.

13 December

1 LCH, p. 182. DK, p. 222 reads: 'bread made from *niamas*, which are roots like big radishes; they sow them and they grow. They plant them all over these lands as their staple diet; they make them into bread and boil and roast them. They taste like chestnuts; anyone eating them would not take them for anything else.' This is probably an editorial insertion by Las Casas, drawn from his wider experience.
2 As Morison points out ('The Route of Columbus Along the North Coast of Haiti and the Site of Navidad', *Transactions of the American Philosophical Society*, Vol. XXXI, 1940), p. 249) this is a gross mistake, as Moustique Bay lies on latitude 19° 55'. He suggests that Columbus had mistaken the star Er Rai for the

Pole Star. See also *American Neptune*, I (1941), pp. 20–4.

14 December

1 'Cape Leg'. Possibly Great Man Point.
2 'Lance-thrust Point'. Possibly Bird Point.
3 The bearing is from LCH, p. 183. The *Journal* (DK, p. 226) has *nordeste*, 'NE'.

15 December

1 The modern Trois Rivières (Morison, 'The Route of Columbus', p. 250

16 December

1 Probably on the site of modern Port de Paix (Morison, 'The Route of Columbus', p. 251).
2 Previously 9.
3 LCH, p. 184, includes the comment from Las Casas, 'a somewhat irreconcilable combination, to be coming from Heaven and to be going about in search of gold!'
4 Dunn and Kelley (DK, p. 233) translate *alguazil* as 'bailiff'.
5 LCH, p. 184, adds the comment, 'He was right about the fineness of the country, but not about the cold. It is fresh, but not troublesomely so; it seemed colder to him being on the sea, and with the rain and wind.'
6 Probably cassava.
7 *pan*, mistranslated by Dunn and Kelley as 'bread'. *Tierras de pan llevar* is a set phrase in rural Spain for cereal land.
8 LCH (pp. 184–5) adds a long and biting passage: 'We may note here that the Indians' natural gentleness, simplicity, kindness and humility, their nakedness and lack of weapons, enabled the Spaniards to despise them and to subject them to the bitter work which they were later made to do; that was the reason for the Spaniards' savage hunger to oppress them and consume them as they did.'

17 December

1 I have omitted the phrase *que llamavan cacique*, 'whom they called cacique', which is probably an explanation by Las Casas. The phrase does not occur in LCH, p. 185, and there is an explicit statement in the DK entry for 18 December (p. 244) that that was when Columbus was told this word. I have therefore translated the

other cases of *cacique* in the 17 December entry simply as 'leader'.
2 LCH, p. 185.
3 LCH, p. 186, adds, 'surely this Baneque [*sic*] must have been the mainland.'

18 December

1 DK has *cacique*; LCH has *rey*, 'king'. See my n. 1 to 17 December, and nn. 4, 6, below.
2 The Feast of the Annunciation was called this in popular usage because the hymns to the Virgin began with the word '*O*'.
3 The ensuing passage is quoted verbatim from the original by Fernando (FCH, Vol. I, pp. 198–200).
4 There is no counterpart to this sentence in the Las Casas text, but see n. 6, below.
5 LCH, p. 186: 'I, who am writing this, have seen and handled it.' FCH, Vol. I, p. 200, describes the medallion as *una medaglia d'oro del peso di quattro ducati*; *excelente* is in DK (p. 242) and presumably in the original, since Las Casas explains it in the margin: 'This *excelente* was a coin worth two *castellanos*.' Fernando has Italianized it. Another variant in this sentence is that the Journal has *unas cuentas mias*, 'some beads of mine', instead of FCH's *un mio portalettere*, 'a portfolio of mine'. *Cuentas* in Spanish can mean both 'beads' and 'accounts'. The FCH version may therefore have mistranslated the phrase in the conversion into Italian.
6 DK (p. 244) here states that 'the Admiral learned there that the king was called cacique in his own language.'

19 December

1 'Two Brothers'. Probably two hillocks west of Acul Bay.
2 'Cape of Towers'. Now Cap au Borgne.
3 Either Marigot Head or Limbé Island.
4 Las Casas comments in the margin (DK, p. 246): 'He has not mentioned the Dos Hermanos or the Cabo de Torres before.'
5 'Cape High and Low'. Now Pointe Limbé.
6 Dunn and Kelley (DK, p. 249) translate this as 'taller than any other'. This is not justified by the text.
7 Cape Haitien, or specifically the Morne du Cap, the mountain range on the Cape

(Morison, 'The Route of Columbus', p. 255).

20 December

1 Acul Bay.
2 The Las Casas text has *cañal* instead of the normal *canal*, which leads Las Casas to comment in the margin: 'I think he means *cañaveral* (cane-brake).'

21 December

1 There is a gap in the text (DK, p. 253).
2 A doubtful translation of *gonza avellanada*, based on Manuel Alvar (ed.), *Diario del descubrimiento*, Gran Canaria, 1976, Vol. II, p. 163.
3 LCH, p. 189.
4 This sentence may be an insertion by Las Casas. It is not in LCH.

22 December

1 LCH, pp. 190–1.
2 LCH, p. 191.
3 LCH, p. 191: 'These must have been the pepper which they call *ají*.'

23 December

1 'Holy Point'. Now Pointe Picolet. Las Casas notes in the margin (DK, p. 270): 'He has not mentioned this Punta Santa before.'
2 Explained by Las Casas in the margin (DK, p. 270): '*Nitayno* meant the most notable lord and grandee of the kingdom after the king.'

24 December

1 LCH, p. 193: 'The Indians were quite right in saying that the province of Cibao was rich in gold; they were saying more than they knew, for there was more gold there than they could have seen or heard of. They had no gold-mining industry, so they never knew or could have known how much there was, which became a matter of amazement later. The distance to Cibao was not great, only about 30 leagues, but the Indians were not used to going far from their homeland, and might well be afraid of that distance and say that it was a long way.'
2 This can mean either 'the Friend' or 'the Mistress'. Now the Île des Rats.
3 *con el tiro de una piedra*, possibly 'a cannonball shot', though this would conflict with the reference soon afterwards to the length of the reef. Dunn and Kelley (p. 275) read *con el ot° de una piedra*

and translate 'at the sight of a stone'.
4 Dunn and Kelley (p. 275) mistranslate
this as 'pass from the western to the
eastern side'.
5 Port des Français.

25 December
1 The ensuing description is taken from
the first-person original as translated by
Fernando (FCH, pp. 202–5). The version
in the Journal differs only minimally
from it.
2 DK, pp. 276–8, addition: 'She grounded so gently that it was hardly noticeable.'
3 Las Casas (DK, p. 278) adds *estava ya la
nao de traves*, 'the ship was now beam-on
to the sea'.
4 Las Casas (DK, p. 178) adds 'towards
the beam sea, not that the swell was very
great.'
5 The Las Casas text (DK, p. 278),
obviously garbled at this point, replaces
the last eight words with *y no la nao*,
literally 'and not the ship'. Dunn and
Kelley (p. 279) translate 'the planking
opened up, but not the ship.'
6 The Las Casas text (DK, p. 278) reads
aun quedava, 'was left'.

26 December
1 This is from LCH, p. 196. Las Casas
(DK, p. 282) has *chuq chuque*. A normal
scribal abbreviation of the period is to
omit the *ue* of the combination *que*,
putting an omission mark above.
Columbus or the later scribe probably
forgot the omission mark on *chuq*.
2 LCH, p. 196: 'The reason was that the
Indians of this island, and of all the
Indies, are very given to dancing, which
they do a great deal, and to assist their
voices and songs as they dance . . . they
had bells, most cleverly made of wood
with a few pebbles inside, which made a
noise, but a dull and harsh one. When
they saw the bells so big and shiny and
clear sounding they were taken with
them more than with anything else.'
3 LCH, p. 196: '. . . *de los que habían
llevado la ropa de la nao a tierra*'. This could
possibly mean 'those who had taken the
ship's canvas ashore'. DK, p. 282 has
simply 'a sailor returning from shore'.
4 LCH, p. 197. This paragraph, or some
of it, could be an amplification by Las
Casas based on his own knowledge.
5 Las Casas comments in the margin:

'Cibao was a province of the same island
of Española, where there were very rich
mines.' He amplifies this in LCH, p. 197:
'When the Admiral heard the name
Cibao his heart was happy, for he
thought it was Cipango, the island on his
map, which he was expecting because of
what Paolo the physician had told him.
He did not understand that this place was
a province of this island, but thought that
it was an island in itself.'
6 Mistranslated by Dunn and Kelley
(DK, p. 285) as 'they rubbed their hands
. . . they did it.'
7 *espingarda*. Either an uncommon or an
obsolete word, to judge by LCH, p. 197:
'. . . a lombard and an *escopeta* [i.e.,
'musket', now 'shotgun'] or *espingarda*,
as it was called in those days'.
8 *la vasija*, one meaning of which is given
by the Academy Dictionary as 'collective
term for the barrels and wine jars in a
bodega'. Dunn and Kelley (p. 291) translate it as 'storage jars'.

27 December
1 LCH, p. 199.
2 LCH, p. 199. Las Casas then explains
Columbus's decision to leave men on the
island. This description almost certainly
corresponds to a lost passage of the
original Journal (a telling piece of evidence is the phrase *vuestra fortaleza*, 'your
fort'; evidently addressed to Ferdinand
and Isabella, which LCH is not), but the
cumulative style and orderly presentation are perhaps more those of Las
Casas than of Columbus. The allusion to
the completion of the fort in 10 days is
hardly something of which Columbus
would have written on 27 December, so
Las Casas is doing more here than simply
turning the first person into the third:

At this time the Admiral decided to
leave some men there, for several
reasons. The first and principal one
was what he had seen of the joyous-
ness, freshness and amenity of the
land, and its richness, manifest in the
considerable and valuable examples of
the great quantities of gold there, with
the consequent possibility of settling
great numbers of Spaniards and
Christians with such profit and pros-
perity.
Secondly, in order that while he was
going to Spain and returning they

might learn the language and make enquiries to find out the secrets of the land, its lords and rulers, and the mines of gold and other metals, and whether there were riches other than what he had seen, and especially what he believed there to be, namely spices.

Thirdly, so as to leave a kind of token so that people in Castile, hearing that some Christians had remained on the island of their own accord, would not be afraid of the distance, or of the perils and hardships of the sea; though this was hardly necessary, for merely on hearing that there was gold and so much of it the men of Spain would not be afraid to go to seek it.

Fourthly, the Santa María had been lost, and it would have been very difficult for everyone to sail home in the caravel.

Fifthly, because of the great desire the men all showed to stay there, and their pleas to the Admiral, in which they said that they wanted to be the first settlers there.

He was greatly encouraged and strengthened in his resolve by seeing the kindness, humility, gentleness and simplicity of all these people, particularly the great charitableness, humanity and virtue of King Guacanagarí, and the remarkable welcome he had given them so far, which was as great as one could have had in one's own parents' home anywhere, and the love he had shown them and his constant offers to do more for them.

With this resolve, then, and to provide them with whatever protection was possible at that time, he decided that a fort should be built out of the planking, timbers and fastenings of the Santa María, with a moat around, which was as strong a defence against the Indians of this island as Salses is against the French, or stronger. He therefore ordered his men to make haste, and the King ordered his vassals to help, and with almost countless people coming to help the Christians they worked so hard and so well that in around ten days your fort was well built, to the extent necessary at that time.

He called it Villa de la Navidad [Christmas Town], because he arrived on Christmas Day, [from now on this is certainly Las Casas] although there is now no memory of there ever having been a fortress or any other building, the trees being as thickly grown and tall (and I have seen them myself) as if fifty years had passed.

28 December

1 LCH, pp. 200–1: *en una silla, con su espaldar, baja, de las que ellos usaban, que son muy lindas y broñidas y relucientes, como si fuesen de azabaja, que ellos llamaban 'duhos'.* The imperfect tense in *usaban* and *llamaban* suggests that at least part of this is taken from the original Journal; the present tense of *son* may indicate that the comparison with jet has been added from Las Casas's own ethnological knowledge.

29 December

1 Las Casas adds in the margin: 'These were not islands, but provinces of Española' (DK, p. 294). In LCH, p. 201, he expands the comment considerably, explaining that Guarionex was a king.

2 LCH, p. 201: 'which must have been of brass or tin'.

30 December

1 LCH, p. 201 (as part of a direct quotation from the original Journal).

2 Las Casas includes in LCH, p. 202, a description of the making of these plaques which could conceivably be based on the original Journal, but is more probably based on his personal observation: 'These plaques of gold were not cast, nor were they made from many grains, for the Indians of this island had no melting process. When they found particles of gold they beat them between two stones to spread them out, and the large plaques were made by beating out large grains or nuggets which they found in the rivers.'

3 This plant, obviously different from what we now think of as rhubarb, was thought by Columbus to be an oriental plant used in medicine. His interest in it was probably aroused by Marco Polo; in the margin alongside the point where Polo mentions the plant Columbus wrote *Reubarbarum*, just as he wrote *aurum, argentum, cinamomum*, etc. alongside Polo's other allusions to natural

wealth (see *Raccolta*, Part I, Vol. ii, p. 452).

31 December
1 Dunn and Kelley (DK, p. 299) translate *por saber . . . el transito de Castilla a ella* as 'in order to know its distance from Castile'.

1 January
1 LCH, p. 202: 'The Admiral thought the pepper called *ají* from this island a fine spice, saying that it is better than the pepper and *manegueta* brought from Guinea and Alexandria.' *Manegueta* may be a kind of pepper, or possibly the fruit of the *amomo*, a plant related to ginger. See Alvar, Vol. II, p. 185 n., and Morison, 1963, p. 142 n.

2 January
1 LCH, p. 204.
2 Dunn and Kelley (DK, p. 301) translate 'a skirmish between the armed men of the vessels [and the men remaining behind]'.
3 FCH, Vol. I, p. 209.
4 The ensuing passage has been somewhat modified in the light of Las Casas's fuller account in LCH, pp. 203–4.
5 LCH, p. 203.
6 Morison (*Admiral*, Vol. I, p. 401 n.) suggests that the speech which follows (taken from LCH, pp. 203–4; not included in the Journal) is an invention by Las Casas 'on the theme "be kind to the Indians and a good example to them" '. I have accepted it as at least fundamentally genuine on three grounds: first, it is generally free from the rhetorical bombast which characterizes Las Casas's emotional interpolations; secondly, Las Casas departs from the content of the speech at one point to say how ill founded the Admiral's confidence was; thirdly and most tellingly, although Las Casas is ostensibly reporting the speech rather than quoting it, it includes one of the cases, quite frequent in the Journal but relatively rare in LCH, of a careless failure to eradicate the use of the first person: *tenían por cierta opinión que éramos enviados de las celestiales virtudes*.
7 This is where Las Casas digresses, commenting on the failure of his countrymen to fulfil Columbus's faith in them.

3 January
1 Las Casas says in LCH, p. 205: 'I do not know how many he took from this island, but I believe he took some, and he took 10 or 12 Indians to Castile in all. I saw them myself in Seville, though I . . . do not remember counting them.'

4 January
1 'Snake Cape'. Possibly Pointe Jacquezi.
2 'Mount Christ'. Now Monte Cristi.
3 FCH, Vol. I, p. 212. This replaces 'etc.' in DK, p. 306, after which Las Casas goes on to say 'but because the land and the area are now well known I am omitting it'. Fernando (p. 212) comments on Columbus's motives: 'The Admiral thought it fitting to mention these details in order to make known the location of the first Christian settlement and possession in that western world.'

5 January
1 LCH, p. 206: 'I am amazed that he does not mention finding salt there, for there are excellent salt fields on this island; perhaps they were some distance away from him.'
2 'Calf Cape'. Possibly Punta Chica.
3 *Sic.* LCH has the same (p. 206).
4 The Journal has *a la quarta del este al nordeste*. Dunn and Kelley (p. 311) translate 'to the northeast by east', which would normally be *al nordeste cuarta del este*. E by N is usually *al este cuarta del nordeste*.
5 LCH, p. 206: 'He would certainly have given a good reward to anyone who had told him where he really was, for he was on the doorstep of the Cibao mines, in the middle of the great *Real Vega* . . . All the hills he could see from there were Cibao, where the world's riches in gold lay and still lie.'

6 January
1 This is contradicted by Las Casas in LCH, p. 207: '. . . he had certainly not experienced them, for these are the wildest, roughest, most stormy and violent winds on the face of the earth, which sink the most ships and bring devastation to these lands.'
2 LCH, p. 207.
3 In LCH, p. 208, Las Casas launches into a 2-page attack on Pinzón, quoting the evidence of the *pleitos*.

4 Jamaica. Las Casas comments in the margin (DK, p. 314): '. . . and in Jamaica a piece of gold was found as big as a great Alcalá loaf or a *quartal* of Valladolid. I saw it myself. Many others of 1 pound, or 2, or 3, or even 8 were found in Española.'

8 January
1 Morison, 1963, suggests that the *sursueste* (SSE) of the text is a mistake for *sursudueste* (SSW).
2 Las Casas comments in the margin (DK, p. 316): 'This river is the Yaqui; it is very powerful and rich in gold. It may well be that the Admiral found gold as he claims, the river being then virgin, as they say, but I think much of it must have been marcasite, which is plentiful there, and perhaps the Admiral thought all that glistered was gold.' See also LCH, pp. 209–10.
3 'River of Gold'. Now the Río Yaque del Norte.
4 Las Casas comments in the margin (DK, p. 318): 'It is bigger than any of these.' In LCH, p. 210, he expands this: 'I say that it is bigger than the Guadalquivir at Cantillana, or even Alcalá del Río, for I know it well.'
5 LCH, p. 210: 'He would have welcomed the news that it was not even 4; he was close to the mines of Cibao, not 4 leagues away.'

9 January
1 *lesnordeste*, mistranslated by Dunn and Kelley (DK, p. 319) as 'north-northeast'.
2 'Red Point'. Now Punta Rucia.
3 Dunn and Kelley (DK, p. 321) print *manegueta* with a capital. DK has a small *m*, a fact of no significance in itself, but compare LCH, p. 210: '. . . on the coast of Guinea, where they gather the *manegueta*'. The mermaids were probably manatees.

10 January
1 'Grace River'. Probably now Puerto Blanco. Las Casas tells us in the margin (DK, p. 320): 'This is the river called Río de Martín Alonso Pinzón, five leagues from Puerto de Plata.'
2 The text has *bruma*, which means 'mist'. This would hardly justify the next sentence, and is probably a mistake for *broma*, 'shipworm, teredo'.

11 January
1 'Fair Meadow'. Now Punta Patilla.
2 'Silver Mountain'. Las Casas comments in the margin (DK, p. 322): 'He called it Monte de Plata because it is very high and the summit is always covered in mist which makes it look white or silvery; at the foot of it is the harbour, which he named after the mountain.' The harbour is still Puerto de Plata.
3 'Cape Angel'. Either Punta Payne or Punta Sosua.
4 LCH, p. 211: '4 fathoms, and it is horseshoe-shaped'.
5 'Iron Point'. Now Punta Macoris.
6 'Dry Point'. Now Punta Cabarete.
7 'Round Cape'. Now Cabo de la Roca.
8 'French Cape'. The name survives.
9 'Fair Weather Cape'. Possibly Punta del Aguila.
10 'Sheer'. The name survives; alternatively, Punta Sabaneta. LCH, p. 211: 'None of the names of these headlands survives today.'

12 January
1 *dado resguardo al navio.* Dunn and Kelley (DK, pp. 325–7) translate this as 'having looked carefully at the ship's performance'. See Guillén Tato, p. 111: *resguardo*, 'distancia prudencial'.
2 'Cape Father and Son'. Now Cabo Cabrón.
3 LCH, p. 211: 'Puerto Sancto'.
4 'Cape of the Lover'. Now Cape Samana.
5 Samana Bay.
6 Cayo Levantado.

13 January
1 Las Casas comments in the margin (DK, p. 328): 'This shows that the Admiral knew something about astrology, though these planets appear to have been confused by poor copying.' Astrology and astronomy were inadequately distinguished at the time. For an explanation, see Morison, 1963, p. 152 n.
2 LCH, p. 212: 'It is not charcoal, it is a dye made from a certain fruit.'
3 Las Casas writes in the margin (DK, p. 328): 'They were not Caribs; there never were any on Española.'
4 LCH, p. 212: 'of San Juan'.
5 LCH, p. 212: 'and he was right; the island was a rich source of gold for a time; it is not so plentiful now.'
6 The Las Casas text (DK, p. 330) reads *al*

alambre o a un oro baxo, '*alambre*, or a base gold'. *Alambre* now means 'wire', but used to be applied to copper or its alloys.
7 LCH, p. 212.
8 Journal: *que es oro o alambre*.
9 Las Casas comments in the margin (DK, p. 330): 'This *guanin* was not an island, I think, but the low grade gold which the Indians of Española said had a smell; they set great value on it and called it *guanin*.'
10 A garbled note by Las Casas in the margin (DK, p. 332) explains that this weapon was made from palm wood and called a *macana*. He explains it more fully in LCH, p. 213: '. . . a palm wood sword, very hard and heavy, shaped like this: [drawing] It is not sharp at the end, but rounded, about two fingers wide along its length. It is as heavy and hard as iron, and will cut through a man's skull to his brain even if he is wearing a helmet.'
11 Las Casas (DK, p. 332) comments ruefully: 'The first fight between Indians and Christians on the island of Española.'

14 January
1 LCH, p. 214. The word, again, is *alambre*. Las Casas adds: 'I think he means copper.'

15 January
1 *alambre*.
2 The Las Casas text (DK, p. 340) reads: *toda la gente*, 'all the people'. Las Casas comments in the margin: 'By the people he must mean the Christians.' LCH, p. 214: 'the people in the caravels'.

16 January
1 'Bay of Arrows'. A point on the north shore is still called Punta de las Flechas.
2 Las Casas writes in the margin (DK, p. 344): 'I think this Cape of San Théramo must be the one now called Cabo del Engaño.'

18 January
1 The Las Casas text (DK, p. 346) reads *un pescado que se llama rabiforcado*. *Pescado* means 'fish', nowadays in the culinary context only. Dunn and Kelley, reasonably, suggest *pescador*, 'fisher', 'fishing bird'.

22 January
1 The arithmetic does not add up. See Morison, 1963, p. 158, 22 January, n. 1.

2 The Las Casas text (DK, p. 348) reads *seys leguas por hora*, '6 leagues per hour'; this is outlandish, and must be a mistake for 'miles'.

6 February
1 LCH, p. 216: NE.

10 February
1 LCH, p. 217, describes the later life of Roldán, 'who subsequently lived many years in the city of Santo Domingo in Española. We used to call him Roldán the *piloto*; he was rich, and had many pairs of houses which he built or ordered to be built in the four streets of the city . . .'
2 A gap in the manuscript.

14 February
1 The shrine and monastery of Santa María de Guadalupe in Extremadura was and remains one of the best known Spanish centres of the worship of the Virgin.
2 The Las Casas text (DK, p. 366) continues: 'which is a house where Our Lady has done and continues to do many great miracles'. I have omitted this on the assumption that it may be an addition by Las Casas.
3 FCH, Vol. I, p. 221: 'Santa María de Santoña'.
4 LCH, p. 218: '. . . for that too is a house for which seafarers, especially those of the *Condado*, have a special devotion'.
5 Dunn and Kelley, p. 367, translate this as 'shirtsleeves'.
6 Dunn and Kelley, p. 367, translate this as 'because of their greediness during the prosperous time they had in the islands'.
7 The rest of this entry continues with the version in FCH, Vol. I, pp. 222–4, which is in the first person singular.
8 Fernando gives the figure as 1,000 ducats. Earlier in the Journal (DK, p. 242) Las Casas says that an *excelente* (translated into Italian by Fernando as 4 ducats), was worth 2 *castellanos*.
9 FCH, Vol. I, p. 224, reads *verità*, 'truth'; the editor suggests *avidità*.
10 The Las Casas text (DK, p. 376) reads: *andaria a popa*, literally 'he must have sailed astern'. My translation assumes the omission of *con el viento* after *andaria*. To sail astern in such conditions under just a forecourse seems not only unseamanlike but impossible.
11 This could conceivably mean 'unbent

the *papahigo*', though to unbend a major sail in such storm conditions would be a demanding task.

15 February
1 FCH, Vol. I, pp. 225–6.

16 February
1 This entry covers 16 and 17 February. Columbus was probably unable to write up the Journal on the first day because of a combination of heavy weather and exhaustion.

19 February
1 This is the Castilian spelling. The Portuguese form would be 'Castanheda'.
2 The 'etc.' is in both DK and LCH. It is impossible to tell if it was written by Columbus or if it represents an abbreviation of the text by Las Casas.

21 February
1 The Las Casas text (DK, p. 382) has *estuvo a la cuerda*. Dunn and Kelley translate 'he jogged off and on'. See, however, DME, p. 196, *estar a la cuerda*; p. 140, *capa*; p. 515, *temporejar*.
2 He means through stress of weather.
3 LCH, p. 223.

22 February
1 *dioles de lo que tenia*, literally 'he gave them some of what he had'. Dunn and Kelley (p. 385) translate 'he produced for them what he had'. It may mean simply that he showed them the documents.

27 February
1 FCH, Vol. I, p. 232.

28 February
1 FCH, Vol. I, p. 232.

5 March
1 In modern Spanish *patrón* means 'owner, boss', and also 'captain of a vessel, especially a small one'. Dunn and Kelley translate this as 'master', which obscures what is evidently a difference from *maestre*, which I translate as 'master' in the following paragraph. This *patrón* is presumably of subordinate rank to the Portuguese *capitán*, whose emissary he is. One possibility is that he is not only the master of the Portuguese vessel, but also its owner, and that the ship was chartered by the Crown. Juan Niño was

both owner and master of the Niña, and Juan de la Cosa was owner and master of the Santa María, though subordinate to Columbus.
2 Possibly Bartholomew Dias, the explorer.
3 These are long, straight trumpets of Moorish pattern.

8 March
1 The Castilian form; the Portuguese would be 'Noronha'.
2 The Portuguese form is 'Sacavem'.

9 March
1 The Portuguese form is 'Valparaiso'.
2 LCH, p. 227, continues: '. . . the King was speaking cautiously and formally, but he must have been raging in his heart at losing such an enterprise, which he had had in his own grasp; he must have been planning to raise all possible obstacles . . . so as to prevent Castile from holding on to the Indies.'

10 March
1 In LCH, pp. 227–8, Las Casas recounts that in a conversation between himself and unnamed persons it was said that 'the King had a plate of beans brought and put on a table beside him, and he told one of the Indians to draw or depict all the islands in the waters of his homeland which the Admiral said he had discovered. The Indian, with no hesitation, laid out the islands of Española and Cuba and the Lucayos and others which he knew. The King looked carefully at what he had done, and then, as if by accident, disarranged the beans with his hands. A while later he asked another Indian to do the same . . . the Indian readily set out the beans to show just the same as the other, and added many more islands and countries, explaining it all in his own language which nobody understood. Then the King, realizing the full extent of the discoveries and the riches which he now imagined them to hold, could no longer conceal the misery within him . . . at losing things of such inestimable value.' Las Casas (LCH, p. 228), using information from García de Resende's *Chronicle of King John II of Portugal*, also says that the King's advisers pressed him to let them seize Columbus and kill him, and that only the King's fear of God saved him.

Notes

11 March

1 The Spanish form of Portuguese 'Vilafranca'.

2 The Las Casas text (DK, p. 398) has *Llandra*, then *Allandra*. The Portuguese form is 'Alhandra'.

15 March

1 Las Casas ends: 'These are the final words of the Admiral Don Christopher Columbus about his first voyage to the Indies and his discovery of them. *Deo gracias.*'

Appendices

Appendix I

1 See my n. 22 to Ch. 4 of the Introduction.

Appendix II

1 This partial payroll was published by the Duchess of Berwick and Alba in *Nuevos autógrafos de Cristóbal Colón*, Madrid, 1902, pp. 7–10. The document is in Columbus's own handwriting, with the exception of the material between oblique strokes.

Select Bibliography

Alegría, Ricardo E., *Cristóbal Colón y el tesoro de los indios tainos de la Española*, Santo Domingo, Dominican Republic, 1980.

Alvar, Manuel (ed.), *Diario del descubrimiento*, 2 vols, Gran Canaria, 1976 (Alvar).

Alvar, Manuel, and others, *Atlas lingüístico y etnográfico de Andalucía*, 6 vols, Granada, 1961–73.

Anzoátegui, Ignacio B., *Los cuatro viajes del Almirante y su testamento*, 3rd edn, Buenos Aires, 1958.

Benzone, Girolamo, *Historia del Nuovo Mondo* (Venice, 1563), facsimile edn, Graz, 1962.

Berwick and Alba, The Duchess of, *Nuevos autógrafos de Cristóbal Colón*, Madrid, 1902.

Carta: see Salazar, Eugenio de.

Chapman, Paul H., *The Man Who Led Columbus to America*, Atlanta, 1973.

Codex Mendoza, ed. James C. Clarke, 3 vols, London, 1938.

Columbus, Christopher, *Libro de profecías*, ed. Francisco Alvarez Seisdedos, Madrid, 1984.

Columbus, Fernando, *Historie della vita e dei fatti di Cristoforo Colombo*, ed. R. Caddeo, 2 vols, Milan, 1930 (FCH). English translation by Benjamin Keen, *The Life of the Admiral Christopher Columbus by his Son, Ferdinand*, New Brunswick, 1959.

Cortesão, Armando, *The Nautical Chart of 1424*, Coimbra, 1954.

Crawshay, L. R., 'Possible Bearing of a Luminous Syllid on the Question of the Landfall of Columbus', *Nature* 136 (1935), p. 559.

Diccionario marítimo español, Madrid, 1831 (DME).

DK: see Dunn, Oliver, and James E. Kelley, Jr.

Documenti: see Genoa, City of.

DME: see *Diccionario marítimo español*.

Dunn, Oliver, 'Columbus's First Landing Place: The Evidence of the Journal', *Terrae Incognitae* 15 (1983), pp. 35–50.

Dunn, Oliver, and James E. Kelley, Jr, *The 'Diario' of Christopher Columbus's First Voyage to America, 1492–1493*, London and Norman, Oklahoma, 1989 (DK).

Edwards, Emily, *Painted Walls of Mexico from Prehistoric Times until Today*, Austin and London, 1966.

FCH: see Columbus, Fernando.

Fonseca, Quirino da, *A caravela portuguesa*, Coimbra, 1934.

García de Palacio, Diego, *Instrucción náutica para el buen uso y regimiento de las naos*, Mexico, 1587.

Genoa, City of: *Cristoforo Colombo: Documenti e provi della sua appartenenza a Genova*, Bergamo, 1931 (*Documenti*). English–German edition, Bergamo, 1932.

Gil, Juan, *Colón y su tiempo* (Vol. I of his *Mitos y utopías del descubrimiento*), Madrid, 1989.

Select Bibliography

Gil, Juan (ed.), *El Libro de Marco Polo anotado por Cristóbal Colón. Versión de Rodrigo de Santaella*, Madrid, 1987.

Gould, Alice, 'Documentos inéditos sobre hidalguía y genealogía de la familia Pinzón', *Boletín de la Real Academia de Historia* XCI (1927), pp. 319–75.

Gould, Alice, 'Nueva lista documentada de los tripulantes de Colón en 1492', *Boletín de la Real Academia de Historia*, Vols LXXXV, pp. 34–49, 145–59, 353–79; LXXXVI, pp. 491–532; LXXXVII, pp. 22–60; LXXXVIII, pp. 721–84; XC, pp. 532–55; XCI, pp. 318–75; XCII, pp. 776–95; CXVII, pp. 145–88.

Guaman Poma de Ayala, Felipe, *Nueva crónica y buen gobierno*, ed. John V. Murra and others, 3 vols, Madrid, 1987.

Guillén Tato, Julio, *La parla marinera en el diario del primer viaje de Cristóbal Colón*, Madrid, 1951.

Hawkins, Clifford W., *The Dhow: An Illustrated History of the Dhow and its World*, Lymington, Hampshire, 1977.

Ife, Barry W. (ed.), *Christopher Columbus: Journal of the First Voyage*, Warminster, 1990.

Jourdain Cathalà de Sévérac, *Mirabilia Descripta*, ed. Henri Cordier, Paris, 1925.

Kelley, James E., Jr, 'In the wake of Columbus on a portolan chart', in Louis de Voysey, Jr and John Parker, *In the Wake of Columbus: Islands and Controversy*, Detroit, 1985.

la Roncière, Charles de, *La Carte de Christophe Colomb*, Paris, 1924.

las Casas, Bartolomé de, *Historia de las Indias*, in *Biblioteca de Autores Españoles*, Vol. 95, Madrid, 1957 (LCH).

LCH: see Las Casas, Bartolomé de.

Livre des merveilles, Bibliothèque Nationale, Paris, MS Fr 2810.

Lollis, Cesare de, and others (eds), *Raccolta di documenti i studi publicati dalla R. Commissione Colombiana pel quarto centenario della scoperta dell'America*, 14 vols, Rome, 1892–4 (*Raccolta*).

Jane, Cecil, *Voyages of Columbus*, London, 1930.

Jos, Emiliano, 'El Libro del Primer Viaje: Algunas ediciones recientes', *Revista de Indias*, Vol. X, 1950, pp. 719–51.

McElroy, John W., 'The Ocean Navigation of Columbus on his First Voyage', *American Neptune* I (1941), pp. 209–40.

Manera Rodríguez, E., *El buque en la armada española*, Madrid, 1981.

Manzano Manzano, Juan, *Colón y su secreto*, Madrid, 1976.

Manzano Manzano, Juan, *Cristóbal Colón: Siete años decisivos de su vida, 1485–1492*, Madrid, 1964.

Marco Polo: *The Travels of Marco Polo the Venetian*, ed. John Masefield, London and New York, 1907 (MP).

Martínez Hidalgo, José María, *Columbus's Ships*, ed. Howard I. Chapelle, Barre, Mass., 1966.

Maundevile, Sir John: *The Voyages and Travels of Sir John Maundevile Kt.*, ed. H. M., London, 1892.

Medina, Pedro de, *The Navigator's Universe: The Libro de Cosmographia of 1538*, transl. Ursula Lamb, Chicago, 1972.

Menéndez Pidal, Ramón, *La lengua de Cristóbal Colón*, Buenos Aires, 1947.

Milani, Virgil I., *The Written Language of Christopher Columbus*, supplement to *Forum Italicum*, Buffalo, 1973.

Mollat du Jourdin, Michel, and others, *Les Portulans: Cartes marines du XIIIᵉ au XVIIᵉ siècle*, Fribourg, 1984. English edn, *Sea Charts of the Early Explorers*, New York, 1984.

Morison, Samuel Eliot, *Admiral of the Ocean Sea: A Life of Christopher Columbus*, 2 vols, Boston, Mass., 1942 (Morison, *Admiral*).

Morison, Samuel Eliot, *Journals and other Documents on the Life and Voyages of Christopher Columbus*, New York, 1963 (Morison, 1963).

Morison, Samuel Eliot, *Portuguese Voyages to America in the Fifteenth Century*, Cambridge, Mass., 1940.

Morison, Samuel Eliot, 'The Route of Columbus Along the North Coast of Haiti and the Site of Navidad', *Transactions of the American Philosophical Society* XXXI (1940), pp. 239–85 (Morison, 'The Route of Columbus').

Morison, Samuel Eliot, 'Texts and Translations of the Journal of Columbus's First Voyage', *Hispanic American Historical Review* XIX (1939), pp. 235–61.

Moule, A. C., *Christians in China before the Year 1550*, London, 1930.

MP: see Marco Polo.

Select Bibliography

Ortega, Angel, *La Rábida: historia documental crítica*, 4 vols, Seville, 1925–6.

Parias, L.-H., *Historia universal de las exploraciones*, Madrid, 1982.

Pérez Embid, Florentino, *Los descubrimientos en el Atlántico y la rivalidad castellano-portuguesa hasta el tratado de Tordesillas*, Seville, 1948.

Pleitos: 'Pleitos colombinos', in the Real Academia de Historia's *Colección de documentos inéditos relativos al descubrimiento*, 2nd Series, 25 vols, 1885–1932, Vols VII and VIII (1892–4). New edn by Antonio Muro Orejón and others, at least 8 vols, Seville, 1964–.

Raccolta: see Lollis, Cesare de.

Ravenstein, E. G., *Martin Behaim: His Life and His Globe*, London, 1908.

Richardson, Philip L., and Roger A. Goldsmith, 'The Columbus Landfall: Voyage Track Corrected for Winds and Currents', *Oceanus* 30 (1987), pp. 3–10.

Rumeu de Armas, Antonio, *La Rábida y el descubrimiento de América*, Madrid, 1968.

Salazar, Eugenio de, 'Carta escrita al licenciado Miranda de Ron, particular amigo del autor. En que se pinta un navío, y la vida y ejercicios de los oficiales y marineros en él, y como lo pasan los que hacen viajes por el mar', in *Cartas de Eugenio de Salazar escritas a muy particulares amigos suyos*, Madrid (Sociedad de Bibliófilos Españoles), 1866.

Sanz, Carlos, *Bibliografía general de la Carta de Colón*, Madrid, 1958.

Sanz, Carlos, *Diario de Colón*, Madrid, 1962.

Sanz, Carlos, 'El mapa del mundo, según el proceso cartográfico de Occidente y su influencia en el de Oriente'; and 'Un mapa del mundo verdaderamente importante de la famosa universidad de Yale', *Boletín de la Real Sociedad Geográfica* CII (1966).

Stevens, Benjamin F., *Columbus: His Own Book of Privileges*, London, 1893.

Thacher, John B., *Christopher Columbus: His Life, His Work, His Remains, as Revealed by Original Printed and Manuscript Records*, 3 vols, New York, 1903–4.

Vázquez, J. A., 'Las Casas' Opinions in Columbus's Diary', in *Topic: a Journal of the Liberal Arts*, Washington, 1971, pp. 145–56.

Vignaud, Henri, *Histoire Critique de la grande entreprise de Christophe Colomb*, 2 vols, Paris, 1911.

Vigneras, L. A. (ed.), *The Journal of Christopher Columbus*, London, 1960.

Villiers, Alan, *The Way of a Ship*, London, 1954.

Whipple, A. B. C., *The Clipper Ships*, Amsterdam, 1980.

Wright, Roger, *Spanish Ballads*, Warminster, 1987.

Yule, Sir Henry, *Cathay and the Way Thither*, 2nd edn, 4 vols, London (Hakluyt Society), 1913–15.

Sources of Illustrations
and Figures

1 British Library, MS Eg 2854,
fols 2v–3.
2 Bibliothèque Nationale, Paris,
MS Res Ge A 276.
3 British Library, MS Add 15760.
4–7 Bibliothèque Nationale, Paris,
MS Fr 2810, fols 51, 84, 87 and 107.
8 British Library, MS Royal
19.D.1, fol. 59v.
9 The larger vessel is from
Bernhard von Breydenbach,
Peregrinationes in Terram Sanctam,
Mainz, 1486; the smaller from the
Estoriador do emperador Vespesiano,
1496.
10–11 Diego García de Palacio,
*Instrucción náutica para el buen uso y
regimiento de las naos*, Mexico City,
1587.
12 Bibliothèque Nationale, Paris,
MS Port 45.
13 National Maritime Museum,
Greenwich, Portolan 14, fol. 15v.
14 British Library, MS Royal
20.E.IX, fol. 4.
15 From the collection of paintings
by John White, British Museum,
Dept of Prints and Drawings,

Catalogue No. 46a.
16 British Museum, Dept of
Ethnography, No. 1949 Am. 22.118.
17–19 From Columbus's *Letter to Gabriel
Sánchez*, Basel, 1493.
20 Part of the Cantino world map of
1502 in the collection of the Biblioteca
Estense, Modena.
21 From a painting in the collection
of the Lázaro Galdiano Museum,
Madrid.
22 From a document in the archives
of the City of Genoa, reproduced in
facsimile in publicity material issued
by the city in 1990.

In-text figures: p. 85: Benedetto Bordone,
Isolario, 1528; pp. 101, 105, 109, 140, 167,
168: Fernández de Oviedo y Valdés,
Historia General de las Indias, Salamanca,
1547; p. 95: Girolamo Benzone, *Historia
del Mondo Nuovo*, Venice, 1563; p. 83:
Martín Cortés, *Breve compendio de la
sphera y del arte de navegar*, Seville, 1551;
pp. 113, 178: Diego García de Palacio,
*Instrucción náutica para el buen uso y
regimiento de las naos*, Mexico City, 1587.

Index

235

Index

Index

Index